To Tom

Our neighbor and good friend
who is such a willing helper!
We appreciate you, Tom!

Sincerely,
Kelly & Gloria Grenga
Feb. 6, 2007

Since you were in the Navy, we
think you will enjoy this book
written by Kelly's sister, Helen.
It is based on their brother's
(James) experiences in the Navy
during W.W.2.

Movies on the Fantail

James B. Grenga

For

Our Parents
Eva and Angelo Grenga

And

Our Brothers James and John

PHOTO ACKNOWLEDGMENTS

Individual photographs used in the "Flashbacks" were provided by the Men of the *Barr* or their families. In addition, those listed below provided photographs used on the referenced pages. Photographs not otherwise acknowledged were attached to James Grenga's diary.

George Budak: pp. 28, 45, 71, 94 (top right, bottom left), 99 (both),
    101 (left), 112, 120, 184 (top), 206 (bottom right),
    210 (top right, bottom left), 218 (bottom), 228
Marvin Cooper: p. 49
Daniel DiBono: p. 2 (bottom)
Harry Gardner: p. 46
John Holdforth: pp. 166, 186
John Hubenthal: pp. 39 (left), 94 (top left), 184 (bottom)
Marvin Johnston: p. 2 (top and middle)
Philip Jones: pp. 142 (right), 191
William Kerry: p.170 (top)
Norman LeMere: pp. 26, 153, 189, 206 (top left), 210 (bottom
    right), 218 (top), 221
Donald Murray: pp. 34, 42, 47 (both), 54, 66 (bottom), 68, 73, 86
    (top), 88, 97
Eric Rosengren: pp. 4 (left), 39 (right)
Andrew Soucy: pp. x, 6, 20 (top), 86 (bottom), 232
Edward Verissimo: pp. 4 (right), 115 (bottom), 124,
    170 (bottom two), 185, 190, 222 (top)
Donald Walker: p. 59
Zenon Wolan: pp. 29 (top), 30, 32, 36, 96, 128, 142 (left),
    222 (bottom)

MOVIES ON THE FANTAIL

**A Sailor's Diary and Memories
from Other Men of the USS *Barr* DE576/APD39**

Yeoman Press
Newnan, Georgia

Library of Congress Catalog Card Number: 2001-131635
ISBN: 0-9709110-0-9

The paper used in this book meets the minimum requirements of American National Standard for Information Sciences--Permanence of Paper for Printed Library Materials, ANSI Z39.48-1984.

FIRST EDITION
Yeoman Press, hardcover, April 2001

Printed in the United States of America

PREFACE

In the Fall of 1997 my nephew David Grenga shared the diary that my brother James Grenga had kept in two log books while serving as a Yeoman aboard the USS *Barr* (an auxiliary personnel destroyer) in the Pacific Theatre during World War II. After reading these in the late summer of 1998 I thought, along with other family members, that we should transcribe and try to publish James' diary. Because many men aboard the *Barr* had autographed these logs with brief notes and their addresses at that time, I became interested in contacting them in the hope that they would contribute their own recollections.

A cherished friend, Miss Sally Bowen, who had been my high school Latin teacher and basketball coach, was instrumental in my meeting her brother Capt. A. Manly Bowen, USN Ret. A friend and contemporary of my older brothers, Manly attended Annapolis and became a career officer who served on two destroyer escorts, USS *Keith* and *Maurice J. Manuel*. He enlisted another Newnan native Robert W. Bridges, a veteran of Iwo Jima and Okinawa who later served on the USS *Cofer* APD at Borneo and Nagasaki.

Together, these friends combined invaluable knowledge and understanding of the *Barr*'s service both as DE in the Atlantic and APD in the Pacific. Manly has supplied introductions to each part of the book. Robert and his wife Martha located some of the veterans of the *Barr*. Their generosity has brought understanding and a sense of immediacy to James' account of events that happened before I could hardly even read.

My memories of World War II include brief impressions of H.V. Kaltenborn on the radio, news reels at the movies, air raids, President Roosevelt's voice on the radio--and the consciousness that my brother James was not at home (Christmas of 1945 Mother said James would soon be home, so I sat at the window watching for hours at a time--until he finally arrived!). Not only that, transcribing and editing a diary of events that occurred during WWII represents a radical change after a career spent teaching engineering at Georgia Tech and publishing the results of my research. Manly, Robert, and the Men of the *Barr* have afforded me an adventure as well as an education in a different field.

Much the most pleasant and gratifying part of this project has been the contact with the Men of the *Barr* and their families. They have been extremely helpful and willing to share their experiences, photographs and related materials; they have been most encouraging and just a great joy to work with; they are indeed a great generation! At the same time, I must acknowledge with deep regret the pain that I have sensed from many of these men who say that their experiences were "burned into memory." I can only hope that their bravery in remembering and sharing will help others to understand what it cost them to live--and re-live--experiences that guarantee all of us our freedom.

Helen E. Grenga, Ph.D.
Professor Emerita, Georgia Tech
Newnan, Georgia, 2001

Notes on the text:

James' diary has been divided into seventeen chapters based, as much as possible, on subject areas or events. Except for introductory, transitional, and explanatory notes by Dr. Helen Grenga and Capt. Manly Bowen, Movies on the Fantail is a transcription of James Grenga's diary along with selections written by his shipmates. As such, the manuscripts appear "as is." The stories (flashbacks) of the men of the USS *Barr* were theirs to tell as their experiences dictated.

"Men of the *Barr*" in this book includes all of those who are a part of the *Barr*'s proud history--officers and crew of the *Barr*; UDT 13 men, who were aboard for only three months and were a major "weapon" of the *Barr*; and the British Royal Marines, who were aboard for a couple of weeks to become part of the first occupational forces in Japan. The ratings and ranks that are given for these men are the highest they held while on the *Barr*; many achieved higher ratings and ranks by the end of the war or later.

The photographs in this book were selected from a total of about 700, some of which were found in James' diary and many of which were generously contributed by other men of the *Barr*. A number of other items, e.g., poems and *Barr* histories, which were attached to James' logs, are also included without attribution as he used them. Among Mother's papers were found a few letters that James had written her during the battle of Iwo Jima; these are included in that chapter.

All photos and "flashbacks" from the Men of the *Barr* are used by permission of the owners/authors. Complete photo acknowledgments are appended.

ACKNOWLEDGMENTS

First, a special thanks to those who shared their equipment and expertise that facilitated my ability to send volumes of materials to the men of the *Barr*: William Thomasson, Jeanette Kirby, Winston Skinner, Emma Hinesley, Glenna Thomas, Jeannie Baggett, and Maureen Kilroy.

I am very grateful to those who read the manuscript and provided helpful suggestions as well as encouragement for this project: Guy C. Arnall, Judge W. Homer Drake, Linda S. Long, Claire A. Sickel, and Dr. James J. Thomasson (LCDR MC USNR),.

My special thanks to a Georgia Tech colleague Dr. Maxine Turner, a writer and independent scholar of naval history, for her valuable technical advice and encouragement throughout the project.

Capt. A. Manly Bowen and Robert Bridges, acknowledged also in the Preface, are due further recognition here for contributing their time, experience and expertise in this effort--as are their wives Delly and Martha for their gracious hospitality and unfailing support for the project.

My deepest gratitude to the men of the *Barr* and their families whose memories have immeasurably enriched this book.

A project that began with family appropriately concludes with grateful acknowledgment of their work as well as their patience and encouragement: James' sister Louise, James' brothers Angelo and Kelly, along with their wives Eloise and Gloria, John's widow JoBess, James' widow Joyce and her husband Burris, and James' children Rene and David.

INTRODUCTION

USS Barr *DE576 Model by MM2cVertes*

The USS *Barr* was named for PFC Woodrow Wilson Barr, who was born in Keyser, West Virginia, on June 30, 1913, and was killed in action on August 7, 1942. On January 13, 1942, Barr enlisted in the United States Marine Corps at Pittsburgh, Pennsylvania. PFC Barr was awarded the Purple Heart; Presidential Unit Citation, 1942; Asiatic-Pacific Campaign Medal, 1942; and the SILVER STAR posthumously for conspicuous gallantry and intrepidity in action while serving with the First Marine Raider Battalion during the attack against enemy Japanese forces on Tulagi, Solomon Islands, on August 7, 1942.

The U.S. Navy's Destroyer Escort (DE) shipbuilding program during World War II was prompted by a shortage of open ocean convoy escorts needed by the Allies for the Battle of the Atlantic. As the allies gained the upper hand in this battle, many destroyer escorts were either converted to or completed as High Speed Transports (APD) for use in amphibious assaults. This is a book of recollections by the men of one of these ships, the USS *BARR*, built as a DE, converted to an APD while being repaired after severe damage sustained in the Battle of the Atlantic, and employed in that second role in the invasions of Iwo Jima and Okinawa in the Pacific theater. It isn't a history, though they were making history. Instead it is a recounting of what it was like to be a young American Navy man living the often dull, but sometimes electrifying, shipboard life during a war at sea. Their stories range from high drama to the frequently tedious life in a ship when nothing is happening and the high point of the day is "movies on the fantail."

A. Manly Bowen, Capt., USN Ret.
Annapolis, 1999

(Captain Bowen's introduction continues in each major division of the book)

CONTENTS

PART I: USS *BARR* DE576--BATTLE OF THE ATLANTIC

> Once out and she was wounded but not out of the fight. . . . . she was not a quitter. True to the words, she was and still is a fighter.

PART II: REDESIGN AND PREPARATION FOR NEW MISSION

> Again we practiced boat drills all day. This is all new to me and some-what very interesting. I am finding that living on a ship is not too bad. The boys are all friendly, maybe more so than boys on a shore station. We know now that someday we will all be in battle together.

> I have always heard about the great "ditch" and now I have passed through it. Truly, it is a great accomplishment of man. There was such pretty scenery all along the "ditch". It was a sight that I shall never forget.

I had a strange feeling this afternoon when we passed under the 'Golden Gate'. I was standing out on the Boat Deck and I watched the Gate fade away on the horizon. Somehow, it seems that we are now leaving everything. But duty calls - and there is a war to be won.

Today we practiced with the demo's. They seem to be getting plenty of practice, and fast, too. And it is about to wear Ship's Company out to keep up with them. These swimmers sure can swim a long way. They practically stay in the water all the time.

PART III: BATTLES OF THE USS *BARR* APD39

This is it! This morning at 0700 we pulled up anchor and are under-way The Captain has just passed the word over the speaker that we are underway for Iwo Jima. . . . we would arrive there about 0400 on the morning of the 16th and would start immediately carrying out demolition work.

Hundreds of little small boats swarmed ashore. Planes were all over the air over the island diving down strafing the beach. Battle wagons, cruisers and destroyers opened up with all their might. I have never seen anything like it. It seemed as if all hell had broke loose.

This morning the U.D.T. boys were put off on Asor Island, for a rest. . . Have been laying around at anchorage and enjoying liberty, such as it is, for the past few days. . . . We are headed for Okinawa. . . . The Captain said that this one was not going to be a picnic like Iwo Jima for us.

Today is Easter and what a parade I saw this morning. Never have I seen anything more pretty than hundreds of the little boats in the water. It was pretty but was sad when you think of their job. . . By noon you could not see anything for all the smoke and dust.

Had a recreation party this afternoon, and it was good to get on land again, and rest for a little. Had ice cold beer, too. . . . At 2115, all hands observed five minutes of silent prayer in memory of our late Commander-in-Chief and President of the United States - Franklin D. Roosevelt.

They say that the Navy is losing more than the Army who landed on the beaches. That doesn't seem possible. It must be true that the enemy are trying to knock out our Navy to avoid another quick invasion. But this Navy has made camp here and will never leave until we have won.

Had recreation yesterday and also again today. I went this afternoon. And when I returned to the ship I had mail. More letters from my girl. O, she is sweet. Everything at home is fine and that helps out a lot.

We have had "K" rations all day - really been rolling. The wind has been very strong. Waves look like they are going to swallow up the ship. They really are high. And you can feel the bow of the ship plunging into them - and the whole ship just shivers and you think it is going to fall apart. Sometimes I think the bogeys are better.

PART IV: POST WAR SERVICE

What a happy day this has been. This morning, we got underway at 0500 to join the Third Fleet off Tokyo. . . . We are now underway at full speed. Like we are going to a fire. And we have just found out that we are going into Tokyo to evacuate the POW's there.

Entered Tokyo Harbor around noon today with the REEVES leading. . . .*BARR* was first U.S. Vessel to tie up at the docks of South Tokyo, something that the whole U.S. Navy has been planning on for four years. . . . we are to have a movie on the fantail tonight. How about that. A dream come true - right here in Tokyo Bay.

This afternoon I saw - and I still can't believe it - I saw destruction and death at its worst. I am sure that there has never been anything like this in the history of the world. It is almost impossible to conceive that one little bomb did all of what my eyes saw this afternoon.. . . Then the loud speaker barked - the Captain said - "We are going home."

Gosh, what a big ocean this is. . . . We go so slow. . . .Yes, a victorious ship is coming back with all its men. But we can't forget those ships and those men that will never come back. . . It is so hard to believe that in the morning when I awake that I will see "God's country" in the distance. A dream comes true . . . God has been with us and I will forever be thankful.

Movies on the Fantail

PART 1

USS BARR DE576-- BATTLE OF THE ATLANTIC

The German threat against Britain was so severe that by 1940 Britain's Prime Minister Winston Churchill had convinced US President Roosevelt of Britain's urgent need for ocean escorts to defend the convoys ferrying supplies both from America and from Britain's Colonial Empire, to the British Isles. Roosevelt first sent fifty twenty-year-old US "reserve" destroyers to help, but more escorts would be needed.

After Congress passed the Lend Lease Act in March 1941, Roosevelt authorized the Navy Department to design and build ocean escorts for Lend-Lease to the Royal Navy. The British selected a Navy Department design with a formidable antisubmarine battery, but otherwise less capable than a fleet destroyer. Roosevelt authorized construction of fifty Destroyer Escorts to be designated BDE. Facing a two ocean war when the Axis powers declared war on the US after the Japanese attack on Pearl Harbor, the US expanded the DE building program. In all, 504 DE's were built; almost all served in the US Navy.

Ocean escorts like the US built DE performed two basic missions in the Battle of the Atlantic: first as close defense, primarily against submarines that took a toll on merchant shipping, and later in 1943 on an offensive mission as the "killer" in a "Hunter Killer Group". "Hunter" airplanes on a small aircraft carrier were specially equipped to locate and attack surface submarines. Several "killer" DE's serving with each carrier had the endurance and weapons to "kill" the submerged submarines. Allied success in breaking the German codes supplied knowledge of submarine locations and communications that dramatically increased the effectiveness of the hunter-killer groups and sharply reduced the effectiveness of the German submarines.

DE's compiled an enviable record as submarine killers, being responsible for the destruction of more German submarines than any other type ship. One of those DE's was the USS *Barr* DE576, one of five DE's assigned to a Hunter-Killer Group organized around the escort carrier USS *Block Island* CVE 21 operating off the African Coast. On May 29, 1944, the German submarine U-549 torpedoed and sank the *Block Island*; *Barr* was struck in the stern by another torpedo, killing seventeen and wounding fifteen men.

The *Barr* was towed to Casablanca where eighty feet of her stern was removed and a steel plate was welded in its place so that she could be towed back to Boston for repair and conversion to the high-speed transport APD39. In all, she had operated as a DE just more than three months.

Introduction cont'd., Capt. A. Manly Bowen

Mr. & Mrs. Barr Christening the USS Barr

USS Barr *after christening*

USS Barr *with damaged stern at Casablanca*

The Barr at 306 feet long and 39 feet wide amidships hardly gave the appearance of an impregnable floating fortress, but an amazing amount of "gear" had been built into her streamlined hull. Topside were one 5-inch gun, three 3-inch, 50-caliber guns (our big artillery), a 1-inch antiaircraft battery, ten 20 Mm AA guns, plus "hedgehogs", depth charges, torpedo tubes, surface and air radar, underwater sound detection devices, fathometer, a mass of radio gear, and the usual bewildering electrical wiring.

Eugene L. Swearingen, Ensign, from his journal, "My Ramblings Aboard the Barr APD39"

CHAPTER 1

THE OLD 39--NOT A QUITTER

Once out and she was wounded but not out of the fight. . . . she was not a quitter. True to the words, she was and still is a fighter.

The USS BARR (APD39), formerly (DE576) was built at Bethlehem-Hingham Ship Yard, South Boston, Mass. Her keel was laid November 5, 1943, and she was commissioned February 15, 1944 - a mighty ship to join our ever growing Fleet.

At this time the Navy Department was seeing the need of ships of the DE class (fast little ships) as a protection against the submarine menace that was prevailing in the Atlantic at that time.

After a short shakedown cruise to Bermuda, she set sail from Boston to join a "killer group" in the Atlantic waters. The "killer group" of which the BARR was a member was composed of the USS BUCKLEY, USS AHRENS, USS ELMORE, USS PAYNE, USS BLOCK ISLAND, and, of course, the mighty BARR.

The "killer group" was in the Atlantic for 25 days before it pulled into Casablanca for supplies. After a few days there, the "killer group" got underway. After being out for about seven days they were attacked by a "wolf pack". This was on the night of the 29th of May, 1944. The USS BLOCK ISLAND (CV) took three "fish" and the BARR, one, during the engagement which followed. The USS BLOCK ISLAND sank (incidentally, the only carrier lost in the Atlantic waters). Reports stated that only six men were killed on the "BLOCK". However, the BARR suffered greater - with 5 killed, 12 missing and 14 wounded. The ELMORE and the AHRENS came together and sank the sub.

The BARR with 80 feet of her fantail wrecked was towed back to Casablanca where she received temporary repairs. Then she went under tow from Casablanca enroute to Boston, Mass. The recent fate was not enough for the BARR. About 600 miles out from the coast of Norfolk, she encountered a North Atlantic hurricane. The BARR was rocking like a cork in the water. (One of Bowman's famous sayings.) The course was diverted to Bermuda; the BARR stayed afloat.

One week's stay in Bermuda and she was towed on to Boston, Mass., where she underwent major repairs, and the conversion to a brand new fighting ship for the Pacific Fleet -namely an (APD). An APD is a high speed troop transport ship.

Incidentally, the "killer group" of which   the BARR was a member sank six German subs prior to the fatal engagement.

RM2c Bowman and SM1c Rosengren
Boston, 1944

WT1c Verissimo and friend visiting
cultural sights on leave

This is where I came in. Some of the information above was contributed to me by my friend, Bowman. From now on, it is my story, for on the 23rd of August, 1944, I came aboard the USS BARR.

The foregoing history of the BARR is almost enough to make any fellow feel proud to be of the crew to sail her again. Once out and she was wounded, but not out of the fight. For now she was being patched up and made ready for another cruise. For days after she was hit, they half expected her to go down at any time. But she was not a quitter. True to the words, she was and still is a fighting ship.

BUCKLEY CLASS DE CHARACTERISTICS

Crew: 220

Length overall: 306' (about the length of a football field)

Beam (Widest Breadth): 35' 10"

Draft: 9' 6"

Displacement, fully loaded: 1720 tons

Main Propulsion: 12,000 HP steam turboelectric power plant

Maximum Speed: 24 Knots (About 28 statute mph)

Guns: Three 3"/50 cal dual purpose guns*
    One quad mounted 1.1" rapid firing AA Gun **
    Four 20 mm AA machine guns

Torpedoes: One triple 21" torpedo mount ***

Antisubmarine Weapons: One "hedgehog" mortar (fired 24 small depth
    charges in a circular pattern ahead of the ship)***
    Two Stern mounted depth charge tracks (for rolling 300#, or 600#
    Depth charges over the stern)
    Eight "K" guns (for projecting 300# depth charges off the side of the
    ship far enough to avoid damage to the ship itself and, with the stern
    dropped charges, create a "pattern" to increase the sea volume lethal to
    a submerged submarine ***

* *Replaced by one 5"/38 Cal DP gun during conversion to an APD*

** *Replaced by a twin 40 mm rapid firing AA gun during conversion*

*** *Removed and not replaced during conversion*

About eight o'clock on the night of the 23rd of August, 1944, I arrived in Boston, Mass. along with a draft of about 50 men from Philadelphia, Pennsylvania. We were all men destined for the BARR. As soon as we arrived a big Boatswain Mate had a big truck outside South Station ready to take us to our new home. Later we were scuttled into a large building that looked more like a hotel than a barracks as we soon found out. This was the Fargo Building. We were all hoping that we would put up there for the night for it appeared to be a pretty nice place. But just as that thought was entering our minds, we got orders to load our sea bags back into the truck. We were all very disappointed.

Then off we went down to the Docks to find the USS BARR. We rode and we rode around and around the docks. No one seemed to know of a ship by that name. Finally, we came across her. It was dark and we could not see much what she looked like.

Later the O.O.D. instructed the driver to take us up to the Barracks where the rest of the BARR crew were quartered. That night I found all the crew of the BARR to be very congenial and I knew then that I was going to like sailing with such a fine bunch of boys.

The liberty in Boston was wonderful. Everyone was so nice and friendly. So unlike Norfolk, Virginia where at one time I was stationed. The Buddies Club there was one of my favorite amusement centers. It was a U.S.O. but was called the Buddies Club. Many an enjoyable liberty I spent there.

USS Barr *DE576 crew members at Casa Manana in Boston, 1944, while ship was being converted to APD: GM1c Purgatorio, FC2c Shannon, SoM3c Yarenbinsky, GM3c Storms, WT3c Pheiffer, WT2c Soucy, MM1c Owens, BM2c Howk, GM2c Skotko, SoM3c Borgeld and BM1c Gallant (All but Pheiffer stayed with the* Barr *APD39)*

One of the favorite establishments that the crew of the BARR frequented was "Leonardes", a little Italian place by the Tremont Hotel. A fellow there played the piano every night while the crew of the BARR sat around talking, laughing and drinking beer. You could find some of the crew in there every night. They did not have dancing but overhead there was a nice little restaurant where you could get good spaghetti. Not as good as I used to have at home, but very good.

The ship was being converted as rapidly as possible. During the time I found that there was plenty of back work for the yeoman to do in the Ship's Office. So with hammers and riveters blasting away, we yeomen worked on.

Whitman was Chief Yeoman and in charge of the office. Max Glaser, Bill Stein, Michael Flannery and myself were the assistants. Time rolled on by and the BARR was looking more like a ship every day.

On November the third 1944, the BARR got underway from Boston, Mass. enroute to Norfolk, Virginia.

Now, I shall put down a day by day account of my trip from home to Tokyo and back.

Y1c Grenga in Yeoman's office

FLASHBACKS

──────────── *The Shakedown Cruise* ────────────

The Barr at 306 feet long and 39 feet wide amidships hardly gave the appearance of an impregnable floating fortress, but an amazing amount of "gear" had been built into her streamlined hull. Topside were one 5-inch gun, three 3-inch, 50-caliber guns (our "big" artillery), a 1-inch antiaircraft battery, ten 20 Mm AA guns, plus "hedgehogs", depth charges, torpedo tubes, surface and air radar, underwater sound detection devices, fathometer, a mass of radio gear, and the usual bewildering electrical wiring.

Complete with two engine rooms, two fire rooms, turbo-electric drive with twin propellers, somewhat crowded but adequate living quarters, cafeteria-style mess halls, a 26 foot motor whaleboat, and tons of stores and miscellaneous supplies, the Barr was ready for her shakedown cruise.

Eugene L. Swearingen, Ensign
from his journal, "My Ramblings Aboard the Barr, APD39"

*   *   *   *   *

We took her down to Bermuda and tested the ship throughout on the way down there and back. We fired all the guns; we ran the engines at slow and high speeds. The Barr was a sharp ship; she was very clean and everything went well on the shakedown. Everyone enjoyed the trip. I was only 19 years old and on the day she was commissioned I was 20 years old, for my birthday was the 12th of February. Shortly after returning from the shakedown, I was transferred to another ship which I had volunteered for. It was an LST crew forming to go to the Pacific. I was aboard the LST, which we called a "Large Slow Target" for the remainder of the War.

Warren G. Quinn, Seaman

*   *   *   *   *

On our shakedown, we were with another DE near Bermuda and we each fired torpedoes (without warheads and too deep to strike) at each other. We could not track their torpedo and, as the captains were talking, our captain said, "It must have stopped off at the Red Barn" - a lounge the two captains went to near Boston.

John A. Earle, Fire Controlman

We were leaving Bermuda when the bearings of the main turbine were wiped because someone didn't turn up the oil. The Engineering Officer asked who could scrape down the new bearings and no one knew how. I said I did. After the repair job was complete, I guess you could say the Engineering Officer considered me his boy.

Armand J. Marion, Machinist's Mate

— Baptism of Fire —

The ship then proceeded to Norfolk, VA, and we were assigned to an "Anti-submarine" hunter group, consisting of the USS Block Island CVE21, USS Buckley DE51, USS Ahrens DE575, USS Elmore DE686 and the USS Barr DE576. During the next few months of criss-crossing the Atlantic, chasing down sub contacts, and investigating reports of any enemy activity, the Block Island continued her air patrol daily looking for any U-boats. One night the planes caught a U-boat surfaced and the USS Buckley was dispatched to attack. The Buckley found the sub and was forced to ram the sub, disabling it. A close hand to hand battle ensued, and finally the sub was sunk with POW's taken aboard the Buckley.

Andrew C. Soucy, Water Tender,
from his personal diary and album

*   *   *   *   *

We departed Boston on Shakedown Cruise to Bermuda. We were all seasick. I was raised by the water and boats, but seasick became a way of life. We departed Boston for Norfolk, Va. to join TG21.11 with the Block Island and DE-51, 575-576-686. We chased many reports, sub contacts. The Block Island aircraft had sighted a sub and directed the DE-51 to follow up on the sighting. After a long period of tracking her, she surfaced and they exchanged gunfire. After some time they decided to ram her, heaving her on top of the sub. A battle began between the two ships, using everything possible at hand. As luck would have it she backed down off the sub and she wasn't seen again. Upon her return to the Task Force, we could see her bow curled around below the water line as she rode the waves close to our ship. This is the story as we knew at the time.

On the 29th of May we heard two explosions from the Block Island. Little did we know that we were next. We were on the outside of the group as the Block Island lay dead in water without power. The next acoustic torpedo (sound wake in the water) changed course from the Block Island to the Barr, which was under power and took this torpedo into the stern. We lost all the depth charges and men on the K guns at that time. The General Alarm sounded throughout all this time. I always remembered the sound. We transferred to the 686 and slept in the bunks of the crew as they performed their duties and moved on as they changed shifts Port and Starboard to other bunks.

Austin J. Page, Seaman

*   *   *   *   *

I was only on the Barr until it got torpedoed. I had an eye injury and am a lifetime member of the DAV. I was a radioman at the time and was inside all the time. I didn't even see the Block Island go down nor the survivors picked up.

Joseph G. Dalesandry, Radioman

*   *   *   *   *

Normally, I would have been stationed in the evaporator section, after fire room, in the middle of the ship. But at the time of the torpedo hit, we were at general quarters and so I was assigned to the forward repair crew. Because of this, I luckily managed to survive the incident. The day we were torpedoed, James Mack, a friend of mine was transferred to my repair crew from the aft end repair group. Needless to say, the entire aft end repair group was lost when the ship was torpedoed. Because he was with me that day and not in the aft of the ship, Jimmy Mack always referred to me as his "Good Luck Charm". We stayed together throughout the war and returned to be discharged together.

Armand J. Marion, Machinist's Mate

*   *   *   *   *

It was a very unusual day that we lost the Block Island. The ocean was like glass (no waves or anything). The Barr was the lead DE on the Starboard side when we went into flight quarters to land and launch planes. . . . We were always at general quarters during flight quarters. My GQ station was on the Flying Bridge with Captain Love.

The sub fired two more acoustic type torpedoes (attracted by sound) and one hit us astern and the other hit the Block Island astern. When I turned around I saw one of our shipmates, named Bennett and two depth charges about 50 feet in the air. The explosion blew all of our depth charges overboard and since we lost our rudder and propellers, we were dead in the water. We took a real beating from our own depth charges. When the Block Island went down it drifted toward us and their magazines exploded and as far as I could see the ocean seemed to rise up about four feet. If we had abandoned ship, I don't think there would have been any survivors.

Marvin A. Johnston, Electrician's Mate

*   *   *   *   *

Michael Gorchyca and I became friends at the Electrician's Mate School at the Naval Armory in Detroit. Mike never returned from the war because he became one of the missing on that fateful night in May of 1944. Mike's story had effects not only at his parent's home in Philadelphia, but also in Detroit where he left a wife and child. . . . Mike was on the stern that night on the "K" guns. I saw him briefly going to General Quarters, and I know he was sad, because he was worried about what he had left behind. I think often of Mike, knowing that he did not want to be where he was, and that maybe he had become associated with a new life and that the Barr and the Navy were not it.

At the time we set our depth charges, my partner and I moved toward the ready boxes which were between the three-inch gun tub and main deck cabin. That's where we were when the Barr took an acoustic torpedo on the stern. The noise was deafening, and I recall that my whole life unreeled before me. When I came to, I realized I was in the water alongside my partner. When I looked at him his whole face was covered with blood and he lay still. I thought he was dead, so I got up and moved toward the forward section of the ship on the starboard side until I found someone. I found it difficult walking, and my back was very stiff and painful. I climbed the steps toward the stack, and at that moment I heard the noise of our horn and a voice saying to me to go to the ladder to turn the horn off. It was Mr. Dickie, our Exec. I said I couldn't climb a straight ladder because I had pain in my legs and back, and he then proceeded up the ladder to quiet the noisy horn.

Daniel L. DiBono, Electrician's Mate

*   *   *   *   *

I was in the forward engine room when the fish hit. We lost both screws and being a turbo-electric drive I was on the throttle. We got a signal from the bridge to shut down and that's what I did.

Fred A. Carver, Electrician's Mate

When the torpedo hit, I was at my battlestation, which was aft - on the torpedo tubes. I was thrown around some and landed on the deck, but was not injured. A good friend, Brady, who was a gunner's mate was stationed on the aft gun. The impact of the torpedo bent the screws and fantail over on top of him, and he was buried in the debris. My friend, Tom Ellis, was missing in action.

Harold E. MacNeill, Torpedo Man

*   *   *   *   *

At the same time the torpedo hit our ship, the horn was blowing and couldn't be shut off. It was impossible to communicate because of the noise. Our Executive Officer, who was later made Captain, jumped down two decks and climbed up the smokestack to the horn and turned it off by hand. At the same time, there was a valve below deck in a compartment full of oil and water that had to be turned off. One of our Quartermasters, whose station is on the bridge, went down into that compartment and turned off the valve. The next time I saw him he was covered in oil. I recall his name as Armstrong. He received a Commendation Medal for his action as did the Captain at the time.

Erik L. Rosengren, Signalman

*   *   *   *   *

I was on the way to my watch duty. I think it was about a quarter to eight. I left the fantail, climbed up the ladder and the torpedo hit when I was about halfway up the ladder. I looked down and all the fantail was gone. All my clothes were in it; I didn't have a stitch of clothes except what I had on. And all my buddies that were down there - they just went - and we did not find any of them. I finally got up where I relieved the watch by the gun. After we reached the states I got a month's leave. After that, we became an APD and shipped down to the Pacific.

Francis J. Skotko, Gunner's Mate

*   *   *   *   *

My husband [George Sark] did lots of cooking on the ship, for most of the guys were seasick. He never got seasick. They wanted him to go for cook striker but he told them no. He was a fireman; that is what he did.

When they got hit, George said nobody lost their head. They got busy and did what they had to do to keep the ship afloat till help came. The men used blankets & mattresses from their beds to plug up the holes to keep it from sinking. My husband was 3 ft. away & never got hurt. When it hit he was thrown into the air & came down in a sitting position. First thing was plug up the holes & take care of wounded. Some got washed overboard. After they moved them, they went back to see about them & they were gone. Some asked how bad they were hurt. They told them they weren't hurt too bad. Some were hurt badly; they never told them that.

He got a 30-day leave and was sent home. He was put on another ship when he went back.

Wavolene Sark, wife of George P. Sark, Seaman

*   *   *   *   *

When we were torpedoed, I was on a gun just forward of where the damage was done. It was a 1.1 gun. All the debris went flying up over the top of us. A depth charge fell down on the deck right beside one of the fellows who was up about mid-ship. Depth charges are very heavy, and this one missed him by only three or four inches.

Joe Purgatorio, a gunner's mate, was on the depth charge rack. He was called forward to fix a gun just before the torpedo hit. All the men left on the racks were killed when the torpedo hit.

Ned J. Marrow, Seaman

*   *   *   *   *

One of the men aboard the Block Island told me he was about to abandon ship facing the Barr when we were hit by the torpedo; and he could see light under the Barr as it was blown completely out of the water. My memory of that instance in my life, over 55 years ago, is etched in my mind and caused me many sleepless nights. I had just been assigned to the sight control of the three-inch guns on the bridge from the aft sight of the 1.1 gun. As I looked aft as we were hit, I saw one of our crew still strapped to his 20 mm cannon on the starboard side of the ship about 40 feet in the air. I don't know who he was, but perhaps I'll see him again with my Lord.

John A. Earle, Fire Controlman

*   *   *   *   *

On May 29, I had just been relieved of my watch and I remember two loud explosions and GQ immediately sounded. On the way to my battle station, I could hear some of the men saying the Block Island had been hit. I was at my station in the No. 1 repair party when we encountered this loud explosion and the ship lurched violently to one side. We knew then that we had been hit. Many of the men assisted the injured and prepared for abandoning ship. Fortunately, we were able to stay afloat. The very next morning, the injured and the men that were killed were taken aboard the USS Elmore. The men that died were given a burial at sea with military honors by the Captain of the Elmore.

Andrew C. Soucy, Water Tender from his personal diary and album

*   *   *   *   *

I was back on the torpedo rack but I wanted to be on the 3" gun. Another fellow was up on the 3" gun, and we traded places. That was on the day we got torpedoed. He got killed and I didn't. So I always thought the good Lord was looking after me - it wasn't my time. The other guy was from Rocky Mountain, West Virginia. Later a couple of guys and I went to West Virginia and visited his parents. They lived way up on the side of a mountain.

They kept 80 people aboard the ship and I was one of them. They took us into Casablanca, and the rest of the DE's went in for the invasion of Normandy.

Clarence I. Priest, Seaman

Casablanca

And so our first trip finally ended in Casablanca, Morocco. We had time to go on liberty, buy souvenirs and eat. I remember buying a shiny bronze-like ring, which I later discovered to be nothing more than copper tubing. I was sure of the ring's "value" when in a few days it turned green on my finger. I guess this is the way you learn the lessons of life, and for me, it was my time to grow up. All of the souvenirs, the ring included, were never taken home.

Daniel L. DiBono, Electrician's Mate

*   *   *   *   *

We made it to Port Casablanca. We slept on the docks in a large building, receiving new clothes to change into. I believe they were army pants & shoes, soap, toothbrush. That is the time the Dr.'s examined us. Later on three carriers arrived, unloaded their cargo, and loaded on over a thousand men from the Block Island plus the Barr Crew. During this time I met George Page Sark. We were good friends from the Barr. He stayed with the Barr crew to Boston and she was converted to APD. We traveled together to Manitowoc for our second ship.

Austin J. Page, Seaman

In towing the ship to Casablanca, a skeleton crew was maintained to protect the ship. While most of those who stayed were volunteers, I was told by the Engineering Officer to "Step Forward." I guess I didn't have any choice in staying. When I stepped forward, so did Jim Mack. He didn't want to risk losing his "Good Luck Charm." I presume I was asked to stay because of my mechanical skills.

Armand J. Marion, Machinist's Mate

*   *   *   *   *

After being towed to Casablanca, a rudder of sorts was attached. This was steered by hand when needed. A man was stationed at a wheel wearing headphones and received instructions by phone from the bridge. This was necessary to prevent the ship from drifting too far left or right as it was being towed.

While waiting for the ship repair, I befriended a U.S. Sailor who had shore duty at Casablanca. He invited me to dinner at his girlfriend's house who had lived there before the war. When the war started she taught Arabic and English to the French, then to the Germans and to the Americans. She lived on the fifth floor of a six-story apartment house. You had to walk up as there were restrictions on the use of electricity for the elevator. When dinner was served we each had two squabs on our plates plus vegetables. After dinner I said the squab was delicious. The girlfriend said it wasn't squab - it was pigeon. I said where do you buy them - she said I don't, I put some breadcrumbs on my windowsill and when the pigeons come I catch them. Some days later my friend took me to a black market restaurant where we had steak and french fries. I learned several days later that it was camel steak.

Finally the ship was ready to be towed back to the States. I was one of a skeleton crew to stay with the ship. A sea going tug took us in tow. It was a scary trip because we were sitting ducks for any submarine. I don't remember how long it took us to get back. It must have been many weeks, we were going so slow. We were heading for the Boston Navy Yard. When we approached Boston, we were in the middle of a heavy fog. Unfortunately, a commercial fishing boat was heading out to sea at the same time. We were later told that the boat got in between our ship and the tug, and the towline decapitated a fisherman.

Erik L. Rosengren, Signalman

*   *   *   *   *

On my first liberty at a restaurant in Casablanca, I ordered steak and eggs (not on the menu), and the waitress came back and told me the cook did not understand. I asked if I might go to the kitchen and show him. The other three sailors with me laughed; but I went and came back with my steak and an egg sunnyside up in the middle of it. Our next liberty we went back to the restaurant, and on the menu was "Steak and Eggs, American Style."

John A. Earle, Fire Controlman

Back to USA

While enroute to the States we ran into a hurricane on about the 16th day of July and were ordered by Washington to proceed immediately to Bermuda for protection. Here we stayed for five days during which time we spent a liberty in the quaint city of St. George, Bermuda.

Manuel Verissimo, Jr., Water Tender
from his journal, "Manny's Excellent Adventures"

*   *   *   *   *

The Barr had a new transom and rudder welded on in a French dry dock and was ready for sea. With a skeleton crew aboard and being towed by a sea-going tug, we headed for Boston. We rolled and tossed like a fish out of water all the time and once I thought we were going to take water down our stack - no place for a person prone to seasickness. We did a little cleaning up, but mostly played cards to pass time away. I made TM2/c because our Chief torpedo man, Riley, said I made good coffee. A storm was brewing as we neared Boston and to avoid it we were pulled into Bermuda - a little R&R and then to Boston and a 30 day leave.

Harold E. MacNeill, Torpedo Man

*   *   *   *   *

After several weeks of repairs and removal of the damaged stern, she was returned to the United States by the USS Cherokee AT66, a sea-going tug. Enroute we encountered a hurricane in our path and we were diverted to Bermuda to evade the storm. I believe at this point our orders were changed to proceed to Boston, MA instead of Philadelphia, PA. It was there in Boston we were converted to an APD. Little did any of us know what an APD was, but we later found out. A new crew was assigned in Boston, and we were ready for sea duty again.

Andrew C. Soucy, Water Tender   from his personal diary and album

*   *   *   *   *

One of the officers wanted us to paint the places where the ship was chipped, using yellow paint. We couldn't understand - here they were bringing in half a ship, all kinds of wreckage, and we were painting the chipped places yellow. Well, we found out that when we were torpedoed all the paint we had aboard at the time, which might burn, was thrown over the side. So, we didn't have any gray paint. We pulled into New York with the ship all spotted yellow. The officers thought this looked nicer than a rusty old ship.

Clarence I. Priest, Seaman

Regrouping

When we got in to the Navy Yard, I was able to call my fiancee. She was relieved to hear me as she had not received any mail for quite a while. I told her briefly what had happened and that I was getting a thirty-day survivor's leave and also being transferred to Miami, Fla. for additional amphibious training. I said, let's get married, so we did. We had been childhood sweethearts since we were 16.

You couldn't get air passage during the war so I went to Grand Central Station in New York to get a train to Miami for our honeymoon and then report for training after. I then found out that as a serviceman I could not get seats without travel orders for that date. As luck would have it the ticket agent was a woman who had a son in the Navy. She said let me see what I can do. She came back and said I have made a reservation for you and your wife in the name of Admiral & Mrs. Erik Rosengren. In addition I didn't have to pay for the tickets because she used my travel orders. After two months I rejoined the Barr.

Erik L. Rosengren, Signalman

    *   *   *   *   *

Fargo Barracks memories - it was probably home to a majority of Barr APD men for some (or all) portion of their '44 Boston stay. Conveniently located at a South Boston shipyard entrance, it was a multi-story ex-warehouse. Rooms in the BOQ portion were small and clean and the cafeteria excellent. It's always mentioned at reunions and always favorably. We officers even had a neat going away party there - wives, music, dancing, dinner and libations - whole nine yards. Cy Aldinger, enjoying the sociability, regaled my mother, who was visiting at the time, with many Germanic expressions and witticisms.

Philip P. Jones, Lieutenant

German U-550 blown to the surface by a DE depth charge attack
Courtesy of USNI Photo Archives

PART II

REDESIGN AND PREPARATION FOR NEW MISSION

In the summer of 1943 the submarine menace in the Atlantic began to wane as the Allies gained control of the sea-lanes and DE building was curtailed. (Contracts for over three hundred DE's were canceled outright, and naval planners sought other uses for excess DE's already in the fleet.) A number of obsolescent destroyers similar to the ones Roosevelt gave to the royal Navy had been converted to High Speed Transports (APD) for amphibious operations, but more were needed. In excess and easily convertible, the DE was chosen to meet the need.

The purpose of an APD was to ferry an advance scouting party, or an Underwater Demolition Team (UDT), to a landing site before the main amphibious assault in order to reconnoiter the beach and remove obstacles. While the UDT performed its mission, the APD remained nearby to counter any opposition from the shore and to recover the team when they were finished. DE's converted to APD's could carry up to 162 men and all their equipment. Conversion normally took about 69 days, though *Barr's* conversion took longer because the torpedo damage had to be repaired at the same time.

The conversion involved enclosing the main deck amidships to create the troop compartments and adding boat handling davits for four landing craft and a cargo handling derrick with two booms. Antisubmarine armament was removed, except for depth charge tracks on the stern. A single 5" gun replaced the three 3" guns that had been considered adequate for antisubmarine work. The 5" was considered more effective for dueling with shore batteries and opposing air attacks. Further reflecting combat experience in the Pacific, heavy antiaircraft machine guns were installed on every available location topside. Although lacking radar control, the result was a fairly respectable antiaircraft capability that proved useful before the end of the war in the Pacific.

The *Barr* sailed from Boston for the Pacific on November 15, 1944, 169 days after being torpedoed in the Atlantic. The *Barr's* shakedown training had been severely shortened to one week in the Chesapeake Bay. Arriving in Pearl Harbor on December 9, the *Barr* crew trained for a month in Hawaii in their UDT support role and embarked the 98 man UDT #13, her primary weapon during the invasions to come. This crucial process occurred just in time for the ship to sail in company with other units for Ulithi, the staging area for the invasion of Iwo Jima.

Introduction cont'd., Capt. A. Manly Bowen

USS Barr *APD39*

USS Barr *APD39*

When the ship was ready, it was taken out for a shakedown, and I can remember this was my first seagoing experience and I got seasick.

Timothy P.J. Nolan, Electrican's Mate

CHAPTER 2

SHAKEDOWN CRUISE--PREPARATIONS AND TRAINING

Again we practiced boat drills all day. This is all new to me and somewhat very interesting. I am finding that living on a ship is not too bad. The boys are all friendly, maybe more so than boys on a shore station. We know now that someday we will all be in battle together.

November 3, 1944.

At 1500 today we pulled up the anchor. Underway for Norfolk, Va. Sea is calm. We are at Full Speed. The ship is rolling on.

November 4, 1944.

Today finds us steaming from Boston, Mass. to Norfolk, Va. The sea has been calm; so much unlike the stories I have heard of the North Atlantic. Maybe we are not out at sea far enough. This afternoon at 1300, I had my first taste of General Quarters. It was a drill. The captain barked over the loud speaker, "This is a drill, this is a drill, All hands man your Battle Stations."

Our captain is Lt. Cdr. P.T. Dickie and our Executive Officer is Lt. W.H. Gordon. Both seem to be pretty good men, however I am still a little peeved at the X.O. for not letting me go on leave while in Norfolk, but I suppose he knew what he was doing.

We only stayed at G.Q. for about 15 minutes today. It was exciting to see how all the men moved swiftly about the ship getting to their Battle Stations. My Battle Station is on the Flying Bridge. I am a port lookout. I like this position for I am able to see out and to know what is going on. We are out of sight of land. First time I have ever looked out and not seen that. O, there have been times though when I was flying that I was up behind a cloud and couldn't see land. But now, I am in a different outfit. Maybe today I am a sailor.

November 5, 1944.

During the night the ship must have rolled in closer to land, for this morning about eight o'clock, we could see land. At 1000 we were moored starboard side of the BATES at the Conway Escort Pier, Norfolk, Va.

We took on supplies and fuel. Thought that we would get liberty, but this afternoon we got orders to stand by to get underway. Didn't even get off the ship.
November 6, 1944.

0800 - Underway. We are off on shakedown training. The Captain announced that we would take our training up around Cove Point in the Solomon Islands area.
November 7, 1944.

0750 - Anchored in Chesapeake Bay off Solomons, Maryland.

0800 - Had General Quarters Exercises.

During the morning and afternoon we held all kinds of boat drills.
November 8, 1944.

0800 - General Quarters Drill.

Again we practiced boat drills all day. This is all new to me and somewhat very interesting. I am finding that living on a ship is not too bad. The boys are all very friendly, maybe more so than boys on a shore station. We know now that someday we will all be in battle together.
November 9, 1944.

Hold it - Had G.Q. Drill at mid-nite last night. Lowered all boats and practiced some more. This is becoming rather tiresome. We have heard that we were going to be a part of the Amphibious Forces in the Pacific. Can't say that I like this very well. I also heard today that we may have to compose an Underwater Demolition outfit of our Ship's Company. I saw the organization book and it does not look like a job that I would care to have.
November 10, 1944.

0800 - G.Q. Drill again.

This morning we practiced Shore Bombardment. What a noise there was with all the guns opened up. Sounds like we are already on the front lines. We fired on Bloodsworth Island which is the little island all ships practice on.

1700 - Underway for Norfolk, Virginia.
November 11, 1944.

Passed Old Point Comfort Light abeam to starboard.

1200 - Anchored in Norfolk Bay.

Called home this afternoon and was very glad to talk to my mother again. Last time I saw her was around September 2, 1944, and even a couple of months seems like an eternity.

Tried to get a three day pass this afternoon but had no luck. The Captain seems to think that we may have to pull out at any time. Sure hate it, for I would certainly like to see home again before we leave.
November 12, 1944.

Today was spent doing nothing much. We took on supplies and fuel. I am still a little peeved because I am not on my way home - no matter if I would have to turn around as soon as I got there and come back. The Captain said that we would probably pull out on the 15th.

November 13, 1944.

Last night I had liberty. Did not go into Norfolk. Whitman and I went out together. Visited Ocean View, and then we went down to "Tinty Town Club" (a club that I could usually be found when I was stationed at Armed Guard School). Saw many people that I knew and certainly enjoyed seeing them again. Harry, the owner, was still there.

From "Tinty Town" I called out to the Armed Guard School, and found that Al Coury, a good friend, was still there. So, Chief Whitman and I went out and paid our respects. I found out that Chief Cassidy, Morrison and Casey were still there. The Waves had run most of the other ones out. The old place was looking better.

Today went by as usual.

November 14, 1944.

Whitman was transferred this morning. Flannery Y1/c took over the office.

This morning I went over to the Naval Air Station to take a test for the Air Corps; but because I did not have my Service Record with me, they would not give me the test. I did not have the time to go back to the ship and get it in time to take the test. The test started at 0900. The next test, I was informed, would be given on the 16th. I don't think we will be here on the 16th. Darn all the red tape.

This afternoon some Marine Guards brought about 50 men down to the ship. (They were men who had been in the brig, and were being shanghaied out of the States). Now I know that we may not be here long. Something is in the wind.

Y1c Grenga

*The following poem was attached inside Yeoman Grenga's diary with note by him:
"Have never been told, but I think my good friends, Bowman and Stein, drew up this."*

*Dedicated to Jim Grenga,
May his merry P-38 rest in peace*

ME AND MY P-38
*In my merry P-38
I will reach the Golden Gate
Just sit me in the cockpit boys
and I will show you all my poise.*

*You doubt my chances of making it fly
All I can say is, it's a big lie
For with my high powered P-38
I will reach that Golden Gate.*

*The year and time means naught to Jim
Just as long as he can bring her in
There is but one Golden Gate you know
Two to one Jim lands in Tokyo.*

*He's been in pipers and aeronicas too
He's had them all in the sky of blue
But all in all there's none so great
As Jim, the yeoman, in his P38.*

*Now he's flown bombers far and late
He's thumbed his nose at fate
The nips will know him by his rate
Jim, the yeoman, in his P-38.*

FLASHBACKS

I was assigned to the USS Barr DE576 which was being towed to Boston to be converted to an APD39. The crew was berthed in barracks while the work was completed. When the ship was ready it was taken out for a shakedown and I can remember this was my first seagoing experience and I got seasick. A deckhand who had 2 stripes on his uniform which meant 8 years of service said to me "What's the matter? We haven't even lost sight of land yet." This was my beginning adventure aboard the Barr.

Timothy P. J. Nolan, Electrician's Mate

*   *   *   *   *

After about four months at indoctrination schools at Tucson, AZ and Ft. Schuyler, NY, I was sent to amphibious boat training at Fort Pierce, FL. After about four months of it, I was assigned 16 enlisted men to train for boat crews. We were a unit from then on. After they graduated, we all went together to Philadelphia and were there assigned to an AK, USS Allegan, in Baltimore being made ready for service. . . . Finally, we were commissioned and went on shakedown cruise in Chesapeake Bay. It was all very interesting, but the Allegan did not carry landing boats; and as we came into Norfolk at the end of the shakedown, we got a message transferring me and my gang off the ship and we were to proceed at once to Boston. . . . I was assigned to the USS Knudsen, APD 101. The skipper was the only other person there and nobody else had been assigned as the keel had barely been laid and the ship was a few months from completion. He was furious when I showed up - called Washington immediately and started the ball rolling for my next assignment. So, after about a week in Hingham, I was returned to the Fargo Building and assigned to the USS Barr APD39, which was being repaired from torpedoing and converted from DE to APD right there in South Boston Navy Yard real close to the Fargo building. Soon my boat crews also showed up and that's how we started our Barr career. These boat crews were a brave and very capable bunch of guys.

C. Richard Keys, Lieutenant (jg)

Panama Canal locks from aboard the Barr

The canal was a beautiful sight. As we approached it from the Atlantic side, around noon of the 23rd, we came upon the first set of locks after running through a mile or so of narrow channel, shaded on both sides by heavy tropical growths. These first locks brought us up in the air about 100 ft. and out into a beautiful man-made lake. We spent two hours or so in and out of small islands before reaching the second set of locks. These locks brought us down about half the distance we had to go to sea level. Again we passed thru narrow channels, but this time instead of undergrowth, the banks rose abruptly from the water to form gigantic cliffs and even mountains. In this section there were areas that were blasted thru solid rock. Thus we came upon the third and last pair of locks which brought us to the city of Balboa and giant Pacific.

Manuel Verissimo, Water Tender from his journal, "Manny's Excellent Adventures"

CHAPTER 3

PANAMA CANAL--FROM SEASICK TO OLD SALTS

I have always heard about the great "ditch" and now I have passed through it. Truly, it is a great accomplishment of man. There was such pretty scenery all along the "ditch". It was a sight that I shall never forget.

November 15, 1944.

Yes, at 1300 this afternoon we got underway. We are enroute to the Canal Zone. We are in company with the USS TETON (AGC14). This afternoon about 1430, we passed the Old Point Comfort Light abeam to port. It is a strange feeling now to be pulling out. We have known for weeks that we would be leaving - and now here we go.

November 16, 1944.

Enroute Norfolk, Va. to Panama Canal Zone. TETON had a breakdown and put out number "five" flag at 1500. The sea is pretty rough. We are now going down by Cape Hatteras. The ladder as I try to walk up it seems to be going up and down. I have been in many "air pockets". I suppose this is what they call a "sea pocket". Some of the men have been sick today. I did not feel so well. I suppose this is my first taste of "sea duty". We have been hitting swells all day, and it seems as if the ship is rising too far out of the water. You can feel the big waves as they beat against the bow and on the foc's'le [forecastle] each time the ship comes down.

November 17, 1944.

Enroute Norfolk, Va. to Panama. Sea has been rough again today. We had a heck of a time eating today. The trays won't stay on the mess table. What a life!!

This afternoon at 1500, we had a sub contact. Went to G.Q. The first time that the Captain had not said, "This is a drill." We lost contact on the sub and proceeded on. We all remarked tonight, over and over again, "This is not a drill - this is it - all hands man your Battle Stations." This was my first experience at a real G.Q. and I did not like the feeling that I had. But it was rather exciting after all.

The Barr *at sea*

November 18, 1944.

Passed San Salvador abeam to starboard this morning around 1100. This afternoon we had A.A. target balloon practice. The sea is calming down.

November 19, 1944.

The sea is calm now. Weather is getting a little warmer. At 1900 we had another sound contact. Went to G.Q. Negative results. This is beginning to be a pretty exciting trip.

November 20, 1944.

Still enroute from Norfolk, Va. to Panama. Had a lot of trouble today from TETON about maintaining our position. They are in charge. Already, I would like to be on land again. However, I am not finding the sea too hard to take.

November 21, 1944.

0650 - Land Ho!!

1022 - Anchored in Manganili Bay. Took on board a "pilot" this morning. This afternoon we pulled in and tied up alongside a coaling dock, at Telfers Island, Panama, C.Z. Received fuel and fresh water. Set ship's clocks back one hour.

November 22, 1944.

0800 - Had liberty last night. Went over to Colon with a bunch of boys. We spent most of the liberty eating, looking around and having a beer every once in a while. Very strange, and yet interesting country. The people here, though, act like savages. But I suppose we have left America (the U.S.A.), and I don't suppose any country is like the U.S.A. Obtained some post cards last night and sent out a few. Don't know whether they will go through or not. Hope they do. Most amusing thing was to see how the people acted. Also the buildings were strangely built.

1100 - We got underway at 1000 and are now proceeding through Lemon Bay preparing to enter the locks.

1600 - We entered Gatun lock at 1226. Lines were thrown over the side and little pulley cars on either side of us pulled the ship through the lock.

1800 - At 1619 we entered Pedro Miguel lock. At 1708 we entered Miraflores

Lashing down the anchor in Panama

Liberty boat about to shove off from the Barr

lock. Now we are entering Balboa Harbor. And we are now full speed ahead for Frisco.

Today has been a very interesting one for me. I have always heard about the great "ditch" and now I have passed through it. Truly, it is a great accomplishment of man. There was such pretty scenery all along the "ditch". It was a sight that I shall never forget. The locks were not very wide. I'll bet that larger ships have a time getting through them. They have a good system though, and I don't think that they have too much trouble.

November 23, 1944.

Enroute to San Francisco. At 1300 we went to G.Q. Just a drill. We had all kinds of drills including Fire Drill, Abandon Ship Drill, Emergency Destruction Drill, etc. The TETON had another breakdown. The BARR is sailing right along, no trouble at all. At 1700 the ship's clock was set back one hour.

November 24, 1944.

Sailing right on along, enroute to Frisco. We are all hoping that we will get liberty in Frisco. The Captain doesn't think we will be there long. O, well we joined the Navy to see the world - off the fantail.

Sailors on the Barr *fantail (movie screen in background)*

November 25, 1944.

Refueled at sea today from TETON. It is a sight to watch how they do this job. At 1400 we exercised at G.Q. And this afternoon we had a movie in the mess hall. This was a treat which we all enjoyed.

November 26, 1944.

Enroute Canal Zone to Frisco. Fired small arms from fantail this morning. Sea is calm.

November 27, 1944.

This morning we had G.Q. Exercises. Tested our gas masks. I am on watch in After-Steering. Standing four on and eight off. This is called "War Cruising Watch." Stein is also on watch. Max has taken over the "Log Room"; so there is only Flannery left to run the office. Seems like we are getting ready for war conditions. Well, I suppose that is what we are out here for.

November 28, 1944.

This morning we went off our course to investigate a life raft that was reported off our starboard bow. No one was in it, but there were some birds perched on it. At first we thought they were men. We had G.Q. drill again this afternoon. Still enroute for San Francisco.

November 29, 1944.

At 1000 we exercised at G.Q. Had A.A. target firing at balloons. Day passed off slowly. We are all anxious to see land again and are hoping that we will have liberty in Frisco.

November 30, 1944.

The sea has been a little choppy today, but not too rough. After coming down by Cape Hatteras we feel that we are "old salts", and can take anything. Around noon today we sighted San Nicola's Island. Also saw an aircraft carrier and three destroyers. Sighted San Miguel Island this afternoon.

FLASHBACKS

I *was assigned to Big Diamond, an island off Casco Bay in Maine. (There are 365 islands in Casco Bay.) We were to ship out on the USS Hale, a destroyer. As it turned out, the Hale had enough personnel, thank you. So I went back to the island to await orders. From there I was transferred to Long Island, a whole half mile from Big Diamond.*

I worked in the Navy ship stores before being transferred to the USS Barr. We went to pick up the Barr at Pennsylvania. We stayed there two months but the ship was ordered to Boston to be converted as APD. Out at sea, we encountered an electrical storm at Cape Hatteras and all hands got seasick.

Norman LeMere, Machinist's Mate

> *   *   *   *   *

November 17 This poor account has suffered from neglect and I shame to write it. I have been seasick!!! Here when I thought the days of the perpetual bucket chain from fireroom to head were finally over, I find that I'm wrong - Oh, so very wrong. Just the second day out of Norfolk, hardly out of sight of land, when that old feeling started again. I do have an excuse tho, it was terribly rough. The roughest I have ever seen it - everyone was sick, including officers. Some of the boys on the bridge watch reported rolls to be as much as 32 degrees at times - you couldn't prove it by me tho - sometimes they seemed like 70 degrees or 80 degrees. Today, however, the 17th of Nov. everything is fine. The sun is shining, the sea is calm, and Manny is again at peace with the world.

Manuel Verissimo, Water Tender
from his journal, "Manny's Excellent Adventures"

Sailors in control room

The first day out of Norfolk, we ran into swells off Cape Hatteras. By night-fall we had three-fourths of the ship company and all the passengers feeding the fishes. Jim McEwen and I ate breakfast the next morning, but the others were not so inclined. . . . It is times like this when you realize that you should have joined the army. Just when we were ready to give up the Navy as a career, we hit the tropical waters and good weather.

We stopped at Colon before passing through the canal, and while the men went on liberty, I contacted a dealer and purchased $3,000 worth of perfume, silk stockings, and ladies' purses for sale in the ship's store. The articles made wonderful Christmas presents.

Eugene L Swearingen, Ensign
from his journal, "My Ramblings Aboard the Barr, APD39"

*   *   *   *   *

Today is a day I shall long remember. It would be impossible for anyone to pass through the Panama Canal, or to spend a night in Colon without having some very vivid memories for a long time. Yesterday, the 22nd, we approached the Panama Canal from the Atlantic side and docked just inside the submarine nets to refuel and wait our turn for passage. It was necessary to stay there all night. This was a welcome decision for us of the crew, for this meant a liberty in a foreign port.

I wish I knew how to write about Colon. There were so many strange and interesting things to see, that it is hard to get your impression down on paper. The houses reminded me very much of the ones in Bermuda. They were made of stucco and painted various pastel colors, but the roofs were black, or occasionally dark red.

Manuel Verissimo, Water Tender
from his journal, "Manny's Excellent Adventures"

Next stop was San Francisco - we sailed down thru the Panama Canal up to San Diego and then San Francisco, and I vividly remember as we sailed off to war in the Pacific, going under the Bridge, I was on deck waving goodbye to a group of girls on the bridge waving to us.

We arrived in beautiful Hawaii around Christmas time and enjoyed gorgeous weather quite different from the snow and cold weather I was accustomed to at this time of year in NY.

Timothy P. J. Nolan, Electrician's Mate

"Lt. Murray in Full Dress" at UDT Base

CHAPTER 4

FRISCO AND HAWAII

I had a strange feeling this afternoon when we passed under the 'Golden Gate'. I was standing out on the Boat Deck and I watched the Gate fade away on the horizon. Somehow, it seems that we are now leaving everything. But duty calls - and there is a war to be won.

December 1, 1944.

At 1000 this morning we sighted San Francisco. Sure was great to see her. From a distance out we could see the "Golden Gate", which I have always heard so much about.

1218 - We are under the "Golden Gate". How pretty she looks. Such a great bridge.

1252 - We are passing under Oakland Bridge. This is another beautiful bridge. We are now proceeding on in to San Francisco.

At 1640 we tied up to Pier 54, San Francisco. The Captain has just announced Liberty - so off I go.

December 2, 1944.

0900 - Last night I had Liberty. Got in Frisco about 1800. The first thing that I did was to put in a call for home. I, after waiting for a couple hours, finally got a call through. I was so happy to talk with my mother again. I also talked to my little baby sis, which I also enjoyed very much. Yes, I am a long way off now. And someday, soon, I will be farther.

I enjoyed the liberty in Frisco last night. I think it is a wonderful city.

1600 - Today has been quiet. Did a little work in the office. Now, I am off for liberty again.

December 3, 1944.

0900 - Enjoyed liberty again last night. We went down to China Town, and it seemed strange - like I was already in a new land.

1258 - Underway from Pier 54.

1320 - Passed under Oakland Bridge.

1350 - Passed under "Golden Gate". Underway for Pearl Harbor, in company with the CECIL.

I had a strange feeling this afternoon when we passed under the "Golden Gate". I was standing out on the Boat Deck and I watched the "Gate" fade away on the horizon. Somehow, it seems that we are now leaving everything. But duty calls - and there is a war to be won.

December 4,1944.

Enroute San Francisco to Pearl Harbor. We had A.A. Firing Practice this morning. We really seem to be getting ready to win this war. The sea is very calm. Have always heard that the Pacific was calm - and so it seems.

USS Barr *APD39 at sea*

December 5, 1944.

Only 20 more shopping days till Christmas. Wonder where we will be on that day. We are going the other way from Georgia as fast as we can go. Had A.A. Firing Practice today. Our ship knocked down eight balloons. About twenty were sent up. I wish that I was on one of the guns but the Captain seems to want me up here on the Bridge as a "lookout."

December 6, 1944.

This morning we set the ship's clock back one-half an hour. We are still losing time. But still going away from the States - so time doesn't matter much. The sea is still very calm.

December 7,1944.

Set the ship's clock back another half hour this morning. Had G.Q. drill this afternoon and fired all guns. What a racket.

December 8, 1944.

G.Q. again this morning and more firing. I suppose we have to get in good shape. Maybe we will have the real stuff soon. They didn't seem to lose much time in getting us out here after the ship was converted.

December 9, 1944.

Passed a formation of about 20 ships this morning. Glad to see that some other units of the Navy are out here with us in this big ocean. Had some more firing practice this morning.

1245 - Tied alongside BLESSMAN (APD 48) in Pearl Harbor, Oahu, T.H.

Such a large harbor this is, and very pretty too. You would never know that there had been such a day as December 7, 1941 here. And there are more ships here than I have seen.

December 10, 1944.

Had liberty this afternoon. Went into Honolulu with a bunch of the boys. Saw a hula show and walked around a little. We didn't get into town until about two and had to start back for the ship around 1600. Had to wait in line a long time for a bus. One of the most amusing things was to see how the boys gather around the little photo shops to have their pictures made with a Hula girl. Didn't have my picture made today. Probably will next time we come in.

The following poem, author unknown, attached inside Yeoman Grenga's diary:

A SAILOR'S COMPLAINT

Why do people glower and sneer
Whenever we go ashore?
The girls all turn away in fear
Or does our presence bore?
Before I donned this uniform
To join the U.S.N.
I never failed to find a date;
The girls all liked me then.
But now they turn away in haste
Whenever I come their way.
Their answer always sounds the same;
"I just can't go today."
"I'd like to Bill, I really would,
But mom would have a fit.
If you but had civilian clothes

A Sailor's Complaint cont'd

She wouldn't mind a bit."
Why can't I wear my uniform?
Why do the folks deride?
For when I wear civilian clothes
I'm still the same inside.
The saying goes - or so I'm told
That clothes will make the man.
But they can't change the man beneath
Yet some folks think they can.
I'm proud to wear the Navy Blue;
Why should I be ashamed?
Because one fellow raises hell,
Why should we all be blamed?
Mothers say that folks will talk
If her girl is seen with you.
One thing these mothers all forget....
That we have mothers too...
We're human beings just like the rest,
Not monsters from the sea.
Because one sailor went astray
Why take it out on me?
Civilians go astray you know;
And is it not the same,
Although he's not in uniform
And no one knows his name.
But comes a war, a boy is killed
How do the folks all stand?
How brave and fine a lad he was;
A credit to our land.
Folks just don't understand, I guess
That we have feelings too.
Or else they wouldn't glare and sneer
At the boys in Navy Blue.

*Lt. Kaiser, Ens. Swearingen,
Ens.Hubenthal and Lt. McKinlay
at Waikiki*

*SM1c Rosengren and other sailors
in Hawaii*

December 11, 1944.

What's this. We got underway this a.m. and now we are anchored in Maalae Bay, Maui, Hawaiian Islands. We have been informed that we are here for Underwater Demolition Training. This is what we have been afraid would happen to us - and now here we are.

FLASHBACKS

Pearl Harbor was gigantic. Ships and more ships as far as the eye could see. It was my first real evidence of our great sea and air power. Planes took off and landed at intervals of approximately three a minute. After three days we started out for Maui, but not before making a liberty on the island of Oahu, on which are located Honolulu and Waikiki. Honolulu was a disappointment, but Waikiki lived up to the reputation of a beautiful summer resort on a south sea island. . . .

Then, too, there are the rainbows. One can be seen almost every day - sometimes double - sometimes triple. . . .

The Royal Hawaiian Hotel was beyond my fondest dreams. Once it was probably one of the most exclusive spots on the globe. But for the duration it has been turned over to the Navy as a rest camp for the submarine men. The hotel itself is beautiful beyond description - its large irregular shape, and painted light pink. (It sounds like an awful color, but as the saying goes - on you it looks good.) However, it was the surrounding grounds that left its biggest impression on me. Tall palm trees, shaded tropical gardens. Gardens such as only Hawaii can grow.

Manuel Verissimo, Water Tender
from his journal, "Manny's Excellent Adventures"

*   *   *   *   *

I left the states on November 27, 1944, my 20th birthday, bound for Pearl Harbor. As I recall, I arrived around the 3rd or 4th of December, just about the time the Barr was arriving on her long trip from Boston.

The next few days were spent awaiting assignment to some kind of vessel. I believed I would get some kind of landing craft, because that seemed to be what most newly commissioned officers were getting. You can imagine how happy I was when the assigning officer gave me the Barr, a destroyer type vessel, my first choice on my preference list. To this day, I believe I got the ship because of my Irish name. The assigning officer being a big burly Irishman. My orders were to report to the USS Barr anchored off the West side of the island of Maui. I believe I reported aboard the ship on the 13th of December 1944. I completed the roster of thirteen officers assigned to the Barr. The youngest and least senior to all. Not an enviable position, because I got the duties and assignments no one else wanted. I knew this to be true on all ships of the Navy, so I accepted it as being normal.

It wasn't too long after reporting aboard ship that things seemed normal and routine. In addition to being the youngest officer on ship, I was definitely the most skinny, not only of the officers, but of all the enlisted men too. I was known to my fellow officers as the "Thin Man", a name I didn't relish. Also a name the enlisted men must have known to be correct. So, when our supply officer, Gene Swearingen, suggested he could fatten me up by feeding me peanuts, I was more than happy to try. I believe I ate every last peanut aboard ship, but I didn't gain one solitary pound. I still remained the "Thin Man," and couldn't eat or want to eat a peanut for months.

John J. Reilly, Ensign

*   *   *   *   *

To make a little extra cash aboard ship, I handled the laundry for our department. Each week we sent our clothes to the laundry and it would come back to the department. I would separate it and put it on each of the bunks. I got a dollar extra a month from each one of the sailors for doing this. So that helped me out a little.

Talmadge F. Grubbs, Seaman

Pier at UDT base in Maui

We spent about a month training with our new underwater swimmers off Maui. After learning how they worked, I decided they were all crazy. We carried four LCVP landing craft, and each landing craft carried six swimmers. Each swimmer carried packages of tetrytol explosives and a reel of fuse wire. The four boats would spread out along the reef line and then turn and proceed to the reef. When they arrived, they would turn and travel along the line of the reef. Six times they would drop swimmers. Each swimmer would then plant an explosive charge, connect a fuse line to it and swim to the adjacent swimmer's point of discharge, planting explosive charges along the way.

At the end of his sector, he would connect his fuse line to his neighboring swimmer's first charge, so there was one long connected set of explosives. The full reef line of explosives was then set on a timed fuse; the boats would turn around and go as fast as they could move down the line of swimmers, picking them up as they went. The system involved a rubber boat tied to the side of the LCVP, and a life ring on about a six foot line.

As the boat reached a swimmer, he would be thrown the life ring; as they moved to the next swimmer, the first one would climb into the boat and then throw the ring to the second swimmer. The timed fuse was set so that the entire reef would blow up, just as the boats turned away. The explosion would then cover their retreat to the Barr. It was very spectacular, and very scary since anyone in the water when the explosion took place would probably be killed or seriously injured. Timing and execution were obviously very important.

John W. Hubenthal, Lieutenant (jg) from his autobiography

CHAPTER 5

U.D.T. TRAINING

Today we practiced with the demo's. They seem to be getting plenty of practice, and fast, too. And it is about to wear Ship's Company out to keep up with them. These swimmers sure can swim a long way. They practically stay in the water all the time.

December 12, 1944.

Anchored in Maalae Bay, Maui, T.H. off the Naval Demolition Base. Loaded aboard ten tons of Demolition Explosives this morning. Also took on board U.D.T. #16. The fellows seem all right, but we did not like to see them bring on board all that explosives.

December 13, 1944.

At 0005 this morning we got underway for training purposes. This morning the team went in and practiced reconnaissance; and this afternoon they set off the charge. What an explosion that made. Wonder what it would have been like if it had went off on board ship. Let's not talk about that! I don't suppose we would have known much about it.

December 14, 1944.

We had liberty today and I went in to the town of Waluka with a bunch of boys. There wasn't much to do. I played pool most of the afternoon. We did have a very good meal in town. It is a treat to eat off the ship once in a while.

December 15,1944.

Not much today. I stayed on board. Wrote letters and did a little work around the office.

December 16, 1944.

Underway at 0800 this morning. Stayed at G.Q. practically all day. This afternoon we fired the main battery at a beachhead. The BARR, GREGORY (DD802) and L.C.I. 1024 made simulated beach bombardment all afternoon. At 1700, we anchored in Maalae Bay and U.D.T. #16 disembarked. We had a movie on the fantail tonight. Enjoyed it very much, after such a day.

December 17, 1944.

This morning some small boats came alongside and took off all the explosives. Very glad to get rid of that. Wrote letters this afternoon.

December 18, 1944.

Last night at 2300 we got underway enroute to Pearl Harbor.

0800 - Moored portside to WATERS (APD 8).

This afternoon we had mail on board. First since we left the states, and it was so nice to have. Even though we are a long way from home, it seems closer when we get mail.

December 19, 1944.

Today we had liberty. It commenced at 1200. We had to be back on board by 1930. We went into Honolulu and then on out to a Beach. It was a beautiful place. I also visited the Royal Hawaiian Hotel which is about as pretty as any place you could find anywhere.

December 20, 1944.

This morning I went over to the Naval Air Station on Ford Island where I took a physical examination and flight aptitude test for the Naval Air Corps. I passed the physical 4.0 and made two (B's) on two of the aptitude tests and a (C) on the other. I am very happy over this for maybe someday soon I can go and do what I have always wanted to do. When I came into the Navy, I thought sure that I would get the Air Corps but something went wrong. Ford Island was certainly a pretty place and we have a very nice Air Station set up there.

December 21, 1944.

This morning I had liberty and I went over to Hickam Field. This sure is a large Army Air Base now. And I'll bet that the Japs would not care to attack it again. It took me practically all morning to walk around the place. I have never seen a place so well fortified. Hickam Field is just off the Fleet Landing Dock at Pearl Harbor.

December 22, 1944.

It is beginning to look as if we will be here for Christmas. The Captain seems to think so. Well, I suppose it is better to be here than out at sea. Hope we are.

Last night we had a scare. We received word over radio to Darken Ship. They expected an uprising of the Jap civilians on Hawaii. We were having a nice movie on the fantail at the time. Made us pretty angry.

Today we heard that nothing ever became of the rumor. Gosh, but it was a good little scare at first. Here we were thinking that enemy action was a long way off.

Today in town, I bought some scarves. Sent one to Mother, one to Louise and one to Helen; and one to Kay. Also sent mother a dinner tablecloth set.

December 23, 1944.

This morning I went over with a party to the firing range. Shot a .50 cal. machine gun, a .30 cal. rifle and a .45 cal. pistol. I have always liked to shoot a gun, and I enjoyed this morning very much.

Movie screen on the USS Barr *fantail.*

December 24, 1944.

This morning we took on ammunition. They even got me in on the working party. I am still trying to figure out how they did this to me. I am very tired tonight.

Well, tomorrow is Christmas Day. The Captain has planned a big party for us on the fantail. Not like last Christmas, but maybe it won't be so bad. At least, the Captain is trying to make it as nice as possible.

December 25, 1944.

Today is Christmas Day. I wonder how it found all the folks back home. Fine, I hope.

And today we had mail again. Such a nice Christmas present. I received ten letters and was so glad to get them.

Tonight we had a wonderful party on the fantail. Everything that we wanted to eat. The officers of the Ship served as Mess Cooks. The Captain passed out the cookies. This is a night I will never forget. Next best thing to being home.

December 26, 1944.

Today, I went on liberty again. Back to Honolulu. Went to see a Hula Dance this A.M., and to a carnival this afternoon. Had a very nice time today.

December 27, 1944.

Went over to the firing range today. Fired the guns again. Would like to do this more often. But if things are like they say they are out further in the Pacific, I should get more practice than I want soon. Maybe they will put me on a gun when we get out in action. Rather hope so.

Had a movie on the fantail tonight . This is an every night pleasure of which I do not know how we would do without.

Mail for me again today. That is nice.

December 28, 1944.

This morning I went over to ComAdComPhibPac office with the Executive Officer on business. Spent all morning sitting around and taking down notes and references.

This afternoon at 1700 we got underway for Maalae Bay, Maui, T.H. with USS GILMER (APD 11) for more U.D.T. Training.

December 29, 1944.

At 0830 we anchored in Maalae Bay. At 1630 boats came alongside and discharged U.D.T. #13. More demo's - as we called them. Wonder how long we will have this team. It seems that our job may be to train the boys.

UDT 13 field trip; Gardner looking to side.

December 30, 1944.

Today, we just layed around at anchor. Thought there would be liberty - but no such stuff. Had a movie tonight.

December 31, 1944.

This morning we had liberty. We got over to the Fleet Landing just ten minutes after nine. The bus left at nine, so we had to get in town the best way we could. Thought we would never get a ride, but we finally did. Played some pool this afternoon and had a very enjoyable afternoon.

<u>January 1, 1945.</u>

Here goes another year. And I am still in the Navy. I enlisted February 18, 1942.

At 0800 we got underway for more training. At 0930 we exercised at G.Q.

This afternoon we went to G.Q. right after lunch and stayed until about 1600. The U.D.T.'s went in to the beach for a simulated underwater demolition operation. At 1630 there was a big explosion on the beach. My, what an explosion. Seems like they were trying to blow the whole beach out of the water.

Horned scullies

Horned beach mine

January 2, 1945.

Today was the same as yesterday. Another hard day at G.Q. Know that I will enjoy the movie tonight.

January 3, 1945.

Today, we practiced again with the Demo's. They seem to be getting plenty of practice, and fast too. And it is about to wear Ship's Company out to keep up with them. These swimmers sure can swim a long way. They practically stay in the water all the time.

January 4, 1945.

At 0900 this morning we anchored in Maalae Bay, Maui, T.H. At 1000, U.D.T. #13 started disembarking from the ship. At 1300 this afternoon U.D.T. #19 started coming on board. I see that we will have the same thing to go over again.

January 5, 1945.

We were ready to get underway this morning when we received orders to stand by. What happens now. At 0830 U.D.T. #19 started disembarking. Well, we thought, maybe we will get out of this trip. But then at 1600 this afternoon, here comes U.D.T. #13 back on board ship.

January 6, 1945.

Today, we have just been laying around at anchor. I suppose we are awaiting orders. We will have a movie tonight, so off I go.

January 7, 1945.

0800 - At 0130 this morning we got underway. We are headed for Pearl Harbor. Something is up and we all seem to know it. The Captain announced a little while ago that we would keep U.D.T. 13 on board. And that we would soon, in a matter of days, be heading out across the Pacific. We all seemed to like this team, but at noon when we docked beside LST812 - in Pearl Harbor and started taking on eighty tons of explosives - well, we wished that we had never seen them. Tonight, the talk is about what would happen to us if all that explosives should go off. We don't seem to like to think about that.

This afternoon we also took on supplies and re-fueled. And now we are going to the movies and try to forget about sitting on eighty tons of explosives.

January 8, 1945.

Had liberty today. Went into Honolulu. Seems like all we wanted to do was sit down and drink beer. And I must have got a little silly for I went in and had my picture made with a Hula girl just as big as you please.

January 9, 1945.

Not much today. We took on more supplies, and are standing by now with U.D.T. #13 on board, waiting for orders. Will have a movie tonight so off I go.

UDT 13: 1st row-Hamman, Robinson, Gardner, Harlan, Gleason, Moranz, Walker, Smith, Allen, Long, Cleveland, Hehli, Murray; 2nd row-McIntire, Behrendt, Hoffman, Cusimano, Morrow, Broome, Stone, Tuttle, Grimes, Foreman, Carlson, Emerson, Whelan; 3rd row-VanWagenen, Taylor, Baker, Reimer, Patton, Taylor, U/I, First, Robinson; 4th row-Cooper, Bier, Deringer, Lynch, LaZarr, Blackwell, Shoemaker, Barrett, Butler, Prince, Brummet, Mattson, Musick, A.N. King; 5th row-Wilkinson, U/I, U/I, R. King, Flathers, U/I, McCaw, Rudy, R. Miller, Frey, Crowder, Toy; 6th row-Cline, Ward, Phelan, Taraborelli, Allen, U/I, Bracken, W. Miller, Delgrosso, Rush, U/I, McElwee, Dollinger, Kinsaul. U/I-unidentified.

FLASHBACKS

We (593rd Joint Assault Signal Corps, made up of about 500 Navy radiomen, Navy signalmen, Army radiomen and Marine advisors) trained to go ashore with the Marines on the second wave when making amphibious landings, and set up communication with ships. And guess what! The outfit was busted up a couple of weeks after being sent to Pearl Harbor. Evidently the UDT had been chosen to perform in the landings in place of us. And a wise choice, too. Served with the Radio Maintenance Unit at Pearl until Christmas Day, 1944; then - The BARR! I remember well the Officers serving that great meal!

Guy E. Farley, Radioman

*   *   *   *   *

After thoroughly stuffing ourselves, we gathered around a Christmas tree someone had gotten from someplace (it was decorated too, with colored lights, tinsel, and a little cotton) and sang carols. Some of the boys more talented than the rest did a few numbers on their own. One played the accordion, two the harmonica, and three or four sang. Of course, before the evening was over, most of the officers were brought forth to do their stuff. A few sang, but most could do nothing more than play the sweet potato (they make better officers than sweet potato players.) Anyway, it was lots of fun and helped to bring Christmas a little closer than it would have been otherwise.

Manuel Verissimo, Water Tender
from his journal, "Manny's Excellent Adventures"

*   *   *   *   *

I was transferred from the Naval Base on Caswell Beach at Southport to Solomon's Island, MD. They were making up crews there, and one day someone requested volunteers for hazardous duties overseas. That is how I ended up at Fort Pierce for UDT training. I became part of a group known as "Moore's Hellers". Ensign Moore was our Executive Officer until he left and was replaced by Don Walker. Our training was on Hutchinson Island, which consisted of North and South Islands. We lived on South Island and practiced blowing up everything we could (in and out of water) on North Island. The ones that couldn't make it through Hell Week were transferred out of the teams.

George Gregory, Motor Machinist, UDT 13

The first thing that we did not like about carrying UDT's was the fact that their work was to be done prior to the invasion. We were to take them within 2,000 yards of the beach and "cover" them with our one five-inch gun!

Eugene L. Swearingen, Ensign
from his journal, My Ramblings Aboard the Barr, APD39"

*   *   *   *   *

We bought a few things on the island (Maui), swam in the most beautiful water and coral that I had ever seen, and fished. I caught a large fish about 30 pounds, which we believed to be tuna.

Eugene L. Swearingen, Ensign
from his journal, "My Ramblings Aboard the Barr, APD39"

*   *   *   *   *

During training operations at Maui, I was on the Bates temporarily, when a launch pulled alongside with an admiral and a civilian who requested permission to come aboard. When they did so, I heard my name called and came forward. The civilian was Lowell Thomas, not only a famous war correspondent, but a friend of my family as long as I could remember. He heard I was in the area and asked if he could visit me. Needless to say, my emotions were mixed. I was overjoyed, but terribly embarrassed. We had a nice visit and he and the admiral left. The ship's captain remarked, somewhat testily, "Magee, if you're expecting visitors, please let me know in advance." I mumbled something, saluted, and escaped, hopefully back into anonymity.

Arthur W. Magee, Signalman, UDT13

*   *   *   *   *

The first time I heard about the USS Barr was during the final days of December, 1944. Team 13 was notified to prepare their sea bags because they would be boarding an APD the following morning.

This event is dramatized in my mind because of the events that occurred that last evening ashore on Maui. We lived in tents in an area that was appropriately called the "dust bowl." To the north were a couple of smelly outdoor toilets. To the south were several outdoor showers. It was common practice for a demo when wanting to shower to throw a towel over his shoulder and take a stark naked stroll to the shower area.

That particular evening it was reported that some ships in the area had picked up sonar evidence of a Japanese submarine. This resulted in the Hawaiian Islands being put on an enemy alert. A friend of mine started jogging to take a shower, but a "buddy" of his seeing an opportunity for a big joke, picked up a flare gun and shot my friend right in his exposed rear area. This was very painful and resulted in some minor burns. My friend went on to the showers, but to himself vowed revenge.

After his shower, my friend returned to the tent area, found the same gun and pointed it at his "buddy." He fired, but the flare went skyward. Since we were on enemy alert, in no time at all, guards and the shore patrol were on the scene and my friend was arrested.

When we boarded the Barr the following morning, my friend was in the base brig. Commander Moranz, knowing he would need all his swimmers in the western Pacific, had my friend brought aboard the Barr before sailing. He was demoted one grade, but three weeks later Moranz reinstated his rating.

Marvin Cooper, Gunner's Mate, UDT 13

*   *   *   *   *

 *Prior to becoming Executive Officer of UDT #13, my exposure to APD's involved temporary duty aboard three old WWI four-stackers that had been converted to carry assault troops in Alaskan waters before being assigned to the South Pacific. Compared to those ships, the USS Barr was a luxury liner. My experiences aboard the Barr were the most rewarding and memorable.*

While at Maui, there was advanced training for the invasions of Iwo Jima and Okinawa. At this time we had the good fortune of being assigned to the USS Barr, APD 39!!

Donald M. Walker, Lieutenant (jg), UDT 13

*   *   *   *   *

When the Underwater Demolition Teams arrived aboard the Barr, we became familiar with what their jobs would be. We learned that the men were to swim into the unmarked beaches and, under darkness, to plant explosives under any obstacles that would hinder the landing craft. Also, they were to visually map the layout of the beach area.

While we were undergoing training exercises with the UDT men, we had time to spend many days on the beach area at Maui.

Andrew C. Soucy, Water Tender
from his personal diary and album

PART III

BATTLES OF THE USS *BARR* APD39

The *Barr* sailed on January 10, 1945, as part of an amphibious task force bound for the advance base at Ulithi Atoll (western Caroline Islands) and from there supported UDT #13 in the invasions of Iwo Jima and Okinawa. Iwo Jima was chosen for capture because Japanese aircraft based there interfered with B-29 attacks on the Japanese home islands from their bases in the Mariana Islands. In American hands Iwo Jima would be a useful air base for attacks on Okinawa, the island chosen as the staging base for the assault on Japan itself.

The invasion of Okinawa was qualitatively different from the assault on Iwo Jima. Iwo Jima is a small island four and one half miles long and about two miles wide at its greatest width. The force assigned to capture it, three Marine Divisions, was sizable, but not nearly the size of the forces gathered for the invasion of Okinawa which is sixty miles long, 18 miles wide at its widest point, and was populated by half a million people. The force assembled for Okinawa exceeded in manpower and tonnage the force assembled for the invasion of Normandy.

Sea battles incident to the invasion of the Philippines, which preceded the assaults on Iwo Jima and Okinawa, had all but eliminated the Japanese Navy's ability to oppose US seapower. Instead, their leaders decided to employ land-based airpower to oppose US assaults. The Japanese training system, however, had been unable to keep up with the loss of the well-trained and highly effective pilots who had been such a threat to US ships at the start of the war. Pilots completing training in 1944 were barely capable of flying safely, let alone conducting successful attacks on ships in the face of intense antiaircraft fire.

The measure chosen to make up for this lack of skill was the suicide attack, the dreaded "Kamikaze" or "Divine Wind". Sworn to the glory of dying for his country, the pilot crashed his bomb-laden aircraft into his target ship. US sea forces experienced the first of these attacks in the Philippines. More occurred during the Iwo Jima assault. The full force of this Divine Wind blew at Okinawa as the Japanese became more and more desperate.

The US response to this development called for stationing air defense "pickets" in the path predicted for incoming attacks to extend radar warning coverage and to break up attacking groups by gunfire. The intensity of kamikaze attacks soon placed a premium on small ships for the picket lines.

After UDT #13 completed pre-invasion activities at Okinawa, the *Barr* was ordered to offload their UDT shipmates to a regular transport. Then she, along with other APD's that had transferred their UDT's, was assigned to picket duty for the remainder of the fighting for Okinawa. Occasionally the *Barr* was relieved of that duty to convoy escort assignments.

Introduction cont'd., Capt. A. Manly Bowen

Funeral of Ray LeBlanc, UDT13

I lost a very dear friend, Ray LeBlanc, with whom I trained at Fort Pierce and worked with thru UDT Able. Ray was a welder by trade and had volunteered to help build additional gun mounts. While welding a mount, a wave from a passing ship splashed upon him and his equipment, resulting in his death. Services were held on the Barr with burial on the beach at Ulithi (a very sad experience).

Donald M. Walker, Lieutenant (jg), UDT 13

While we were at Ulithi, one of the UDT men went over the side to do some welding. While watching him doing the welding, I saw a wave come up and short his electrode and I noticed that he was going to be electrocuted. I jumped overboard to try to save him, but was unable to reach him before he was electrocuted.

Armand J. Marion, Machinist Mate

CHAPTER 6

ANCHORS AWEIGH

This is it! This morning at 0700 we pulled up anchor and are underway. . . . The Captain has just passed the word over the speaker that we are underway for Iwo Jima. . . . we would arrive there about 0400 on the morning of the 16th and would start immediately carrying out demolition work.

January 10, 1945.

At 0633 we got underway from Berth W-1, West Locks, Pearl Harbor, T.H. We waited around this morning for the Heavies to join us in a convoy. At 1030 we were all formed and heading out to sea. The ARKANSAS, the NEVADA, and the TEXAS were with us and many more ships. About fifty in all.

About 1100 we had A.A. Firing Practice at a sleeve that was towed over us by a plane. Boy, those BB's sure have the fire-power. They shot down every sleeve that passed over them.

Yes, we are traveling in style with all these battle wagons and other ships. The Captain told us this afternoon that we are headed for Ulithi. God knows where that is. I have never heard of the place. Well, here we go anyway. Clocks set back 1/2 hr. this afternoon.

January 11, 1945.

Enroute Pearl Harbor to Ulithi [in the Caroline Islands about 1800 miles south of Tokyo]. This morning we went to G.Q. and had an anti-submarine drill. We have been zig-zagging all day long. We are a screen for the large ships. This afternoon, we set the clocks back another half hour. Still losing time. Already, I am wishing, in a way, that we would go back the other way, but on the other hand, this is all new and exciting to me.

January 12, 1945.

Today has been dull. Same old thing. We are still zig-zagging all day long.

January 13, 1945.

The WATERS, BATES, and ESTES are also along with us. Set clocks back

1/2 hour this morning. Exercised all afternoon at simulated submarine attacks. Just glad that it was not the real thing.

January 14, 1945.

We are a part of Task Group 52.11. This morning we went alongside the NEVADA and took on fuel. All hands were standing outside looking over this mighty ship of our fleet. She certainly is an independent looking contraption. Looks as if she could take care of herself. The sea was calm and we did not have any trouble fueling at sea.

January 15, 1945. & January 16, 1945.

Today is not today but it is the 16th. It was the 15th up until nine o'clock and then they started calling it the 16th. So by rights this heading should be the 16th. This morning at nine we crossed the 180° meridian, and now I am a member of the "Golden Dragon."

This afternoon we had G.Q. drill and had some firing practice. Seem to be getting ready for the "little men."

Set the clocks back 1/2 hour today.

January 17, 1945.

Today we passed by three groups of ships all going in our direction. See that we are not out here alone. This afternoon we went to G.Q. and practiced simulated Air Attacks. Maneuvered at high speeds and sharp turns. This old baby can still get around.

January 18, 1945.

Another year has slipped by me. Today, I am 23 years of age, Today is also my father's birthday, and how I would like to be home today. We always have a good meal on that day. Good spaghetti - I can taste it now.

The TEXAS launched two planes this afternoon. We went to G.Q. and fired at a sleeve that was towed by the planes. More noise. It is a sight to watch those big guns open up on the battle wagons. This afternoon after G.Q. drill, we had a movie in the mess hall. We all enjoyed it very much.

January 19, 1945.

Nothing much today. Same old day. Set clocks back 1/2 hour this afternoon.

January 20, 1945.

Same as yesterday. Days are just rolling on by. We are just sailing on along. We are supposed to arrive at Ulithi on the 23rd.

January 21, 1945.

Set clocks back one-half hour this morning. Zig-zagged practically all day.

January 22, 1945.

Same as yesterday. Set clocks back another half hour. I am on watch and some times this half hour is to my good and sometimes it isn't.

January 23, 1945.

This morning when I went out on deck, I could see ships for miles around.

We were coming into Ulithi. The people in the States had been wondering where our fleet is. Well, there are enough ships right here to beat Japan.

This afternoon, we took on fuel and at 2000 we tied up alongside the BATES.
January 24, 1945.

This morning we had MAIL, and we were all made very happy. This afternoon I had liberty. We went over on the island and had a nice, enjoyable beer party. We had our own beer as the ship loaded up before we left the States. Tonight we will have a movie on the fantail so I think I will go. Big Day.
January 25, 1945.

Had mail again this morning and we were all very happy. Yes sir - we can take that at any old time. Spent most of the afternoon catching up on some work and looking out over the harbor at all the Ships. Yes, we do have a mighty fleet. The Japs can't win.
January 26, 1945.

Not much today. I did not go on liberty. But this afternoon I went for a swim off the fantail. Sure was refreshing for the weather is hot here. You would never know that back in the States they were having Winter.
January 27, 1945.

Today I went on liberty again. Nothing to do over on the island. Have only seen sailors. No populated place around where we go for our beer party. But we do enjoy sitting around talking and drinking beer. This afternoon I had my first taste of taking the wrapper off a coconut. Boy, that was a job.
January 28, 1945.

Went to church aboard the CASCADE this morning. This is a large supply ship, and they had all the comforts for a nice church service. Enjoyed this very much, for on our ship we only have church music played over a speaker on Sunday morning.
January 29, 1945.

Took on ammunition this morning. Also had more mail. This afternoon we had a tragedy on board. One of the Demo's was welding a piece of metal on the side of the ship near the water-line. Somehow, it grounded him and he was electrocuted. He fell off the board and went under the ship. The body was recovered and everything possible done for him but he never came back to life. His name was LeBlanc. We all were very sorry. The Ship's Company and the Team are getting along swell together. This is our war together.
January 30, 1945.

At 1000 this morning we held funeral services for LeBlanc. This afternoon Flannery Y1/c was transferred, and I was placed in charge of the ship's office. This afternoon LeBlanc was taken over to Asor Island for burial.

> *In Flanders Field the poppies grow*
> *Between the crosses, row on row ...*
> *So sang the minstrel long ago.*
>
> *We honor those whose graves are known,*
> *For whom the crystal notes were blown,*
> *In ceremony, not alone.*
>
> *But what of those who died at sea,*
> *Destroyed by our, then, enemy?*
> *No graves for them -- just memory.*
>
> *And though for them the bells have pealed,*
> *Beneath the seas their fate is sealed --*
> *For them there is no Flanders field.*
>
> *Copyright 1999 by Rima Magee*
> *Published with her permission*

January 31, 1945.

Had liberty this morning and when I came back tonight I found that I had six letters. Boy, how they do help. Would almost take anyone out of a blue mood. Had movie on the fantail tonight.

February 1, 1945.

Nothing much today. Had a swimming party off the fantail this afternoon.

February 2, 1945.

Still at Ulithi. My, the way we had come across, I thought we would be in Japan by now. There is talk that we may leave soon. But now all we are doing is having liberty and movies. Received some more mail this afternoon.

February 3, 1945.

At 0730 this morning we pulled up the hook. Went out to Mugai Island and at 1000 went to G.Q. The BLESSMAN and the BATES went with us. All morning and all afternoon we practiced Underwater Demolition work. At 1600 this afternoon we anchored again off Ulithi.

UDT 13 Team meeting on the fantail; Lt. Walker in center

February 4, 1945.

This morning I went over to the CASCADE with the Church Party. This afternoon seemed like a Sunday at home. So peaceful and quiet.

February 5, 1945.

Had liberty this afternoon. Enjoyed it very much. Even if it is on a little old island, it is good to get off the ship once in a while. Also had five letters this afternoon after I returned from liberty. Off to the movie.

February 6, 1945.

0800 - Anchors Aweigh. We are off on some more simulated landings. Looks like we are getting rehearsed for something. There is talk that there will be an invasion some place some time this month.

At 1400 this afternoon we went to G.Q. We practiced simulated Underwater Exercises. And around 1600 we fired at a sleeve which was being towed by a plane. At 1800 we anchored back where we came from.

February 7, 1945.

The crew had liberty this morning, but I did not go over. Worked this morning. Went swimming and wrote letters this afternoon.

February 8, 1945.

This morning I went over on liberty. Don't know why I do such. There is nothing to do over there. I suppose it is that I just like to get off the ship. This afternoon I had some more mail. Good to get. Off I go now to the movies.

February 9, 1945.

This is it! This morning at 0700 we pulled up anchor and are underway. The Captain made a speech this afternoon over the loud speaker. He informed us that soon we would be in action. He said that we are underway now for an invasion. Well, I suppose we do have to fight a little too. We have been hanging around here quite a spell. But with the force that we have I don't believe there is any place that we couldn't go. We have ten battle wagons, about fifteen cruisers and many destroyers and other type ships. Yes, I suppose we are going some place.

February 10, 1945.

Steaming along - don't know where we are going - but we are going. It is a funny feeling - I can say that. And we just can't help but think of that eighty tons of explosives that we are riding on. That is the worst part of the deal. But we can't back out now - we have a job to do. Just have to hope and pray that nothing hits us.

February 11, 1945.

This morning the Captain told us that we were going to stop at Saipan [in the Marianas about 1400 miles south of Tokyo]. But from the way we are going - from one direction to the other - I don't know where we will wind up. We have been zig-zagging all day. Thought that by now we would be running into some subs but no - maybe they know who we are.

From Frisco to Pearl Harbor and from Pearl Harbor to Ulithi we acted as the screening ships for the large ones. But you should see who is getting all the protection now. All the APD's are in the middle of the group. Maybe they don't want to take a chance of us getting hit with all these explosives on board. We think it is a good idea too.

February 12, 1945.

This morning we sighted Tinian [in the Marianas about 50 miles north of Saipan] about 0700. Also took on fuel this morning and met with rest of APD's to take up screening station (inner screen) for overnight. Thought that we would anchor tonight but it looks as if we will stay underway.

February 13, 1945.

Today, we practiced simulated beach landings, and Demolition Exercises. Seems to be a last minute check up. The Captain has not said as yet, where we are going. We are a little excited and would just like to know. Well, we will probably find out soon. Just two more days.

2000 - The Captain has just passed the word over the speaker that we are underway for Iwo Jima. Said that it was a small island about 700 miles from Tokyo. Gosh, I didn't have any idea that it was going to be that close. He said that we would arrive there about 0400 on the morning of the 16th and would start immediately carrying out Demolition work. Also said that "D" Day was on the 19th. Here we have to go in three days before the invasion. Does not look too good. I wonder if

I could back out now. We will probably be seeing plenty soon for they say it is a well fortified little island.

February 14, 1945.

Steaming enroute to Iwo Jima for our big day - the one we have been preparing for. Today we went to G.Q. at 1300 and practiced all kinds of drills. Only one more day will go by and we will see what it is all about. Everything is so peaceful now. The NEVADA is right by us, and all those other "big boys". Well, anyway, we have plenty with us. We are sure going first class. The Captain said today for all men to stay alert.

February 15, 1945.

Nothing much today. Same as yesterday. Things are too quiet. Had G.Q. drill. It is now 1900. In the morning at 0400 we will be within a few miles from the little rock. I wonder what I can say in my book tomorrow at this time.

FLASHBACKS

UDT 13 and USS Barr crewmen immediately bonded as a unit which made it easy when it came time to carry out orders. We usually met on the fantail each morning for updates or changes. As I recall, both C.O./X.O.'s were able to get their messages across verbally each AM with rare exceptions of written follow-up reminders. Cdr. Dickie was the most competent skipper when in formations, docking, training drills and special skills while refueling while underway in both calm and rough seas. Oh, yes, we usually got the ice cream and other goodies that we requested from the mother ship when refueling was terminated.

As for food supplies in general, you might check with Eugene Swearingen to confirm that we may have been the only APD that had an ample supply of ripe olives which was to his liking.

Donald M. Walker, Lieutenant (jg), UDT 13

*   *   *   *   *

Once, while in the Pacific, I was stationed on the steering watch during General Quarters. I didn't have my glasses and couldn't see a thing. As a result, the ship ended up going everywhere but the right direction. After that, I was never asked again to do this battle station.

Max Glaser, Yeoman

*   *   *   *   *

The food on the Barr was good. The ship was a little too warm, but we managed. We spent the days at sea mostly on the fantail either exercising or playing cards. We also made up charges to be used underwater.

George Gregory, Motor Machinist, UDT 13

*   *   *   *   *

On the way to Ulithi, the Barr had to take on fuel. It was a dark and stormy afternoon. We pulled alongside the Texas and connected. And connected. And connected. The hoses kept breaking as both ships tossed in opposite directions. To help our ship's crew endure the miserable job, the Texas' band came on deck and played all our favorite songs. Unfortunately, the wind took most of the sound away from us. But we appreciated the effort they made. Especially when they sent over ice cream and movies to us.

Arthur W. Magee, Signalman, UDT 13

Just forward of the enlisted men's quarters on the starboard side was the enlisted men's mess hall. During the afternoons and evening, it became a game room. The games were mostly draw, five card stud, and seven card stud poker. We were not allowed to have money on the table, so cards torn in half were used for chips. Each chip was usually valued at five cents, and a fifty cent limit was usually in force. Of course, this varied with the wealth of the players.

On our long trip west to Ulithi, I played poker most every night. One time my buddy, Sherman Prince, had a run of bad luck, so I loaned him $20 to stake him for awhile. Paydays were few and far between in the middle of the Pacific. Sherman's luck changed and he met me on the fantail just as I had unwrapped a stick of doublemint gum. Sherman handed me a $20 bill to repay his debt. We talked for awhile, and I threw the gum wrapper into the ocean. Sherman left and I looked down at my hand still holding the gum wrapper. I had thrown a half month's pay into the briny deep!

Marvin Cooper, Gunner's Mate, UDT 13

*   *   *   *   *

We arrived in Ulithi Jan. 23rd in the early morning. What a surprise when I first saw it. I expected a few small islands and a few ships. Yet here before me spread hundreds of ships. I thought to myself, the second Pearl Harbor (except these were all fighting ships). I was soon to find out that Ulithi was as active as Pearl. We had a few nice beer parties here on one of the smaller islands.

Manuel Verissimo, Water Tender
from his journal, "Manny's Excellent Adventures"

*   *   *   *   *

Ulithi was caused by a partially submerged volcano. A rim of coral almost completely encircles the anchorage. Thus it is easy to protect ships from enemy attacks by a simple submarine net. There are a few small coral islands, none of which are over 25 feet high. We were literally amazed to see the vast number of ships in the anchorage. It greatly exceeded the number we had seen in Pearl Harbor. For once we realized that we were a very small part of a very huge fleet.

We went over to Pug-a-Lug Island and there we established the Pug-a-Lug Officers' Club. Tom Kaiser (ship's doctor) found a most amazing limb (or root-- we never decided) from a dead tree, which we used as a bench. An old crate served as the table. The routine was to have a drink, then go for a swim. . . . We borrowed swim fins and face masks from the UDT's and had a wonderful time swimming in the coral. You have never really enjoyed swimming until you swim with fins and a mask in a coral sea.

Eugene L. Swearingen, Ensign
from his journal, "My Ramblings Aboard the Barr, APD39"

We did lose one UDT man. He was welding an eye hook alongside the Barr to tie up the PT boats. A wave crashed into the ship, catching him off guard. He was electrocuted and washed overboard. It took us an hour to retrieve the body. We buried him on a nearby island.

Norman LeMere, Machinist's Mate

*   *   *   *   *

While we were at Ulithi, one of the UDT men went over the side to do some welding. While watching him doing the welding, I saw a wave come up and short his electrode and I noticed that he was going to be electrocuted. I jumped overboard to try to save him, but was unable to reach him before he was electrocuted. After that I was one of the boys with the underwater demolition men. I could never do anything wrong with them because I tried to save one of their companions.

Armand J. Marion, Machinist's Mate

*   *   *   *   *

Although it was mid-winter when we arrived at Ulithi, the days and nights had become hot. As we approached Ulithi, I and some of the others decided to take our hammocks into the LCPR's where we could enjoy the breeze caused by the moving Barr. Of course, this was not permitted, so we had to wait until after dark to make this move. I remember one night when the sea was rather rough, I heard a flapping noise in the bottom of the boat. In the dark, I finally found a flying fish that had flown into the boat. I spent many nights, when we were close to the equator, sleeping in the reconnaissance boats.

Marvin Cooper, Gunner's Mate, UDT 13

*   *   *   *   *

Small world department! One night at Ulithi, I was loafing on the bridge, chatting with Lt. Don McKinlay. Discovered he was college mate at Dartmouth with my cousin, Mutt Ray who, at this time, was skipper of a PT Boat.

Arthur W. Magee, Signalman, UDT 13

*   *   *   *   *

On the way to Iwo Jima, I met my brother-in-law at Ulithi and got permission to go over and sleep on the carrier deck. While I was over there, the bombs started coming down and I wired the Captain to get me back to my ship. I figured I'd be better off on my own ship than on the carrier.

Francis J. Skotko, Gunner's Mate

February 12th we passed Guam. We thought it would be blacked out, but it wasn't. When they found out we were going by, two spotlights were switched on and swung into the sky to form a huge V as they knew what was up. Feb. 12th we arrived off Tinian and Saipan. We spent that day and the next on our final maneuvers. Feb. 14th just before we left Saipan, four Marines that had been aboard for some of our maneuvers off Maui, came aboard. We were off! This was no drill. The captain told us where we were going and what to expect. Everyone took the news calmly. We had known since Ulithi thru the rumor channels and they were surprisingly correct.

Manuel Verissimo, Water Tender
from his journal, "Manny's Excellent Adventures"

D-Day at Iwo Jima from the Barr

Iwo Jima is an island that God must have donated to Satan many years ago. A little over six square miles it had over 20,000 vicious Japanese soldiers dug into its lava formed surface. Mt. Suribachi to the south and a high ridge to the north were the distinguishing topography of the island. The ocean water was about 59 degrees compared to the 85 degree water at Ulithi and 80 degree water at Maui. We knew that the "Naked Warriors" would be very uncomfortable.

Marvin Cooper, Gunner's Mate, UDT 13

D-Day, LCIG one mile off Green Beach and Mt. Suribachi

CHAPTER 7

IWO JIMA--THE LITTLE ROCK

Hundreds of little small boats swarmed ashore. Planes were all over the air over the island diving down strafing the beach. Battle wagons, cruisers and destroyers opened up with all their might. I have never seen anything like it. It seemed as if all hell had broke loose.

February 16, 1945.

This morning we were all up at 0400 on our battle stations. About 0700 we could see fire works in the distance. Planes were giving the Japs hell on the island. About 0800 we saw two Jap ships that were firing at our planes. Next thing we saw explosions on the Jap ships and they went up in flames. What an explosion that was. And I just can't imagine what an explosion there would be on this ship if it ever gets hit by a bomb. O, well, I don't suppose we will know it if one does hit.

This morning when we got in, we split up. The big stuff went right on in to the beach. What a sight it was to see our "big boys" laying off the shore bombarding the little island. And what a small piece of rock it is.

This afternoon we closed in. Our job was to put up a Navigational Light on Higashi Rocks. (These were a bunch of little rocks about a half mile off the southern end of the island.) The U.D.T. boys had the light put up on the rock and had just started getting back in the little rubber boats when Jap batteries opened up on the rocks.

The Captain then ordered all hands to hit the deck, and turned full speed ahead to close the batteries. About this time, our five inch started barking. And I have never heard so much noise. After we had shot about 15 or 20 rounds on the beach, the Japs stopped firing. Our fire and also some air coverage must have knocked the gun emplacements out. Or either the Japs stopped firing, being afraid of giving their gun position away.

Our U.D.T. boys all came back. Not a scratch on one of them. Only lost one rubber boat. I now know that they are the lucky "13". They told us how close the shrapnel came to them and how afraid they were. O, yes, I forgot around 1000 this morning we had a sound contact. Two destroyers took over. Don't know how they made out. And at around noon we had a Flash Red. "Bogeys" were in the area, but our fighters must have got them for we didn't see any. This ends today - and this must be what they call war. And I hate it already. We stayed at G.Q. and Condition 2M. practically all day.

February 17, 1945.

This morning we proceeded to Eastern Beaches for reconnaissance by the U.D.T. About 1000 we sent our boats in to the beach with U.D.T.'s. Around 1100 we started to go back in close to the beach to pick up the demo's but after we got in we were ordered back to the retirement area because there was intense motor fire going on.

UDT 13 in LCPR to recon Green Beach at Iwo Jima

There were about 12 LCI's that were giving our Demo's fire support, and all of them were knocked out of action. They are the bravest little ships in the Fleet. They went right almost up on the beach to give fire support, and it was really a hard thing to take to see them coming out all shot up. About four of them I could see, were sinking right in close to the beach. Destroyers then closed in to give support. Also low flying planes strafed the beach.

About 1230 we went back in to the beach to pick up the Demo's. We met some opposition but finally got the boats aboard and took off. The Destroyers closed in around our ship and blasted away at the Japs. We fired only a few shots. Our main concern was to get the boats aboard and get the hell out of there. Shrapnel hit all around the ship but none hit the ship. Both boats got back and all the Demo's were safe. We then went around to the Western Beaches where we sent the boys in for reconnaissance. About 1500 they went in. We layed off about 2 or 3 miles and Destroyers went in and gave fire support.

An air attack was made on the island by about four or five raids of B-24's about 1300. What explosions. All day long our planes have been bombing the island and our ships have been blasting away. You can hardly see the island for all the smoke. All last night the island was lit up by star shells and the "big boys" blasted away.

James Grenga wrote the following to his mother:

CENSORED   *17 February 1945*

My Dearest Mother:

Have a few minutes off now, so I suppose I will try to write you a few lines. Have been working fairly·hard for the past few days. And not getting as much rest as I should have. But this can't last forever.

Hope that all at home is well and happy. I am fine. Just get a little lonesome at times. I do think of you and home frequently.

I have passed all my tests - including short-hand - for first class; and I expect an advancement at the first of the month.

Have not had any mail for several days and am getting very anxious to hear from you. It may be a few days yet before I do hear from you. Just hope that you and all the family are well - then I have nothing to worry about.

You would be surprised to know where I am now. Maybe you will hear soon. As I told you before I can not talk about the ship or anything that it does. Not now, anyway. But I am all right, and have all the confidence in the world.

Well, mother, there is not any news that I can divulge so I suppose I will close for this time. Hoping to hear from you soon; and praying every night that God will take care of you and the family; and bring me safely home some day, tomorrow. Give all the family my love. Tell Helen that I love her lots. Good-night for now. And I do mean good-night. I am about to fall asleep. I love you, mother, always.

Your loving son,
James

February 18, 1945.

Last night there were enemy planes around. We did not open up but all around we could see and hear the Destroyers and larger ships firing away. They have radar control and don't have to see the planes to hit them. On small ships we don't have radar control fire, so we don't suppose to open up unless we are attacked.

This afternoon we returned to replace the light that we put up day before yesterday. It had been shot out. Did not have any trouble until boats started back to the ship. Then the Japs opened up on them, with machine guns. I could see through my glasses that the bullets were hitting all around the boats. We started in but were given orders to retire.

D-Day at Iwo Jima; Lt. Aldinger,
Capt. Dickie, and Lt. McEwen on the bridge

We were just standing by and shrapnel started hitting all over the ship. No one was hit with it. The Captain sure did not have to holler for us to hit the deck this time. When we heard that stuff hitting all over the ship we went right down and stayed there. What a day this has been.

February 19,1945

Last night around dusk at about 2120 we went G.Q. "Bogey" was reported in area. About a couple minutes before that a Jap plane had been sighted off our port side, about two or three hundred yards away and very low to the water. Our ready guns did not open up for some reason. About five minutes after we got to our battle stations, the USS BLESSMAN (APD 48) which was about a couple miles behind us was hit by a bomb. I suppose we were just lucky that he did not come in on us.

This morning we proceeded close to the beach. This was it. 0900 - Hundreds of little small boats swarmed ashore. Planes were all over the air over the island diving down strafing the beach. Battle wagons, cruisers and destroyers opened up with all their might.

*Ensign Reilly adjusting radio on
the flying bridge*

I have never seen anything like it. It seemed as if all hell had broke loose. By the time the little boats got to the beach, the island was covered with smoke. You could hardly see the island at all. I don't see how anyone could live through it. Our boats went in along with the second wave to give Demolition support, if necessary. We lost one of our boats this morning but none of the boys were killed.

When the first wave went in, we were standing off about 2 or 3 miles. I could see through my glasses as plain as day our tanks getting knocked out - seemed as if nearly all of them were getting hit. Saw several of them blown up in the air. And it was a terrible sight to see bodies of men falling through space. All up and down the beach where they were landing was nothing but a cloud of dust. Shells were hitting one after the other. Our ships moved in close and pounded away at the Jap batteries with all their might. Our planes filled the sky - but still the beach where our boys were landing was covered with shells.

The worst place seemed to be the gun emplacements at Mt. Suribachi. They shelled and bombed that place but still the Japs were shooting. This kept up all day long and tonight when we were pulling away they were still pounding away. War couldn't be more terrible.

2100 - Just came back from G.Q. Had Flash Red at 1900. Had a big air attack. Most of the time we were concealed under a smoke screen. Ships about a mile from us fired away for about a half hour. Reported that three were hit. We did not see any planes as we were in smoke. Will retire now and hope I can sleep the rest of the night. Gosh, I don't see how I can. Am really all excited. This is all new to me and it does not look so good. Am very tired. We stayed at G.Q. from 0600 this morning until about 2045, with the exception of about two hours we had off about dusk.

February 20, 1945.

Was up last night for G.Q. Doesn't look like the Japs are going to take it sitting down. We stayed under a smoke screen practically all night and did not open up. The "big boys" fired all night long. Star shells lit up the beach. Went to G.Q. again this morning as we were expecting a big air attack. We saw no planes.

And what do you suppose happened this afternoon. We had mail. I never thought we would receive mail right up at the front. Was sure nice to hear from my family and enjoyed hearing from a girlfriend, Kay. Had six letters from her. It is now 2000.

February 21, 1945.

I don't see how they can bomb a place so much. All day long and all night our ships are pouring it in. And our planes fill the air. You can hardly see the island for all the smoke. They say our boys are really having a hard time on the beach. And I have certainly seen that from where I am. They say that one out of every two that hit the beach on the 19th was a casualty. It all looks so easy for the Navy. I know it could be worse.

2000 - Just got back from G.Q. We went to our stations around 1700. Enemy aircraft were in area. Saw a lot of anti-aircraft firing, but we saw no planes and did no firing.

CENSORED   *21 February 1945*

My Dearest Mother:

Have been pretty busy today and hardly feel like writing letters, but will try to write you a few lines to let you know that I am all right. We have been having a lot of excitement lately and still are as far as that goes. I am all right and hoping that I can come through this war just as I went in it. Maybe I can tell you soon where I am now - or at least where I have been. Gosh, I could write a book on the things that I have seen. But I suppose you will hear more in the newspapers than I could ever tell you. However, I agree with Sherman when he said that war is hell.

I hope that all at home are well and happy. I think about you and the family often and pray every night that God will take care of you; and that I may see you again someday soon.

I am still unable to get any mail, and don't know how long it will be before I will have any. I haven't sent any off in such a long time. Hope that you have not worried about it too much. There is a reason, and I am sure that you would understand.

How is Dad? Tell him that I said hello and that I hope he is well. He is the best dad in all the world. We've had a few little arguments in our life but they never meant anything - I am sure.

And give my little sis a big hug and kiss for me. Tell her that I am coming back to see her some of these days - and I am hoping that it will be soon.

Must go for now. Write soon and often, and I promise that I will get as many letters as I can off to you. Be good sweetheart, and remember that I am always thinking of you and always loving you. Bye for now-

Your loving son,
James

<u>February 22, 1945.</u>

This morning around 0300 we had a Flash Red. No firing was done by this ship. This afternoon we had a Flash Red from 1500 to 1830. Planes all around. All ships around opened up. No ships were hit but four planes shot down. We are still on our screening station. Don't like this job at all. If one of these dern planes ever hit us, I don't have any idea as what will happen. Will probably be pretty bad. Our "big boys" are still blasting away day and night. It is now 2200.

Robinson and Lt. Murray on 50 cal. gun station

CENSORED   *22 February 1945*

My Dearest Mother:

Have a little time now, so I think that I will try to write you a few lines. And I don't think that there is anything new that I can say. I suppose that you are reading enough in the papers. Probably more than I myself could tell you.

Certainly is a bad day today. It has rained all day, and also yesterday. I am glad that it is raining--if you know what I mean. Visibility is very poor, ceiling zero. But old days like this make me feel awful blue and lonely. Of course, I have all my ship-mates to keep me from getting too lonely, but there is still that little something lacking.

Well, it is not long until the first of the month. Although military duties come first, I am still having to get out all the reports on time. Between the two of them, I stay fairly busy most of the time. But have already started working on the monthly reports and don't think that I should have too much difficulty in getting them out.

I am also looking for an advancement the first of the month. I don't see how they can hold me down now. I have passed all the tests, and I certainly have enough time in my present rate to warrant promotion. Hope that I will get it the first.

How is everyone at home. Fine, I hope. I hope that dad is not having to work too hard these days. It is a good thing that he sold the other cafe. Trying to run two businesses is too much for him. He is getting on up in years. Of course, you would never know it to look at him. He has taken pretty good care of himself during his life, hasn't he.

I have not had any mail in a long time. When we do get in the position to receive mail, we should all have plenty. And I hope that I will have my orders for the air corps by that time. I think that when I get in that it will be just about the right time.

Well, mother, there is not much to say. Same old thing every day. But I try to write as often as I feel like writing even if just to let you know that I am thinking of you.

Tell all hello for me and give them all my love, and here's hoping to see you all again someday soon. Must go for this time. Bye now.

Your loving son, forever,
James

February 23, 1945.

This morning at 0400, a "skunk raid" was reported. Found out later, it was a sub and some of our ships got it.

This morning at 1035 we saw "old Glory" being raised on the "hot rocks". It came over the radio that the Marines were advancing on the top of the "hot rocks" and were going to put a flag there. Was really a grand sight to see that old flag waving there. This afternoon we went to G.Q. at 1500. Enemy planes around. And again tonight at 1800. Lots of aircraft fire but we did no firing as no planes came in our range. Gosh, this G.Q. stuff is getting old. Now, we just wonder how long we will be as lucky as we have been. The old "39" is three times 13, maybe that is our luck.

Old Glory being raised on Iwo Jima
Photo by Steve Hill

February 24, 1945.

This morning we went on a search for survivors reported by a plane, but when we got to the life raft we found it empty, with the exception of some birds perched on it. The "big boys" are still laying it on all day and all night. I wonder how much longer they can hold out. We have reports that the Japs are weakening. We also found out today that our Demo's (U.D.T. #13) was the only team that suffered no casualties at Iwo Jima.

2300 - Just back from G.Q. Enemy planes have been in area since around 2000. Not many got in close. Our C.A.P. are sure taking care of most of them.

CENSORED   *24 February 1945*
My Dearest Mother:

I hope that these few lines will find all well and happy. I am feeling very well, but am a little disappointed in not getting my rate the first of March. My division officer recommended me for the rate, but the Executive Officer on board the ship for some reason wants me to wait another month. He said that he wanted to be sure he knew what he was doing when he did rate me. I suppose that he is right in a way; but I know a lot of boys that have been rated, and they did not even have all the tests in let alone qualified for the higher rate. But I did not get the break. Breaks count a lot sometimes.

Anyway when I do get rated, I suppose that he will be satisfied in his mind that I am fully qualified to take over the job of Yeoman first class on any ship or shore base in the Navy. And I probably will be. I am reading a little of the "books" every night, now, and studying more on my shorthand.

I passed the test with a mark of 3.8. 4.0 is perfect in the Navy. Well, I don't suppose another month will make much difference. I have waited this long. But if I get to go to the air corps, I will still be Y2c. That is what I am thinking about when I want to get the rate the first of March. Maybe something will happen to me in the air corps, my eyes go bad or something like that. Then I will have to go back to the fleet as a Y2c, and will probably remain Y2c throughout my naval service.

One consolation, and that is that the war is not going to last forever, and I think that I can fair better on the outside than I can in the Navy. I would not stay in this Navy if they gave me a Captain's rate. Too much petty nonsense in it.

I suppose that you will receive the $50 the first of March. Write me and let me know if the money has been sent? You should still be getting a bond each month outside of the $50 each month.

Hope that everyone at home is well and happy. How is my little baby sis. Give her a good hug and a big kiss for me and tell her to be a good little girl.

Has Louise gone off to her new destination yet. I have not heard from her in a long time. Maybe I will get a letter from her the next time that we have mail on board ship. Sure hope so. How is Angelo doing in Tech now? Is he still making the grade all right. I sure do hope that he will be able to stay there.

Please excuse this typing. It is very hard to try to type when you almost have to hold on to the desk with one hand while you are typing. It does get pretty rough out here sometimes.

I think that we are going to get some mail off tomorrow. Sure do hope so. It has been such a long time since I have sent off any. I know that you are beginning to wonder what has happened to me. I can not tell you anything about where I am or what I am doing. But I am all right, and that is all that matters.

Tell all hello for me and give them all my love. I am always thinking of all of you and hoping that every one is all right, and hoping that I will see all of you soon. I feel sure that my orders will be waiting for me when I get in. Must go. I have a lot of monthly reports to get out. Bye for this time. I remain

Your loving son, forever,
James

February 25, 1945.

Easy day today. No G.Q. all day. Maybe the Japs have given up hope. Sure hope so; for this stuff can get on your nerves. Just wish it was all over so all us boys could come back. We have lost a lot here at Iwo. Reports say it is the worst battle the Marines have ever fought. Had time to write a few letters this afternoon.

February 26, 1945.

This morning we found the body of Pvt. Lester C. Martin of the Marines floating in the water. Body was inspected and weight tied to it. We had an excitement this afternoon when sub was reported two miles from our station. Other ships took off for it and dropped depth charges. Don't know whether they got a hit or not. No air attacks today. Really, they must have given out - or given up hope. It looks like we have taken over.

February 27, 1945.

Calm day. And a happy one. We had mail this afternoon and a movie in the mess hall, too.

It's wonderful how mail can make a fellow feel. Lots of it was from a sweet little girl I know in La Grange. Good to know the girls have not forgotten me. We are still screening. We hope to leave here for the rear areas soon. Our main job was done before the landing, but they keep us around here anyway.

February 28, 1945.

This morning around 1000 we went in to the transport area and dropped the hook. Received more mail on board. Out again around 1800 - back to our screening station. Ship ahead of us had sound contact, but they think it was false. Fighting still seems to be going on the beach. Had a movie this afternoon. Really is nice.

February 29, 1945.

I'm sorry - this is a new month.

March 1, 1945.

This morning at 0200 we went to G.Q. Had a large air attack. Enemy planes all around. All ships were firing but we didn't seem to hit anything. Several bombs were dropped from the enemy planes. One ship was hit. No bombs dropped within two or three miles from us. Gosh, and I was beginning to like it here. Really was exciting to go to G.Q. again after laying off for a few days. We secured from G.Q. about 0430 this morning.

This afternoon all was calm. We had more mail on board and saw another movie. We have to have our enjoyment along with the war, don't we? 2000 - all calm.

March 2, 1945.

This morning we had a sound contact. Later verified as non-sub. This afternoon we got orders that we are assigned now to a "killer group" to investigate all sound contact. Meanwhile we are to remain on our station. Now 1600.

2200 - At 2100 we went to G.Q. Enemy planes reported in area. All ships made smoke. And no planes were seen by us, and no firing. I think our C.A.P. got them all.

March 3, 1945.

All calm today. Had a movie this afternoon. Still on our screening station. Sure hope what I hear is correct. They say we may leave tomorrow or the next day.

FLASHBACKS

D-Day Minus 3

D-Day minus 3   When the bombardment had first started, our planes had also started to bomb the island. Now in the early afternoon they were dive bombing. It's an unforgettable scene to see them come screaming down, their guns banging away, and then drop their bomb and head for the sun.

Manuel Verissimo, Water Tender
from his journal, "Manny's Excellent Adventures"

*   *   *   *   *

We arrived at Iwo 3 days before the landing and watched as our naval and air force bombarded the island. While on patrol we were fired on as our UDT team was securing a marker for a navigational light. We all ducked when the Japanese fired at us, but returned fire when the Captain told us we should shoot back.

During the invasion we provided picket duty station to warn of any submarines and aircraft in the area.

I was also lucky enough to fire our 40 caliber machine guns on deck to sink a large rowboat (empty) but for fear of explosives or mines we sank it.

Timothy P. J. Nolan, Electrician's Mate

*   *   *   *   *

When we carried the Frogmen in toward the beach, they fired at us from the beach and scared the heck out of us. That was the first time I was ever fired on, and I hit the deck like I was on dirt, trying to get out of the way. But we came through that O.K. - didn't get hit. We opened fire on them, and we knocked out that bunker that was doing the firing.

Talmadge Grubbs, Seaman

*   *   *   *   *

Three days before D-Day at Iwo, our team had to install a light on a group of rocks about a thousand yards from the island in broad daylight. Our swimmers were walking around the rocks setting up the light when they came under machine gun fire from the Japanese.

Then things happened quickly. Capt. Dickie, the commander of the Barr ordered flank speed and turned the Barr directly into the beach. I was standing on the boat deck during this time and it was apparent to me that Capt. Dickie was going to run the Barr right up on to the beach, but what he was doing was putting the Barr between the UDT men and the Japanese. Of course, the crew of the Barr were firing their guns at the Japs the whole time. Capt. Dickie's action enabled our men to return safely.

Edward N. Deringer, Quartermaster, UDT 13

*   *   *   *   *

The light (navigational light) was set in a box affair that looked exactly like a dog house with the opening for the light pointing out to sea, so that you can see it just if you were in the right spot. . . . You've got to hand it to those UDT men, they're all right. They had taken a sign with them, and had set it up on the rocks. You could see it plain from the ship in large red letters. "750 MILES TO TOKYO" compliments of the UDT 13. Some of the fellows had returned with a few shells and a star fish for souvenirs.

*Manuel Verissimo, Water Tender
from his journal, "Manny's Excellent Adventures"*

*   *   *   *   *

Ensign Hehli was in a boat after dropping men on Higashi Rocks and I watched him turning and dodging machine gun fire from the enemy. Twin spurts of water kept following him - probably from one of their twin small caliber weapons.

Donald H. Murray, Lieutenant (jg), UDT 13

—————— **D-Day Minus 2** ——————

I was seaman-first class. Later I transferred to the engine room, then James gave us our test for Machine Mate 3/c P.O. My G.Q. was on 5" gun.

While we were firing our 5" gun at Iwo Jima we had a new 50 lb. shell with a plastic nose. These shells sat along the bulk head around the gun. One fell, hit the deck and its nose broke off. That day 10 faces turned the color of snow in January.

For his part, the service man loading the shells in the gun did not skip a beat. He picked up the broken shell and tossed it overboard. (More luck!)

Norman LeMere, Machinist's Mate

Bob told me it was so bad - he was so frightened he couldn't talk about it. It seems he and his men left the ship - got on the beach when all hell broke loose - the ship had to leave. The sky was bright with bombs and the noise beyond anything he'd ever witnessed. Early morning the ship came back and they got back safely. I was told later by his son, Robert, that Bob and another man had made the hawser to grab onto into an 8, so that the men wouldn't slip off trying to get onto the boat. I'm very proud of that and of Bob. Bob had said many young men were killed at Iwo - from either drowning or killed by bullets right in front of your eyes. "So many young men," he said.

Frances R. Gleason, wife of Robert E. Gleason, Ensign, UDT13

    *   *   *   *   *

I had GQ assignment on one of the 50 cal. guns on the Barr's fantail. This assignment only applied when I was free of an operational assignment. During the battle of the light I was on my gun station when Captain Dickie ordered the Barr towards shore to protect the light crew. The 5 inch and the 40's blasted away, but the island was far out of reach for the 50 calibers.

On the 17th I had a swimming assignment. Jack Barrett and I and four other sets of swimmers left the Barr on an LCPR. Team 13 had 10 swimmers and Teams 12, 14 and 15 each had 20 swimmers. So 70 swimmers were to swim into the beaches, remove the mines, map the beach, locate obstacles and bring back a sample of beach sand.

The LCPR took us within about a half mile of the beach. The LCIG's had all been knocked out of operation in the morning reconnaissance operation, so all we had for fire support was the destroyer line backed up by some cruisers and a couple of battleships. They added Navy fighter planes to strafe the beaches.

When I rolled into the water, I thought it was all over. The water seemed so cold that I felt I would never live an hour in it. Jack and I started toward the beach, and after swimming a couple of hundred yards our bodies became used to the frigid water. The fire support and its noise were awesome. The far out battleships were firing 16 inch shells over our heads into the beach. When they passed over us, it sounded like a freight train roaring through the air. As we neared the beach, the Japanese started doing their job. What appeared to be rifle and machine gun bullets started zipping the water around us. Jack and I submerged and started swimming underwater, coming up occasionally for air. We soon reached the surf and crawled close enough to get a sample of sand. Fortunately, the beach was clear of mines and obstacles.

By the time we returned to the swimmer pickup line, it was late in the afternoon, the wind had picked up, and the waves were white-capping around us. When I lined up for the retrieval, my LCPR from the Barr missed me. We were operating next to Team 12, and a Team 12 LCPR scooted me out of the water. The Bates' LCPR pulled alongside the Barr, and I quickly scooted up the cargo net to safety.

The old Barr never looked better, and all 10 swimmers met in a conference room for debriefing. Each swimmer was given a glass and the doctor or Pharmacist Mate poured us a healthy glass of brandy.

Marvin Cooper, Gunner's Mate, UDT 13

*   *   *   *   *

On the evening of the day (Feb. 17, 1945) that the twelve LCIG's (Landing Craft Infantry Gunboats) were hit, Tokyo Rose came over the radio and told us that the Japs had sunk the American Navy and that they knew about us UDT people and that they were waiting for us. - Kinda scary - since nobody was supposed to know about us "Demos!"

Bennie M. Rice, MM, UDT13

*   *   *   *   *

Thanks to some fancy maneuvering by our skipper, we landed the swimmers, retrieved them and got out without any damage. (Capt. Dickie was smart enough to realize we could get close and get under the shore battery guns.) We took a couple of advance intelligence men ashore with the swimmers. When we retired out of range that night, a Japanese "Betty" bomber flew within 50 yards of our bridge and proceeded to bomb the USS Blessman which was proceeding at full speed to join us. After this experience, our skipper decided the flyer couldn't see us in time to release his bombs, but he could clearly see the phosphorescent wake of the Blessman. <u>For the remainder of the war, we did not steam at full speed after dark; it probably saved our lives.</u>

John W. Hubenthal, Lieutenant (jg) from his autobiography

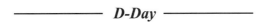

D-Day

I had the luck to draw straws to see who would lead the Marines into Iwo on D-Day. At 8 am I was in a small boat, an LCPR, circling off the beach next to Suribachi. I waved to circle the wagons and on to the beach. Swarms of boats circling behind me formed ranks and followed me to the beach. When they could no longer get lost, I waved them on and went back to an anchored LCIG where I stayed until relieved later that day. We were being shelled and the ship suffered injuries and lost their main gun.

Donald H. Murray, Lieutenant (jg), UDT 13

On February 19, 1945 (D-Day) at Iwo Jima the Baker boat crew, along with Ensign Charles Hamman from Shawnee, OK, led the first wave of Marines to the right beach. We went to about 200-300 yards off the beach and then turned around and left.

Bennie M. Rice, MM, UDT13

*   *   *   *   *

D-Day.   We had our radio cut in on the channel on which a Colonel in the forward C.P. was directing operations, and all afternoon we were grouped around the radio listening. He was a tough old bird, and could he swear when something went wrong. . . . "I've lost about 60% of my men in the left flank. My right flank isn't doing so bad, but the casualties are very heavy. The Japs are well organized. Each time we take a step forward, we encounter new, and more pill boxes, block houses, fortified caves or strong points, but things are really shaping up." All afternoon we listened to him either telling a company to move up or back, calling for Navy gunfire in a center section, or an air strike, or for supplies and ammo. Toward the end of the afternoon he started to call for barbed wire, food and water in preparation for digging in for the night. He also wanted Navy gunfire in a certain section all night long, and ships to fire to keep the front lines bright all night. About this time he got word of a counter attack that 500 Japs were preparing for, and he called for an air strike to break it up before it got started.

Manuel Verissimo, Water Tender
from his journal, "Manny's Excellent Adventures"

*   *   *   *   *

A Team 13 crew (I was not included) led the first wave of Marines into the east beaches at Iwo Jima. The following days were filled with post invasion missions. We delivered explosives from our abundant supply for the Marines to use to blow caves. We worked with Teams 12 and 14 to clear the disabled landing craft from the beaches. This was a process of towing out to sea and blasting them with tetrytol if they did not sink.

Marvin Cooper, Gunner's Mate, UDT 13

─────────── **D-Day Plus** ───────────

I and ten of my men volunteered to go back onto the beaches to clear the beaches of the broached landing boats that had occurred during the first assault wave. The beaches were completely cluttered and the other landing boats with their men could not unload. The first assault men were pinned down in the volcanic ash and the front line wasn't over 300 feet from the water line. My men and I

took two rubber boats loaded with explosives and swam them into the beach. For the next three days, we blew the broached boats into the ocean, opening the beaches for more assault troops.

Harry E. Gardner, Ensign, UDT 13

* * * * *

On the second and third days of the invasion, when so many of the amphibious boats used by the Marines to land on the beach became broached because of the black sand (lava rock), Baker boat crew (UDT13) went in and pulled the boats off the beach into deeper water so bigger boats, LST's and LCI's, could get in with supplies, men, take off wounded, etc. We were under fire from mortar fire mostly. H. John Rice (no relation) should have gotten a medal for his bravery for he stood up and did his job under intense fire and dangerous battle conditions.

One of the ship's crew asked me to bring back a souvenir from the beach. I brought back a 50 cal. machine gun with a full clip in it (50 bullets) and gave it to him. Don't know his name, but heard it got raffled off several times later.

Since the coxswain had to stay on the boat and the radio man had to stay with the radio, the motor mach was the only one who could go on the beach and hook up the boats to be pulled off. And that was me. Every time we pulled a boat off the beach we lost some more rope - so they had to go back to the ship and get more rope. I stayed on the beach until they got back. I had some interesting times dodging mortar fire and talking to the Marines. It's too bad that I didn't have a camera with me - some of it was pretty gruesome.

Bennie M. Rice, MM, UDT13

* * * * *

Feb. 20 Boats over the side with demolition teams and their deadly tetrytol. To go on the beach and blow up obstacles if any. We stood by very close to the beach. Anti-aircraft fire directed at planes started falling all around us. One shell burst no more than 20 feet in front of me. Boy! Did I hit that deck fast. It scared the hell out of me.

Zenon C. Wolan, Electrician's Mate   from his journal

* * * * *

After the K's at Okinawa, my most vivid memories are of 2/16/45, 2/17/45, 2/18/45 & 2/23/45, all 4 dates at Iwo. The 2/18, night before the landings when a Betty bomber went low over us and creamed APD Blessman, perhaps stands out most.

Feb. 23 we watched the flag raising on Suribachi, probably about 1 1/2 miles or so away.

Philip P. Jones, Lieutenant

*   *   *   *   *

D-Day plus 2 (Feb. 21) One-third of the island is ours, but casualties keep piling up. All the UDT men went in to the beach today to help clear the beach for the supplies to land. They brought back some gruesome stories. Marines dead and stacked in mounds lying everywhere. The beach filled with wrecked landing boats and equipment.

Manuel Verissimo, Water Tender
from his journal, "Manny's Excellent Adventures"

*   *   *   *   *

After the invasion of Iwo, we spent about ten days assisting in removing sunken and damaged landing craft from our assigned beaches. On one occasion, when our landing craft had just touched the beach, two Marines signaled for us to get down. We hit the deck and heard a loud bang. When we got up, the Marines were gone; they had taken a direct mortar hit.

Edward N. Deringer, Quartermaster, UDT 13

*   *   *   *   *

March 1 D-Day plus 10. Still fierce fighting on island. CB's working hard on air strip. Was pretty close to island again today--could see plenty of soldiers and Marines fighting Japs. Took fuel off oiler No. 85. Probably will be leaving here soon. Fighting was pretty hard on island tonight. Marines have gained 500 yards in past twenty-four hours.

Joseph E. Purgatorio, Gunner's Mate   from his journal

*   *   *   *   *

From D-Day through March 3, 1945, the Barr screened or anchored while our Underwater Demolition Team No. 13 worked with the beach-masters and removed underwater obstacles. The team that chose the most dangerous assignments, chose No. 13 as their team number, had a black cat as their symbol and had not a single casualty.

Eugene L. Swearingen, Ensign
from his journal, "My Ramblings Aboard the Barr, APD39"

The following poem by Rima Magee (wife of UDT13 member, Art Magee) was written in 1998 for the Black Cat reunion at Fort Pierce, referring to the Iwo Jima invasion.

We all have reached our sunset years --
Remembering days of old
When we were rife with vibrant life,
Reckless, brave and bold,
As we rode upon the waves
In waters warm and cold.
The dolphins, too, remember well
The thunder in the air;
The skies so bright with booming light,
The rocky, treeless lair.
But we strove forward mightily --
All together there!
We muster here in thinner ranks --
Though halt and lame and gray,
We still stand tall upon the mall
To hear the bugler play
The stirring melody of Taps
For those who've gone away.
How joyous now to say "Hello!"
How sad to say "Goodbye."
For God will beckon and we reckon
Parting day is nigh.
But there will be full complement
At the muster in the sky.

Copyright 1999 by Rima Magee
Published with her permission

On shore leave at Guam, I overindulged during the beer bust. I was lying on a flat rock on the beach with the tide coming in, feeling no pain at all. Bill Crandell grabbed me every time the water washed over the rock to keep me from floating out to sea. Do you suppose that's why I don't drink beer to this day?

Arthur W. Magee, Signalman, UDT 13

UDT volleyball game on Asor Island

The Barr's Two "Zekes" on R & R Break
EM3c Copenhaver and EM2c Wolan

CHAPTER 8

GUAM AND ULITHI - R & R

This morning the U.D.T. boys were put off on Asor Island, for a rest. . . . Have been laying around at anchorage and enjoying liberty, such as it is, for the past few days. . . . We are headed for Okinawa. . . . The Captain said that this one was not going to be a picnic like Iwo Jima for us.

March 4, 1945.

O, boy this morning about 0900 we fueled and by noon were underway for Saipan. As we were leaving this morning we saw a B-29 land on Iwo. They say it is the first B-29 to land there. Something was wrong and it could not make it back to its base in Saipan.

Gosh, it is nice to get away. It is just bad that the whole war is not over. At least, now, with the lives of thousands of Marines, we have a base pretty close to Japan. Who knows how many more lives are going to be lost before we reach our ultimate objective - Tokyo. Maybe now we will get a little rest. At least, we are going back for awhile. This past month will always live in my memory as the worst thing I have ever seen.

March 7, 1945.

Changed course this morning at 0300 right out from Saipan for Guam . The ships that we were escorting went in to Saipan.

1600 - Anchored at Guam [about 50 miles south of Tinian]. No mail for us.

March 8, 1945.

Had a beer party and ball game this afternoon. Came back aboard to find I had mail. Lots from my girl; two from home.

March 11, 1945.

This afternoon at 1400 we got underway, enroute to Ulithi in the Carolines. We hear that we are going back down for some more training, with the U.D.T. boys.

March 12, 1945.

Had practice G.Q. drill today. Test fired all guns. The most noise we have heard since we left Iwo.

1600 - Anchored in Ulithi. No mail here for us.

March 15, 1945.

This morning the U.D.T. boys were put off on Asor Island, for a rest. We are still on the ship. Well, maybe they need a rest. Had liberty this afternoon. Went over on Asor Island. Ran across "Shorty", a yeoman I used to work with back in the good old Discipline Office at Great Lakes. Sure was good to see him and talk with him again.

March 17, 1945.

Have been laying around at anchorage and enjoying liberty, such as it is, for the past few days. This morning around 1000 U.D.T 13 came back on board and after dinner a few Army Officers reported aboard. The Captain said we would get underway soon, and also that it was another invasion. Gosh, we have just got through with one. But I suppose it will take a lot of invasions to end this dern war. Had some more mail this afternoon. Just returned from a movie.

Lt. Kaiser and UDT Executive Officer Walker

March 20, 1945.

Still anchored and having recreation parties and getting mail. This is good duty.

1500 - The Captain just told me to have the Sailing Report ready first thing in the morning. Said we were going to Saipan and from there straight on to another invasion. Boy, we are sure winning this war fast. Wonder where this will be. The dope that we are going is all over the ship now, but no one knows where.

March 21 1945.

At 0630 this morning we pulled up the hook. At 0900 we had G.Q. drill.

1600 - We are now speeding along with a heck of a large convoy, BB's, DD's, cruisers, aircraft carriers and other ships. The Captain was on the speaker a few minutes ago and gave us the dope. We are headed for Okinawa. Due there on the morning of the 25th, seven days before the "blowout". The Captain said Okinawa was 325 miles south of Japan. My O, my. I'll bet we get into it this time. The Captain even said that this one was not going to be a picnic like Iwo Jima for us. Warned all hands to keep alert. I forgot, this morning, I found out that I am to man the .50 cal machine gun at the port look out box. Maybe it will be better if anything comes at us, to be shooting back. I like the new job fine for I have always liked to shoot a gun.

March 22, 1945.

Enroute to Okinawa. This morning we had G.Q. drill and fired all guns. I got to fire my 50 cal. Boy, does it kick. It sure does put the lead out. Seems I emptied a magazine in about a couple of seconds. Had a movie in the mess hall this afternoon. Don't suppose we will have any more mail for some time. The U.D.T. group are working all the time going over their maps and charts.

March 23, 1945.

This morning we went alongside the ARKANSAS to fuel. What a big thing she is, and how little we are beside her. Have been zig-zagging all day. Are in dangerous waters now. Lots of "subs" have been reported around. We are not going by Saipan. Orders have been changed.

March 24, 1945.

Enroute Okinawa. This morning "sub" sighted by ship ahead of us; they attacked but I don't think they got the "sub". In the morning, we will be there. Gosh, but it seems that we should be having more trouble than we are. Getting pretty close to Japan, and it seems they would have more to say about our approaching Okinawa. Things are too calm. In the morning, I'll bet I can't say that.

FLASHBACKS

Our ship was anchored off Saipan between our operations at Iwo and Okinawa; the swells were eight to ten feet; we had to stand up to eat; even our food would slide all over our tray. In addition, we slept in bunks that were canvas and five feet high; during this period, we had to chain our bunks up at an angle to keep from falling out.

Edward N. Deringer, Quartermaster, UDT 13

*   *   *   *   *

On March 4, 1945, we were ordered to Saipan, then Guam, for provisions, liberty (BEER!), and on back to Ulithi to stage for the Okinawa invasion.

John W. Hubenthal, Lieutenant (jg)   from his autobiography

*   *   *   *   *

Our sister ship, USS Bates, had an officer for recreation and entertainment by the name of Eddie Duchin. Right, the piano guy. He had his record collection with him and regularly kept us thinking of home with his music. One night, I think it was on Guam he entertained the troops and had fortified his courage too strenuously and had a hard time staying on the piano stool.

Donald H. Murray, Lieutenant (jg), UDT 13

*   *   *   *   *

I remember a beer party on Guam. The beer was warm and some of the younger guys, sort of intoxicated, started playfully throwing empty beer cans at each other. Soon we had a beer can fight similar to the old snow ball fights that we had when we were kids. Fortunately, no one was seriously injured though I do remember seeing some bleeding foreheads.

Marvin Cooper, Gunner's Mate, UDT 13

*   *   *   *   *

We had leave for a few days at our Guam Base. The UDT had a jungle enclosure rest camp. Jordan wanted to visit them and so we got a jeep and headed for the hills. A stockade with corner machine gun posts. After a time they were ready to go back to the ship. They had gunny sacks full of coconuts and on the way Jordan asked me if I was thirsty. Handed me his canteen and I had a swig of pure fire-water. I was very naive and didn't tumble to the makings of jungle juice. Several weeks went by and one morning black eyes and cut lips and scrapes showed at morning muster. The jungle juice was ready. We searched the ship many times with no results. Finally and probably when the juice was gone, we discovered the LCPR water casks were the storage places. I was guilty of bringing fun aboard.

Donald H. Murray, Lieutenant (jg), UDT 13

*   *   *   *   *

Eddie Duchin was the movie officer aboard the Bates. I was his equivalent aboard the Barr. I was stuck with the job because I was the junior officer - never could figure why he got the job because he was a Lt. Commander. He was the CIC (Combat Information Center) officer aboard the Bates. We had a good one with Lt. (jg) Gordie Huber.

I had a few get togethers with Mr. Duchin while trading and swapping movies. His projection man and mine did the detailed work. I am sure he was aboard the Bates from Maui till up to the Okinawa campaign. I don't know whether he was still aboard when the Bates was hit by a suicide plane. Incidentally, the nice young sailor, was killed in this action. It was said that they had a small piano aboard the Bates for Duchin to play, but they could not get him to play it most of the time. This may have just been rumor. I remember that Mr. Duchin was a sun bather. I can still see him lying on the deck sunning himself. He had a real deep tan all over.

John J. Reilly, Ensign

*   *   *   *   *

A sunken Jap one-man sub was a play area of sorts at MOG Fleet recreation area (in Ulithi anchorage)

Philip P. Jones, Lieutenant

*   *   *   *   *

Soon we cruised down to Ulithi, and Team 13 moved from the Barr to the Island of Asor for an R & R leave. We were there for all of two days. I and others visited Ray LeBlanc's grave. We did some swimming in the warm waters. There was a small hospital on the island but we decided there were no nurses attached to the hospital because throughout the base there were pipes with funnels protruding from the sand. These were designed as urinals and were used by sailors, Marines and army personnel.

Marvin Cooper, Gunner's Mate, UDT 13

Team 13 had 13 officers; it took us 13 days to get from Fort Pierce to Hawaii. We considered 13 very lucky, particularly when we had so many near misses and never lost or had a man killed in combat. Ensigns Hehli, Hamman and Murray just about had it in Ulithi when we were exploring outer islands in our rubber boat and a storm blew up. We battered our way back to the ship with a small outboard motor (which repeatedly immersed on the back side of a wave.) PHEW, would have gone to sea without a trace.

Donald H. Murray, Lieutenant (jg), UDT 13

  *   *   *   *   *

We arrived at Ulithi and continued work that had started at Guam, much needed repairs to machinery. I haven't worked so hard as this in a long time, night & day. The deck apes painted the ship. We are no longer the "Green Hornet". Back to battleship gray. Did I say we came back for a rest?

Manuel Verissimo, Water Tender
from his journal, "Manny's Excellent Adventures"

  *   *   *   *   *

March 16 . . . Ship more than half painted. Hull is blue and superstructure is gray. Looks better than that green we had.

Zenon C. Wolan, Electrician's Mate   from his journal

  *   *   *   *   *

March 23 . . . At 2400 we got a flank reverse bell. We just missed a collision with the APD 101 by a hair. At 0400 the same thing happened. Those guys ought to get on the ball.

Zenon C. Wolan, Electrician's Mate   from his journal

  *   *   *   *   *

On the lighter side, there were humorous times. I can't remember their real names, but there were two boys, boat crews, that we called Little Stoop and Big Stoop, one real short, the other real tall. Now, Big Stoop's bunk was right over mine. You probably know how those bunks were made - metal rails, canvas with eyelets, small rope laced thru the eyelets around the sides and ends. Well, to mess up a good night's sleep, all you had to do was cut the rope in one place, and the rope would slowly work loose. Only one way for ole Big Stoop to go - down on me.

Guy E. Farley, Radioman

One time we were in port and, as the cook, I had gotten some supplies off an Australian supply ship - it was lamb. Finally, the guys came to me and said "Priest, we're tired of this lamb. We're butting our heads against the wall." So at night time we went down and threw it over the side.

Then another time we got a lot of canned turkey and we had turkey any which way you could make it - turkey pot pie, turkey and gravy, turkey with vegetables. Sometimes we would get eggs old enough to vote.

Clarence I. Priest, Seaman

Ensign Hubenthal on Deck watch

FC2c Shannon, FC2c Haglan, GM2c Stillwell, and GM3c Dahman at Gun 43 (40mm)

SM2c Krawiec at light signal

QM1c Armstrong in the wheelhouse

CHAPTER 9

OKINAWA - EASTER PARADE

Today is Easter and what a parade I saw this morning. Never have I seen anything more pretty than hundreds of the little boats in the water. It was pretty but was sad when you think of their job. . . . By noon you could not see anything for all the smoke and dust.

<u>March 25, 1945</u>.

This morning EDWARDS which was a little ahead of us opened up on a Jap plane. This was about 0010. From then till about 0230 we had G.Q. We fired at no planes. At 0700, Barr set Condition Two Mike. All guns were manned. At 0900 we went to G.Q.

This morning at 0500, we arrived off Okinawa. U.D.T. reconned beaches at southwest tip of Tokashika. No opposition from shore. Battle wagons, cruisers and Destroyers started opening up with all their might.

We stayed at G.Q. until 1600 today. Retired west of Kerama Rhetto for the night. A pretty calm day with exception of a little excitement early this morning.

<u>March 26, 1945</u>.

This morning, I had all the excitement that I shall ever want. We went to G.Q. at 0530 - sunrise G.Q. We were transferring army officers to the GILMER, which was just off our port bow when we had an air attack. The KNUDSEN, just off our starboard beam, received a near bomb miss. There were two planes attacking us three ships. The planes that dropped bombs at KNUDSEN on our starboard side went into a suicide dive. It came right at us, went right over the top of us, missed us, and crashed into the waters right close aboard the GILMER. The GILMER lost a few men from strafing.

The other plane which was coming in on our port side was taken under fire by a destroyer about a half mile away. It kept coming toward us and my little .50 cal. was the first gun on this ship to open up on it. Later I found out that it was way out of range of my .50 cal and the boys have sure kidded me! Guess I got excited. But I sure was pumping lead at him. - It came on in - heading right for us, all guns were opened up. It got almost on us and made a sharp turn back, and went back for the destroyer that had previously taken it under fire. The destroyer must have hit him for he nosed down and crashed into the water. I don't see how either plane missed us. We sure were lucky.

That attack did not last but about 20 minutes. However, we stayed at our battle stations as planes were reported 40 or 50 miles away, closing. At 0730 we had a Flash Red, Control Yellow. Enemy planes close around again. Could see anti-aircraft firing all around but none closed our ship. 0800 - Flash White. 0830 - Condition 2.Mike. At 1000 we took screening station, in inner screen - E-26.

At 1700 had G.Q. 1745 - secured. At 1842 we went to G.Q. as bogeys were in area again. At 1920 we secured from G.Q. Retired for the night. And what a day it has been. Enough excitement to last me the rest of my life.

March 27, 1945.

This morning we were up at 0430 at G.Q. Flash Red - Control Yellow. (this means enemy air attack imminent, fire at all planes.) None of our planes are supposed to be in the area when such control. Ack-ack all around. No planes close to us. We did no firing. The NEVADA was hit by a suicide plane. What an explosion. Must have been loaded with bombs. At 0645 we secured. We were supposed to reconn Keise Shima this morning but operations are postponed. Took our screening station for the afternoon. Subs were reported sighted by planes a few miles away. We have had no contacts. Underway at 2000 for retirement area.

March 28, 1945.

Early this morning we almost had a collision with the KNUDSEN. All engines were thrown back full and all of us thought we had been hit.

Sailors in the Engine Room

What a scare. At 0530, we went to G.Q. Enemy planes in area. 0700 - secured from G.Q. Around noon we followed the mine sweeps into beaches of Keise

Shima. Went to G.Q. at 1300 because of floating mines. We shot up two mines while waiting for the sweeps to sweep the area. At 1400 demos went in to plant demolition charges on reefs. About three or four tons were planted on the reefs and at 1610 it was set off. An explosion sky high occurred. And I imagine all of us had that empty feeling of what would happen to us if anything ever hit us - as we had plenty of that stuff on board. Really, these are some exciting days. Retired for night.

March 29, 1945.

Enemy planes were in area from mid-nite on last night. We went to G.Q. three different times. Ack-ack fire all around but no planes closed our ship. The closest ack-ack was about 1500 yards away.

At 1030, had Flash Red, Control Yellow. Planes all around. Two ships hit about a mile from us by suicide planes. 1110 - Flash White. 1130 - Explosion on the beach by the demos. 1300 - Flash Blue - enemy air attack probable. 2030 - Flash Red, Control Yellow. All ships opened up on planes coming in low on the water. I saw one ship get hit. And also a pattern of bombs dropped behind another. Retired for the night. Boy, these suicide planes are awful. We have been real lucky so far not having any more coming in for us.

March 30, 1945.

Peaceful night last night. At 0530, we went to Day light G.Q. We do this every morning. Don't want any of them to slip up on us. We realize that when they come in that they come right on in. Our Captain is the calmest man on the ship.

Captain Dickie

At 0805, we had Flash Blue, Control Green. Set condition 2M. About 0900, members of Team #13 and #19 were bombed and strafed by planes. Our boys came back and no one was hit. At 1300, a demolition explosion went off on the reefs and 1310 another. Sky high they were. At 1900 we got underway for night retirement.

March 31, 1945.

This morning we went to G.Q. at 0155. At 0120, heavy anti-aircraft fire was all around. One bomb dropped about 1000 yards on our starboard bow. Another was observed dropped close behind us. Boy, was it a mess when I got to my battle station. The sky was full of ack-ack. And what a feeling it was to be asleep and have something like this to happen.

0751 - Flash White. Everything calm. Spent the day screening LST's while they put the Army and big "tom tom" ashore. They are going to use these big guns to help bombard Okinawa along with the ships. 1716 - Flash Red, Control Green. We saw no planes. Retired for the night north of Kerama Rhetto. Tomorrow is the big day. And what an invasion this will be. Hundreds of ships are standing by waiting for tomorrow.

April 1, 1945 (EASTER PARADE)

At 0300 this morning, enemy planes came in for the attack. Ships to the west of us opened up. Plane came close aboard to our ship but was only sighted a mere second. This plane was shot down by a destroyer off our port beam. We should have opened up on him for he came in real close, but the Captain has given orders to hold fire unless you can see the plane and he commits himself. At 0630, back to G.Q.; planes in area. Anti-aircraft fire all around. 0740 - secured from G.Q.

Today is Easter and what a parade I saw this morning. Never have I seen anything more pretty than hundreds of the little boats in the water. It was pretty but was sad when you think of their job. This morning we must have had all the planes in the air. They were flying over in groups headed in to the beach. And all the ships opened up on the beach with everything that they had. What a sight it was. By noon you could not see anything for all the smoke and dust. We were not in as close to the beach as we were at Iwo but I could still see plenty.

We retired at 1800. And at 1900 we had our excitement. Planes were in the area. One came in on our port side and we opened up on him. He crashed in the water about 300 yards away. At 2000 we secured from G.Q.

April 2, 1945.

Enemy air craft were in area all night. Lots of anti-aircraft fire was going on, but none came in close to us.

0500 - Flash Red, Control Yellow. Went to G.Q. Anti-aircraft fire filled the sky. Three ships were hit. 0700 - Flash White, secured from G.Q.

At noon we took screening station A-34 about 12 miles from Okinawa. About 1800, GRIFFIN who was just behind us opened up on a plane. This plane was identified as friendly. I guess everyone is getting itchy fingers because these Japs really do slip up on the ships. They come in low to the water and it makes it hard for the radar to detect them. They are on us sometimes before we know it.

April 3, 1945.

Enemy planes in area all night. At 0500 we went to G.Q. Flash was red. We saw no firing. 0700 - Secured. Gosh, what a racket all the big ships make. Big guns roaring 24 hours a day. Never letting up. We hear that our boys are doing pretty good on the beach.

Left screening station about 1500, went into the transport area. 1805 - went to G.Q. Never in my life have I seen anything like it. The sky was covered with red tracers. It seems that every ship in the transport area had every gun opened up. Jap planes came in. Several of the ships around were hit. Some bombs were dropped. I have seen anti-aircraft fire a lot and sometimes in the movies. But you could never see fire like this unless you were here. There must have been five or six hundred ships there in the transport area and I suppose all were opened up. We could hear shells whizzing by our ship, as some of the planes were low on the water.

People were firing like mad. I was stooped under my gun firing right on but my knees were really knocking. I have never been so afraid in all my life. I must have aged five years. I felt like the world was at end. This went on for about ten or fifteen minutes, then everything was calm. I came back down here in the office and prayed and thanked God that we came out of that one all right.

We secured at 1900. At 2010, we went to G.Q. again. Flash Red, Control Yellow. Another attack. Ack-ack fire all around us. We did no firing as we saw no planes. At 2045, Flash White. We secured.

RM3c Heaton

FC3c Pennington

<u>April 4, 1945</u>.

Enemy aircraft in area all night. Thank God, none came close to us and we had a nice night for sleep - if anyone could sleep. I was up about 0200 this morning. I just woke up and I walked up on deck and saw ack-ack firing at a distance. Lots of the boys were sitting around in the mess hall drinking coffee. It was no use in losing sleep for we know that we would have G Q. if any planes came in close. But it's just that waiting and feeling that at any minute you will hear that awful sound out of a sleep - that dong, dong, dong. I went back to bed about 0300 and finally went off to sleep.

This morning the Captain read over the loud speaker the result of the battles, in the last 24 hours. Around 15 of our ships were hit, twelve of them by suicide planes. We went back to our old screening station this afternoon.

<u>April 5, 1945.</u>

And guess what happened this morning. We got mail, and O, how welcomed it was. Never have I been so glad to receive anything. While we were in the transport area we saw the NEVADA get hit again. This time by shore batteries. Yes, those dern Japs are fighting back. But our big ships are laying it in to them day and night. 1600 - Anchored in Kerama Rhetto. We heard tonight that a Jap task force is underway headed for here. All ships have been ordered to be ready to get underway. O, my, do we have to put up with something else. These suicide planes are enough.

<u>April 6, 1945.</u>

What good news we heard this morning. They say one of our task force met the Jap Fleet and destroyed it. Said the battleship YAMATO was hit by eight bombs and several torpedoes. That should stop them. They must remember they are up against the best Navy in the world.

At 0308 we went to G.Q. Big air attack over at Okinawa. Few planes reported around Kerama Rhetto. But it is nice in here. When we have Flash Red, we make smoke, and consequently Jap planes can not see us. But we man our stations just the same. At 0630 we secured from G.Q. At 0800, Flash Red, Control Yellow, lots of firing going on just outside of anchorage. Secured around 1000. At 1100, set condition 2 M. Bogeys in vicinity. At 1145, secured. No planes closed.

Around 1500, we went back to G.Q. Big air attack underway. Enemy planes closed Kerama Rhetto. At the time of the attack, we were tied alongside a tanker taking on fuel, and transferring U.D.T. #13 and equipment to an APA. Our fantail was loaded with explosives. What a position to be in for an air attack. Really I felt like two cents.

Then it all started, all around us was like hell. The first thing that happened was I saw a plane low to the water coming down between two ships. And although the two ships were in a bad position to fire at the plane because each was in the line of fire of the other - they opened up. All of a sudden, I saw this plane bank and go right into one of the ships. What a very big explosion. I later found out that it was an ammunition ship.

About that time we opened fire on a plane just off our port bow. Our fire and other ship's fire got him. Next one was coming from our stern, we opened up but he crashed into the water just missing a ship close by. Then there was ack-ack fire all around us. And firing low on the water, for the planes all came in low. Four were shot down close to the anchorage. Just about the time this attack was over, a friendly chicken (as we call our planes) took off from a carrier. He hardly got off the carrier good until he was shot down. I think the pilot was saved.

I suppose all of us had had enough for one day, and just couldn't think before we shot. We were finally well hidden by smoke and were relieved. Finally secured about 2030.

Gosh, how long can we be lucky like this. It seems that things are getting worse. They are really picking on us ships.

S1c Meehan

SM2c Budak at Signal Light

April 7, 1945.

This morning we were up around 0400 at our battle stations. Bogeys closed Kerama Rhetto. I can remember now that I was half way to my gun by the time G.Q. bell rang. O, what a heck of a way to be awakened. I was awakened by gun reports. By the time we got to our guns, every ship in the Rhetto was opened up. Several planes were shot down. I was more afraid of our own ships this morning than I was of the planes. The planes were low on the water and ships were firing into each other. I heard a lot of bullets whizzing by the bridge. We had reports that several of our men on ships in the Rhetto had been hit. Also had a report that one ship just outside the anchorage had been hit by a suicider. Right after we got to G.Q. this morning, we started making smoke and were soon hidden. At around 0630, we secured.

We put off the U.D.T.'s this morning and around 1300 took up screening station Able-27, north of Kerama Rhetto.

This morning the Captain read over again all the ships that have been hit in the last 24 hours. Maybe I had better not tell here. But the story is sad. We hear that we are losing more men than the Army who are on the beach fighting. That doesn't seem to be likely. 1800 - On screening station, Able 27.

April 8, 1945.

This morning, the same old thing. They won't leave us alone. Was up at G.Q. at 0530. Did no firing as no planes closed our station. 0700 - Secured.

Screening station Able-27 all day. At 1400, we went to G.Q., Flash Red, Control Yellow. Bogeys closed. Ship in Able 28 hit by aerial torpedo. Right after we got to G.Q., we observed torpedo wake coming toward us. Executed sharp turn and got out of the path. Two planes knocked down dead ahead. Secured around 1530.

1830 - Flash Red, Control Yellow. Went to G.Q. Plane attacked ship on our starboard beam. Suicider dived into water. Many planes were reported over around Okinawa. We secured around 2045. Back to G.Q. around 2130. We saw no planes and did no firing. 2230 - Secured from G.Q.

FLASHBACKS

──────── *Easter Parade Minus 7 to 6* ────────

Okinawa was the largest of these islands, 60 miles long with a reported population of 500,000 and 100,000 Jap troops. We hoped that it would not have the fortifications of Iwo Jima, and that all we had to fight were the troops. The other twelve or so islands we were to take prior to L-Day were all small and not very well fortified and were to be used as stepping stones. . . . It can readily be seen that we would need this air cover, as Okinawa itself had seven airfields and we were within 30 minutes flying time from hundreds of airfields in Formosa, China and Japan.

Manuel Verissimo, Water Tender
from his journal, "Manny's Excellent Adventures"

*   *   *   *   *

At Okinawa, the skipper decided to serve Easter dinner on Palm Sunday, the day we began our operation. After my morning mission, I discovered Hasbrouk standing on the fantail with a heaping plate of food. "Hey," he said, handing me the plate. "You gotta go out again right away." I gulped, grabbed the plate and dashed across the fantail to the other side where the boat crew was waiting for me. The food was delicious, but did you ever try to eat while bouncing along in a landing craft?

Arthur W. Magee, Signalman, UDT 13

*   *   *   *   *

The Japs had planned to use Kerama Rhetto as a base for suicide boats when Okinawa was attacked. We fooled them by taking the Rhetto first and destroying over 700 small boats.

The minesweepers did a tremendous job. It was the largest area ever to be cleared of mines by the Navy. How dangerous their work is, and how little credit they receive! The papers will only say, "The area around Okinawa is being cleared of mines."

Eugene L. Swearingen, Ensign
from his journal, "My Ramblings Aboard the Barr, APD39"

Intelligence reports said that there were no gun emplacements and very little troops here (Tokashika Shima). To get to the beach where the army was to land, they (UDT 13) had to go through a channel as the beach was inside a cove with high ground on all sides. If they had put any kind of guns on their high spots, they could stop the whole U.S. Army from landing there. A single machine gun would have blasted our boys to hell and they were kind of worried, but to our great pleasure, everything was clear.

Manuel Verissimo, Water Tender
from his journal, "Manny's Excellent Adventures"

*   *   *   *   *

The Barr took us to the Kerama Rhetto islands where Team 13 was to open the beaches of Tokashika Shima. I swam in to the beach on the morning of March 25. The water was colder than the water at Iwo, but no Japanese were shooting at me and I survived. There was a coral reef that extended to the beach. The area was a sheltered bay and there was practically no surf. It was determined that no demolitions were needed because the invading troops were going in on amtracs, and it was believed that the island was lightly defended.

A day or two later, Team 13 made a reconnaissance of Keise Shima. I did not take part in that mission. Keise Shima is about a mile from the Okinawa mainland. It was determined that a demolition operation was needed to blast coral heads to provide a channel to the beach. Team 13 worked to a man placing over 27 tons of tetrytol in three days to blast a channel to shore. I snagged the back of my leg on a piece of coral resulting in a gash several inches long. My buddies yelled for me to get out of the water because I was bleeding profusely. They were afraid I would attract sharks. I boarded the LCPR and our Pharmacist Mate, Emerson, bandaged and taped my leg, and I went back to work. I still carry the scar today.

Marvin Cooper, Gunner's Mate, UDT 13

——————— **Easter Parade Minus 4 to 3** ———————

Our next operation was at Tokashika Shima, west of Okinawa, where we did a recon of the beaches, no big deal. From there we proceeded to Keisa Shima. There we set charges to create a channel that the larger landing craft could use to bring in large cannons to shell Okinawa proper. It was there that on the third and last day of our demolition work, we were attacked by three US Navy planes. They strafed with machine guns and each dropped one bomb. Our men were lucky they missed completely. At the time of the attack we had three tons of explosives in the water.

Edward N. Deringer, Quartermaster, UDT 13

Okinawa - Keisa Shima Island: This small island was one mile off the mainland of Okinawa. The mission was to blow a channel for a company of men and their equipment. I was the officer in charge of this mission. We blew a channel through large coral heads and coral reefs that was 100 ft. wide and 300 ft. long. It was large enough to bring in an LSM landing craft that had 200 men, their fighting equipment and radar station. It took our crew two and one-half days and over 27 tons of tetrytol blocks to blow the channel. Later that afternoon, when the water had cleared, we swam back in to examine our work. The next morning I was carried over to the LSM, had lunch with the Skipper and Commanding Officer of the company and then was asked to steer the boat through the channel and land it. What a thrill! I had never steered a ship before. Mission accomplished!

Harry E. Gardner, Ensign, UDT 13

*   *   *   *   *

March 28 . . . As we passed by one of these islands this morning I saw the DD594 which was sunk by a mine. Her bow was still sticking out of the water. We got a warning to watch out for suicide boats loaded with explosives.

Zenon C. Wolan, Electrician's Mate   from his journal

*   *   *   *   *

On the 28th of March we went in close to Keise Shima, proceeding through areas with possible mines. A destroyer coming through the same area was sunk - only 75 survivors from a ship complement of 350. One battleship, one cruiser, and four destroyers were hit by "suicides."

Eugene L. Swearingen, Ensign
from his journal, "My Ramblings Aboard the Barr, APD39"

*   *   *   *   *

Captain Dickie gave us an unconfirmed report that the USS Halligan DD594 had struck a mine. I had been aboard the USS Halligan DD584 visiting with friends just a few days before, so I went to the log room and asked Jim Grenga to check and see if the Captain had made an error in announcing the DD594. Jim checked with the Captain, and it was the Halligan DD584 which was sunk. Two of the friends I visited were lost and never found. I know their families well and have kept in touch with them.

Andrew C. Soucy, Water Tender
from his personal diary and album

March 28 . . . This morning we passed one of our Destroyers that had been sunk in close to one of the small islands. The Captain just gave us the news on how everything was going. That Destroyer that had been sunk was the Halligan. She had been sunk by an underwater explosion, possibly a suicide boat.

The island we had invaded was secured with light casualties, also 5 other islands were secured. On three others, the Japs were putting up a stiff fight.

Over at Okinawa, the air raid of the previous day had caused a bit of damage. The Nevada and some destroyers had been hit by suicide planes. The Japs lost three planes by A.A. fire, six suicides and two by our fighters. Our losses - 45 dead, 3 missing and 98 wounded. They picked up 75 survivors from the D.D. that had been sunk, 45 of them wounded.

The UDT went on reconnaissance on a couple of small islands just off Okinawa. They found they would have to blast. The army was to put up a battery of Long Toms to support the landings on Okinawa.

March 29 . . . We have captured 145 suicide boats to date. Along with 24 boats captured last night were 99 Japs and 1 Intelligence Officer. Plans for the defense of Okinawa with these boats were also captured.

Manuel Verissimo, Water Tender
from his journal, "Manny's Excellent Adventures"

———— *Easter Parade Plus* ————

April 3 Army men on the island are 12 days ahead of schedule. We had 3 air raids last night. Marines say that 11 Japs attacked them at one point. When the charge failed, they committed suicide. They were women dressed in nuns' clothes.

Manuel Verissimo, Water Tender,
from his journal, "Manny's Excellent Adventures"

In order to protect ourselves from the Japanese aircraft, all ships were ordered to put small craft over the side and circle the mother ship making heavy smoke. We were warned to be on the lookout for Japanese suicide swimmers who were thought to be on the islands. Our Doctor, whose battle station was in the officers' wardroom (Our dining table was used as the emergency operating table) mistook our Filipino mess cook for a Japanese invader, and almost shot him as he came into the wardroom to make coffee for the captain.

John W. Hubenthal, Lieutenant (jg) from his autobiography

In Okinawa, my friend, Shannon, had his infrared glasses shot right off his face; he couldn't believe it - he didn't even get a scratch. I think it was rifle fire from the beach that hit his glasses.

Francis J. Skotko, Gunner's Mate

*   *   *   *   *

The "Divine Wind" was disastrous to the U. S. Navy. The "Divine Wind" was what the Japanese called their suicide plane pilots. These were young men trained to take their small planes off the ground or carriers. They did not need to know how to land them.

Marvin Cooper, Gunner's Mate, UDT 13

*   *   *   *   *

I was the Boat Officer, and John Hubenthal, Assistant Engineering Officer, and I and Gene Swearingen, the Supply Officer, and Jack Reilly, Assistant Communications Officer, bunked together in a little compartment aft and below decks right next to the 45 tons of tetrytol . The UDT guys always told us it wouldn't explode unless set off by a fuse - but we had our own opinion, and sort of felt that if one of those Kamikaze Kooks happened to hit close to it we'd be the first to know. Or not know, more likely.

C. Richard Keys, Lieutenant (jg)

*   *   *   *   *

It took some doing to get us out of the beach battalion, but we were finally enrolled in Class 7 which became UDT 13. I served at Iwo Jima and Okinawa - where the war ended for me. The beach battalion wanted me back when we got to Okinawa and there I stayed when the rest of the Team returned to Maui and the Barr left for other assignments. About a month later, a Jap shell blew me out of the hole where I had taken shelter against the bombardment, and I was out of it.

Arthur W. Magee, Signalman, UDT 13

*   *   *   *   *

The only time I had a chance to fire at the enemy, I was stationed on the flying bridge with Robinson at our 50 caliber machine gun. I saw a Jap plane flying at us and hollered to open fire. Robbie tried, but the gun jammed.

Donald H. Murray, Lieutenant (jg), UDT 13

While in anchorage at the Kerama Rhetto (which means western islands) we were preparing to depart the USS Barr. Our men had brought the remaining high explosives out of the hold and placed them on the deck on the fantail of the ship. About that time I heard over the loud speaker, "Bogeys on the starboard quarter". It was repeated over and over. We knew what it was - the dreaded kamikaze or suicide planes. About that time I stepped out of our troop compartment onto the fantail of the Barr. Again I heard speakers blaring "Bogeys on the starboard quarter". It was then I realized that I was standing on the starboard quarter looking at tons of high explosives. I leaned back against the bulkhead and slowly sat down on the deck. I was so scared I could not stand up.

Edward N. Deringer, Quartermaster, UDT 13

    *   *   *   *   *

We left the Barr after our demolition operations at Iwo Jima and Okinawa. During this time, I had lost my hearing in one ear due to a blast and also had contracted a fungus from being under and in the water so much, so I was sent to a hospital in Oakland and then to Portsmouth, where I was discharged after the war ended.

George Gregory, Motor Machinist, UDT 13

Screening Duty

The following months found us at the invasion of Okinawa. Our job was to protect the beach area and do screening duty around the island. During these days we encountered many GQ's and Kamikaze planes. Several ships were hit, but we were lucky to escape without incident.

Andrew C. Soucy, Water Tender from his personal diary and album

    *   *   *   *   *

I recall the incident when we were on picket duty of a close call (collision) with another ship. I was on duty in the engine room with Chief Electrician Allendorf when we got the signal to reverse engines all stop to all power reverse. The chief carried out the order quickly and saved us from a collision.

Timothy P. J. Nolan, Electrician's Mate

    *   *   *   *   *

April 7 . . . A D.D. came next to us with two gaping holes in her bow. The holes were more than eight feet in diameter. Another D.D. in front of us had her whole fantail ripped to shreds. Both ships were hit by suicide planes.

Zenon C. Wolan, Electrician's Mate from his journal

Mail, just like James said, was all important. Once, while standing just off Okinawa, we slowly drifted between shore and a cruiser. The cruiser would fire occasionally at a called in target. Well, they fired right over the Barr, and I was on the boat deck writing a letter. What I almost did, was - faint.

Guy E. Farley, Radioman

*   *   *   *   *

James also brings the proper emphasis on MAIL!! My wife and I exchanged daily letters during this period, and she had the good sense to save them all. In re-reading them, my comments about mail are very much the same as James'. Unfortunately, we were not allowed to write about our activities due to the strict censorship, so my letters are not very revealing. They do reflect my moods, and when the dates are compared to James' journal they become more understandable. In one letter, I told my wife that I'd had a fight with "the yeoman" about using the typewriter. Since James was the lead yeoman, my fight probably was with him, I don't remember.

John W. Hubenthal, Lieutenant (jg)

*   *   *   *   *

As head of the main control in the engine room and while we were on general quarters one night when the Japanese were bombing us at Okinawa, I heard one of the young sailors that was on the aft depth chargers holler up on the intercom and say, "Slow down, your wake is giving you away!" We immediately got a bell and slowed down. Our skipper pulled our ship out of our patrol formation. The ship behind us went by and was bombed within minutes. We didn't get hit because when we slowed down, we reduced our wake and were not seen by the airplanes overhead. Our skipper was brought up on charges for leaving the formation in time of battle. When he explained what the situation was with the wake, from then on we were allowed to proceed slowly with small wakes and we lost very few ships. I don't know who the young man was, but his observations that night were responsible for saving many men.

Armand J. Marion, Machinist's Mate

*   *   *   *   *

For a time or two, I was stationed at GQ on a 40 mm gun as, I think, an ammunition handler. It was night, the Barr slow speed, no wind, quiet. The sound of a Jap Bogie off starboard. All eyes straining, Captain Dickie saying "Wait 'till you see 'em, boys," and someone's helmet fell off, hitting the deck, sounding loud as a bomb. My legs turned to water, and evidently everyone felt like me. When we understood what had happened, what a laugh! I have no remembrance what happened to the plane.

Guy E. Farley, Radioman

* * * * *

Our orders were to report and shoot. We reported a lot and shot little, because the Kamikazes would dive down the line of the tracer bullets from our guns to the ship, and we did not have the firepower to knock a plane out of the air. . . . Since the fleet strategy was obvious, i.e., "Let the little ships absorb the Kamikazes to protect troop ships and larger vessels in the harbor", I have often wondered if our skipper could have been court-martialed for not being a sacrificial lamb, but I am eternally grateful that he was not "Gung Ho" about it.

John W. Hubenthal, Lieutenant (jg)   from his autobiography

* * * * *

I remember a humorous incident that today remains a classic in my mind. We spent considerable time on anti-submarine screening and had a number of very close calls with disaster. We hated it when Bogies were in the area, but if we were to have them, we wanted them during the daylight hours, where we could see them to shoot at if attacked. At night, it was worse for us, because the Japanese pilots could see us but we could not see them. We always hoped for cloudy skies or moonless nights. Our wakes also helped the enemy spot our ships. Captain Dickie saved us on more than one occasion by always reducing speed, when he could, to *reduce the wake. The wake produced a phosphorus light that was easy to spot from the air.*

We were on screening duty, as usual, on a very bright moonlite night, while at Okinawa, and under the command of an admiral named Blandy. His flagship was a communication ship whose T.B.S. code call was "Wiseman." Now a word of explanation here. Talk between ships was done by signal flags, signal light, or by radio. TBS meant "Talk Between Ships." T.B.S. was short ranged and was to always be used sparingly. All ships had a code name. Ours, as I remember, was "Alameda." We had many over time. Another name for us, was "Marmalade." It was changed often to reduce the chance of being compromised by the enemy.

On this particular night we were at G. Q. with Flash Red, Control Yellow. Many enemy planes in the area. The moon was bright and full, and the conditions were not the best for us. In fact we hated it when it was so bright. We were very apprehensive. Then like some miracle, the night turned dark. We were having a total eclipse of the moon. It was awesome. We were experiencing it, but it just didn't seem real. Then without warning, and in a voice filled with awe and deep respect, the T.B.S. speaker blasted forth with these words. "Oh Wiseman, Oh Wiseman. Are you responsible for this gratuitous eclipse of the moon?" We never knew who was responsible for the question, but it did relieve the strain all of us who heard it felt. We believed the voice summed up all our feelings, and did much to remove our fears and stress. And it was done in a humorous manner that was most welcome.

John J. Reilly, Ensign

Movie screen on the USS Barr *fantail*

We stayed in Saipan on Monday, April 22, and the men got some much needed rest. The men on shore at Saipan thought they were really up "at the front," but when we got back as far as Saipan, we thought we were really safe.

We had movies on the fantail every night, and even if it rained we stayed for the entire movie. Some of them were real "stinkers" and most of them we had seen before in the States, but we enjoyed them. Hollywood says the best movies are at the front, but "the front" to them means Pearl Harbor.

Eugene L. Swearingen, Ensign
from his journal, "My Ramblings Aboard the Barr, APD39"

I particularly remember one that appealed to us all. It starred Alice Faye along with her leading man, John Payne. I believe the title of the movie was "Hello Frisco Hello." In the movie Alice sang a song , "You'll Never Know." No one could sing it like she did. When she was done, there wasn't a dry eye in the crowd. All our thoughts, I am sure, were on our loved ones and sweethearts back home in the states. We were visibly affected. It touched all our longings and desires and made us feel good, but melancholy, at the same time. It brought out our innermost feelings. We were scared most of the time, lonesome, and homesick. At least that was the way it affected me.

As a footnote to this incident, while returning the movie, it was dropped into the water and mostly ruined. Our projectionist managed to save some of the footage. Fortunately, the part with Alice singing the song was saved. It was shown over and over on many occasions to our delight.

John J. Reilly, Ensign

CHAPTER 10

SAIPAN - R & R

Had a recreation party this afternoon, and it was good to get on land again, and rest for a little. Had ice cold beer, too. ... At 2115, all hands observed five minutes of silent prayer in memory of our late Commander-in-Chief and President of the United States - Franklin D. Roosevelt

April 9, 1945.

O, what a happy day. We are now underway with convoy for Saipan. How we have prayed for this day. Now, we will have a chance for a little rest. Since March the 25th has been hell at Okinawa. This must be war at its worst. We are winning just like we always will do, but the Navy is paying a price. We are so happy to leave now. We have done our main job. But we hear we may have to return here as they expect this to be a long drawn out battle.

This morning at 0400, we went to G.Q. Bogeys closed all around. We heard several pass over our ship but did not open up on them. This is the Captain's policy especially on dark nights when we have a good chance of not being detected. But destroyers all around banged away. One ship off our port beam was hit. Saw two planes go down in flames. The destroyers have fire controlled radar. They usually open up every time a plane comes over. They have a lot of fire power, too.

We hardly stand a chance firing at a plane at night. They have all the advantages over us. And even if you hit them, they keep on coming, for now we hear that all planes are suicide planes. It's no happy thought. We stayed at G.Q. from 0400 to 0730 this morning.

It is now 2000, and we have been underway from Okinawa since 1200. No more trouble, although we hear that a big air raid is in progress around Okinawa. But off we go on our well-deserved rest. I don't care to ever see Okinawa again.

April 10, 1945.

We thought we were safe for awhile, but this afternoon, around 1700, we were back at our Battle Stations. The FEIBERLING (DE 640) had sub contact. We joined her to run down the sub. We finally got contact on the sub and rolled off depth charges one after the other. FEIBERLING threw off hedge-hogs. But we finally lost contact of the sub. Steamed around for a while but never regained contact. Sub must have went way down. But our convoy was safe so we joined and proceeded on to Saipan. We secured about 1815.

April 11, 1945.

Enroute Okinawa to Saipan. This morning, FEIBERLING had a sound contact. Left formation to investigate. No results.

April 13, 1945.

At 1742, we anchored in Berth L54, at Saipan. Good to get back. Had movie on the fantail tonight. Best one in a long time. No mail today.

April 14, 1945.

Had a recreation party this afternoon, and it was good to get on land again, and rest for a little. Had ice cold beer, too.

At 2115, all hands observed five minutes of silent prayer in memory of our late Commander-in-Chief and President of the United States - Franklin D. Roosevelt. Will go to bed now, for a good night of sleep.

April 23, 1945.

All good things sometimes end. And so it is. This morning at 0500, we got underway for Okinawa, screening 13 LST's.

We have enjoyed the few days around Saipan. Nothing to do but go on recreation parties, but that can be a lot of fun sometimes. While we have been here, we have had good movies on the fantail, swimming parties, and had a pretty good time. We also had lots of mail. That good old stuff. Mail does mean a lot to us boys out here. For this is the kind of life that is away from everything.

The Pacific is rough duty. We also added two more 20's on our fantail and four more .50 cal. back there. We are hoping like everything that things will be calmed down a little when we get back. Due there on the 29th. Surely, it can't be as bad as it was.

April 27, 1945.

Today, we had a little excitement. Since we left Saipan we have been having drills all day. G.Q. after G.Q., but just practicing except on the 25th. We had several sound contacts that day, but had negative results. They don't seem to want to fool with us, for every time we go after one we soon lose contact.

But today the FIEBERLING who was just off our port bow destroyed a midget submarine before we knew what had happened. We went to G.Q. and had a contact ourselves, but had negative results. This was in the morning around 1000.

This afternoon around 1400 we had another contact and made emergency attack. We must have gotten this one or damaged it, for soon after the attack we could see oil all over the water. Around 1800, one of the LST's reported a periscope sighted ahead of the convoy. All ships made emergency turn and the FEIBERLING took off for the sub. They reported no results.

Tonight we heard over TBS [Talk Between Ships] that a big air attack was underway at Okinawa. I guess we are in for it again. Gosh, how I wish this whole thing was over. But I suppose a million more are wishing with me.

Communication Division on the Barr *fantail*

"A Bunch if Engineers"
WT2c Soucy and EM1c Goldman standing 2nd and 3rd from left

April 28, 1945.

At 0230 this morning, RINGNESS in adjoining station had a sound contact. All ships made emergency turn.

At 1830, a floating mine was sighted close aboard - about 300 yards on the port bow. Gosh, how close we came to it. And it was almost dusk. Sure is good to see it before dark for at dark you don't know they are out there until you hit one. They say they are awful things to hit. I was one of the men ordered to open up on it. Also, the 20 mm on the port side. Finally we sunk it without exploding the mine. It just went out of sight. That thing was too close for comfort.

FLASHBACKS

April 13 Worst news we ever had today. President Roosevelt's death left us all feeling blue.

April 14 275 planes shot down over Okinawa in the last two days.

Manuel Verissimo, Water Tender
from his journal, "Manny's Excellent Adventures"

*   *   *   *   *

April 17 Tied up alongside floating dry-dock and the DMS that got hit at Iwo Jima. She was in sad shape. No.1 fireroom and engine room was a mass of twisted steel. We got two 20 mm guns from her.

Zenon C. Wolan, Electrician's Mate   from his journal

*   *   *   *   *

Entertainment was always welcomed while we served on the Barr. Life could become rather routine despite the ever present dangers that go with fighting a war. We knew we had a job to do and we wanted to get it over with and get back to our loved ones. Movies were a source, a diversion away from the routine and miseries of war. I was responsible for getting the movies to be shown aboard ship. It was a job that required plenty of boat ride travel along with getting plenty wet on many occasions. Then I had to beg, borrow and trade to get the best movies available. Luck had a lot to do with it too. I am sure we all had our favorite movies, although any movie was better than none.

John J. Reilly, Ensign

*   *   *   *   *

When I was a cook, I used to get the guys gallon cans of peaches and sugar. They'd go in a life raft - and we had casks up there made out of wood that were full of water. It was supposed to be used in case we had to use the life raft. They'd dump the water out and fill it full of those peaches and put the sugar in and make brandy.

Clarence I. Priest, Seaman

I came aboard the Barr in Saipan the first part of 1945 - after the UDT men had left. At Saipan I had been aboard a tanker. We watered ships night and day from Iwo Jima and other places. We were constantly waiting with water at Saipan and out amongst the fleet. Then I got pulled off and assigned to the Barr. We took a convoy of LST's loaded with Marines to Okinawa - my first experience with actual combat. We screened for the convoy. We had our own radio frequency in the sonar hut.

Warren T. Pierce, Sonarman

*   *   *   *   *

April 27 . . . Submarine attempted to attack our convoy. Fired two torpedoes at APD 100. One missed her bow by 25 yards and other missed her stern by 75 yards. The APD then made a depth charge attack on it and sank it. Debris and oil was seen to cover surface where sub was. Five more sub contacts were made after that, but no results. Boy there must be a mess of them out here. Men told to keep a sharp look-out.

Zenon C. Wolan, Electrician's Mate   from his journal

*   *   *   *   *

All at once here comes a voice, with no formalities or anything, saying "There's a periscope!" There was a sister ship on the screen. We went to General Quarters immediately. Much excitement - all the ships went to General Quarters. They started dropping depth charges. Before they dropped the depth charges, they started to run - a torpedo was fired at them; they were fortunate enough to maneuver out of its way. Then they dropped depth charges and made a kill. They found human lungs afloat, which was the number one reason they knew they had a kill. And, of course, oil and debris were floating. It was a midget submarine - two-man submarine. We always heard they would be glad to sacrifice their life for their country. They knew they would die, but they wanted to do some damage to the Americans. If they had fired at the convoy, they could not have missed a ship; but thank the good Lord they fired at the screening vessel and it maneuvered out of the way.

Shortly after that, the Captain called me up to his quarters, and he said I would be his talker. I told him, "Captain, I'm just a dumb old country boy; I can't talk." He said "Oh, yes you can; you're following me right now. They're sound-powered phones; you'll be my talker for most parts of the ship - and from them to me for General Quarters purposes." Many, many times we were at General Quarters. Every time we had General Quarters I saw Jim Grenga because he was on the flying bridge, too. He manned a 50 calibre antiaircraft gun. His station was approximately 15 feet from where I stood by the Captain. There were two of those

50 cal. guns on the flying bridge. The sonar hut was just forward of the flying bridge and down about 4 feet lower than the bridge. So, if I happened to be on watch, I could be on duty very quickly. When the Captain decided to have General Quarters, he would flip the switch and the minute that switch would click, it would wake me up. I always slept in my clothes, so all I had to do was slip into shoes and go.

Warren T. Pierce, Sonarman

*   *   *   *   *

April 28 At sea escorting convoy. 1700 came across floating mine. 40 mm and 20 mm fired, but missed. I was called on bridge with rifle, destroyed mine on seventh shot. Big air raid at Okinawa--27 raids. They shot down 70 enemy planes. One suicide plane dove and hit hospital ship Comfort--serious damage to ship and personnel.

Joseph E. Purgatorio, Gunner's Mate
from his journal

The Pacific Ocean is very badly named. It seemed like whenever we wanted to launch or retrieve the boats, the water would be quite rough. They (boat crews) had to become expert at freeing the boat from the hooks, cables and other gear that was used to pull the boats up from the water into their boat davits when launching and just as expert at hooking up when going back aboard ship. And they did these things while the ship was underway at about 3 to 5 knots. When the ship was rolling from one side to the other and the waves were three feet high, it got pretty exciting wondering if they'd make it! The boats were about 36 feet long and weighed 20 tons and were stowed in davits on top of the superstructure deck (over the main deck) so that the Barr was a very top-heavy ship.

C. Richard Keys, Lieutenant (jg)

Boat deck on the Barr

CHAPTER 11

OKINAWA - SUICIDERS ALL AROUND

They say that the Navy is losing more than the Army who landed on the beaches. That doesn't seem possible. It must be true that the enemy are trying to knock out our Navy to avoid another quick invasion. But this Navy has made camp here and will never leave until we have won.

April 29, 1945.

Last night at 2230, we had a Flash Red. We formed A.A. screen. We heard that the Hospital Ship, Comfort, was hit about 25 miles from us last night by a suicide plane. Those dirty Japs. They are crazy. We all know that.

At 0330 this morning we were at G.Q. Planes came in as close as five miles. None closed the convoy. We had no trouble. At 0510 - Flash White. Secured. At 0750, back to G.Q.; Flash is Red, the Control is Yellow. Planes drew fire from ships ahead of us. None closed the convoy. 0810 - Flash White.

At 1500, we were anchored right off transport area. At 2110, Flash Red, Control Yellow, G.Q.; planes came in from the north. Firing going on all around. We saw no planes. At 2250 we secured. At 2330, Flash Red, Control Yellow - three bogeys coming in. All three shot down by screening ships. 2400 - Secured. I see that things haven't changed. Well, we made it before; God will protect us again. It's a hell of a place to come back to.

April 30, 1945.

This morning we took screening station A-36-A. This is supposed to be the worst out here. It is about ten miles north of Point Bolo. Point Bolo is supposedly the landmark that Jap airmen take when coming down here. And when they approach from the north as they usually do, they come right over this station.

I can't understand it, but we have had no alerts all day. It is now 1800. Hope we have a peaceful night too.

May 1, 1945.

Last night at 1930, we had a Flash Red. About 2000, two planes passed over us. It was dark and they did not see us. And we certainly were not going to let them know we were down here. 1810 - Secured. At 0200 this morning, we had a bogey on our scope. It closed to three miles before it was shown chicken. Everything quiet all day until 1900 tonight. Flash Red, Control Green. Bogeys reported but none came in. 2030 - Secured. Still on station A-36-A.

May 2, 1945.

Gosh, what a calm day this has been. No G.Q. Several enemy planes were reported at different times during the day way off, but none came around Okinawa. Sure is a relief. But we know this can't last. The battle is still raging over on the land. Guns firing from our ships 24 hours a day. Flares light up the island at night. Now 1930.

May 3, 1945.

Had an easy night last night. Still on Station A-36-A. Around noon we went to G.Q. Lots of firing going on up north of us. None closed our station. 1245 - Secured. Around 1330, mail boat was alongside with mail. Sure is nice to be screening out here and still have mail every once in a while. Around 1630, back to G.Q. Several planes shot down in adjoining stations. One ship hit by suicider.

1750 - Flash White - secured. 1850 - Flash Red - G.Q. Many planes in area but none closed our ship. 1955 - Secured.

What a time. It is bad to always have to break your neck getting to our stations. I am usually sitting around in the office when the bell rings - ready to go at a minute's notice. Keep my life belt laying right on top of my cabinet, too.

2030 - All calm now. Moon is about a quarter.

Flying Bridge Group during Flash Red
Lt. Cdr. Gordon, Capt. Dickie, Lt. McKinlay, Lt. McEwen

May 4, 1945.

Boy, we had some scares last night. At 2020, I was awakened by the loud report of the G.Q. bell. As I was hopping out of my sack, the Captain barked over the speaker, "Bogey two miles, closing." I grabbed my pants and ran as hard as I could. I was sleeping in my shirt. After I got to my station I found out that I had the left shoe on my right foot.

Just as I got to my gun I saw a bomb explode in the water. It just missed the GOSSELIN who was about four or five hundred yards in front of us. When we got to G.Q., we found that we had about 20 planes on our scope. About an hour at G.Q., bogeys dropped flares right over the top of us. All ships were banging away, but we had a report soon after we got to G.Q. that two ships had already been hit.

Boy, was I afraid when I saw those flares coming right down over top of us. We could hear the motor of the plane but could not see it. And we were lit up like a Christmas tree. I just knew that we could expect bombs any minute. But they never came. Around 0530, we secured and all went down to hit our sacks. I was too nervous to hit my sack then and I came in the office and laid my head on the desk, and finally dozed off.

Around 0800, back to old G.Q. Boy, and was I tired, but that did not slow my actions of getting to my station. Many planes were close around. Two were shot down by two other ships and the Barr. Right after we started action we felt an underwater explosion - sort of rocked the ship a little.

At 0930 - secured. Around 1000, a body was sighted nearby in the water. Later determined to be that of a Jap aviator. We opened up on it and soon it sank. Around 1030 we went back to G.Q. Flash Red, Control Green. We had friendly chickens also in the air. A little while after I got to G.Q., I witnessed a spectacular dog-fight. One of our planes came down and four Jap zeros. They finally got out of sight. No planes closed our ship and we did no firing. 1115 - Secured.

Around noon we got mail again. O, happy day. At 1900 - Flash Red, Control Green. 1920 - Flash White. 1950 - Flash Red, Control Green. No planes came in these two times. 2030 - Just secured from G.Q. All calm now.

May 5, 1945.

Last night at 0225, we went to G.Q. Many "bogeys" came in from the north. Bright moonlight night and what a sight it was. Several planes passed ahead of us about two miles soon after we got to G.Q. We could hear the motors. Funny thing - they tried to fool us by showing their red running lights. Usually when we see a plane in the sky with red lights we take it to be a friendly "chick."

Around 0330, enemy planes made bombing attack on GOSSELIN who was in station A-37-A. We are in station A-36-A. The GOSSELIN was the first ship to open up as they were making the attack on her. The GOSSELIN received several near misses. One of the planes was shot down by fire, one crash dived into the water and the rest went away. Around 0500 we secured from G.Q. Flash White, Control Green. And no bogeys on the screen.

Around 1030 this morning the Captain read over the speaker all the ships that have been hit in the past 24 hours. We get radio reports every morning. We can fully realize that there is a lot more to this battle for Okinawa than we see. It is hard to believe that we have been as lucky as we have. Ships have been hit all around us, but the old Barr is still in the fight.

At 2000 we went back to G.Q. "Bogeys" coming in from the north. Flash Red, Control Yellow. Many bogeys came in and there was a lot of firing all around. None closed our station and we did no firing. At 2345 Secured from G.Q.
<u>May 6, 1945.</u>

During the night we changed stations. Now on Charlie 27. At about 0200 we went to G.Q. Over a hundred planes were reported coming in. Many were reported shot down by CAP's. About 0300 we noticed many explosions over on the beach and we received word that the enemy were bombing Yonton Airfield. Lots of ack-ack was seen at a distance. No bogeys came any closer than seven miles to our ship. The new station that we have is around Kerama Rhetto. And this attack was concentrated on the airfield and ships in that area. We had several reports of ships being hit.

0500 - Secured from G.Q.

0730 - Flash Red, Control Yellow. Bogeys closed Kerama Rhetto. Several shot down by ships close by - none came in on our station. 0935 - Secured from G.Q. The Captain read again of all the ships hit in the past 24 hours. Most all the ships hit were the result of suiciders. It's enough to make anyone afraid. For I have seen them come in on ships - saw them hit - and saw them still come on in. They are really trying to knock out our fleet.

40 mm Guns

I sometimes doubt our chances of coming through. The law of averages would have gotten us long ago. Maybe there is something to the saying that the Barr has had its hit already when she got that torpedo. I pray to God all the time that is so. Around 1900 Flash Red. - G.Q. Nearest bogey was reported 40 miles away but none closed Okinawa. Around 2000 we changed stations to Baker 6. Secured from G.Q. around 1930.

May 7, 1945.

Another terrible night last night. About 0200 we went to G.Q. Flash Red, Control Yellow. Many bogeys in the area. When we got to G.Q., the sky all around was lit up with ack-ack fire. A plane was shot down dead ahead of us just about the time we got to our stations. And it was a pretty moonlight night.

O, how I hate that moon. I'll bet I have said that a hundred times. But out here, a bright moon has no place. We sit up there on our guns and just wish there was some way we could go up and put a blanket on that moon.

This morning just after we got to G.Q., several planes passed over us. We could hear the motors. We did not open up for we could not see them. Later on white flares were dropped directly overhead. The Captain gave full speed ahead and we moved out of the way. Boy, I get so afraid every time they start dropping flares. For we are trying to hide from them. We would really be duck soup for them if we opened up at night all the time.

We had plenty of scares this morning. We would be there and keep hearing reports - Bogey 8 miles closing - Bogey 6 miles closing - bogey 4 miles closing - bogey 3 miles opening. That went on for a couple of hours. It sure tries a man's nerve. Sure a relief when the report comes over the phone that the bogey is opening.

Around 0500 - Secured from G.Q. At 1100 - back to G.Q. Bogeys attacked ships about five miles astern of us. None closed our station. 2000 - All secure.

May 8, 1945.

2000 - This day has been a calm one. Not even a Flash Red. And how, O, how nice that is. But we know that days can't always be like this. It would be Heaven if they were.

As usual the Captain announced over the speaker all the ships that were hit in the last 24 hours. We have really had a battle so far here. They say that the Navy is losing more than the Army who landed on the beaches. That doesn't seem possible. It must be true that the enemy are trying to knock out our Navy to avoid another quick invasion. But this Navy has made camp here and will never leave until we have won.

May 9, 1945.

At 1600 we were relieved on station by USS SWEARER. Went to transport area off main beaches at Okinawa. At 1850 went to G.Q. Bogeys closed the transport area. All ships opened up. Such an array of tracer bullets you don't always see. Several planes shot down. Two ships hit by suiciders. Around 1930 - secured from G.Q. At 2000 went back to G.Q. And around 2015 ordered to get underway to relieve ship on Baker 26 who had just been hit by a suicider. At 2045 - secured from G.Q.

We may have had a chance to get some mail tonight, but this had to come up. Now, we are back on a screening station. O, how I would like to have some mail. But I don't guess war plays any favorites.

May 10, 1945.

Last night around midnight, it started. Flash Red, Control Yellow. However, we did not go to G.Q. until about 0300, when things were really getting rough. About the time we got to our stations, a plane just off the water passed right in front of us. Ack-ack from ship in adjoining station got him. What a splash there was in the water. Also there was ack-ack all around us in the distance. Only this one plane came in close to us. 0440 - Flash White, Control Green. - no bogeys on our screen.

About 0450 just after we secured we were ordered to take station Baker 13; the ship there having been hit by a torpedo. Submarines were reported in area. They said they expected a coordinated attack. And those kind are bad, for when we have bogeys around, we slow our speed to keep from leaving a large wake, but at the same time we make good targets for submarines.

0646 - Flash Blue. 0700 - Flash Red, Control Green. Bogeys reported a long way off. At 0852 - Flash Red. Ship went to G.Q. Many planes came in and a lot of firing. We saw no ships get hit. At 1135 bogeys closed our ship and ship in adjoining station. Ship in adjoining station hit by two suiciders, but after she was hit our fire and hers downed three planes. Another ship up ahead about five miles was hit by a bomb. Around 1430, relieved by LAWRENCE. 1630 - Anchored.

1730 Mail boat returned and O, boy, we had lots of mail. O, how good it is to get mail these days. And what a pile I had. Most of it was from a little girl back in La Grange, Ga. whom I think a lot of. She is writing me almost every day now. That is something for the books. Also a few from mother. She says that she can't help but worry about me. - If she only knew the whole story - how every night and day we just live for the next attack. But it is good that she does not know it all. I know that the papers are not telling how bad it really is over here. That sure would ruin the civilian morale.

At 1920 - back to G.Q. But we had it on them this time. We made smoke. Bogeys were all over us. Several ships next to us (Destroyers) opened up by radar control. At 2030 - Secured.

May 11, 1945.

At 0130 - Flash Red. And it stayed Flash Red all night but we never went to G.Q. Planes never closed closer than seven or eight miles. But last night I was out on the boat deck about 0300 and could see every few minutes red tracers going into the sky. We were in smoke practically all night, but somehow I could not sleep well. Around 0500 - Flash White.

At 0800 - G.Q. About 30 planes coming in from the north. At 0900 we got underway to join A.A. screen around the transport area. Yes, us little ships have to move out of a pretty safe place and go out to protect the larger ships. And O, what a raid we had. But luckily none got through our CAP. We had at one time about forty or fifty pips on our screen - distance 20 to 30 miles away.

This afternoon around 1500 we were tied up to a tanker taking on fuel. At 1630 we anchored in Hagushi Anchorage.

2000 - All Secure.

May 12, 1945.

At noon, we relieved GOSSELIN on station Baker 11. 1340 - Flash Red. High flying snoopers in the air - angels 30,000. None came down for an attack. At 1500, Flash White. We heard of a daring story here. Some of the CAT's went up after these planes. At this high altitude the friendly chicks' A.A. guns would not fire. We heard that one of our aviators downed a Jap plane up there by the use of his propeller. I suppose there's always a way.

1855 - went to G.Q. Flash Red, Control Yellow. Many planes in area. Ship in station Baker 13 hit by suicider. No planes came within five miles of our ship. At 2040 - Secured from G.Q.

2100 - All Secure.

May 13, 1945.

This morning planes started coming in right after midnight and were in area all night. Although several times they came in as close as three and four miles we had no G.Q. This morning when we got up we heard all about it. It just doesn't seem right to be sleeping when enemy planes are around. But the Captain was on the Bridge all night and he was watching out for us.

At 0530 - Flash White.

This afternoon our sound gear broke down. About 1900 we were relieved on station during an air attack. We had just gotten off station good when the ship (CROSBY) who just relieved us was hit by a suicide plane. We had orders to report to the Transport Area; but when the CROSBY was hit, we received new orders to go back and relieve her on station.

May 14, 1945.

We secured from G.Q. around 0100 this morning. But another Flash Red at 0300. Back to G.Q. We are on station Baker 30 now which is 10 miles north of Bolo and planes came all around us and over us. About 0330 all ships opened up. Several planes were close around. One shot down. About 0430 - Flash White.

Around 0630 back at G.Q., because a small native boat was sighted, and the O.D. thought it was a suicide boat. However, most of the suicide boats are supposed to have been destroyed. You can never tell though. My .50 and other 50's and 20 mm guns opened up and sank the small boat.

Sailor at 50 mm Gun

Around 1800, we got underway to meet the USS Hospital Ship SAMARITAN and escort her back to Okinawa. We don't forget what happened to the COMFORT awhile back. But what fools some big shot must be. We reported that we have no sound gear. And when we were assigned this task, we sent another TBS, but no answer but our original orders. So we set course to join the SAMARITAN. That is just like the Navy. They have a job to be done and they just don't seem to care about anything but getting that job done.

1900 - Flash Red, Control Yellow. Enemy planes all around. About 1945 one came in pretty close on us. We opened up and so did a couple other ships close by. The plane turned from us and crash dived into the water pretty close to one of the other ships. About 2030 - Flash White. Secured from G.Q.

2100 - All calm. Underway at full speed to rendezvous with SAMARITAN.
May 15, 1945.

About 1400 today we joined the SAMARITAN. We took station about three miles astern and set course for Okinawa.

2000 - All Secure. Gosh, we wonder if there are any subs around but the only way we would know would be to see them or get one of their fishes. O, what a life.
May 16, 1945.

Had another calm and restful night last night. O, if they could all be like that. What a wonderful world this would be. And we arrived back at Okinawa around 1300 - and guess what reward we get for a task well done - not even an overnight layover in the transport area in smoke. As soon as we got in, we were assigned Baker 30. The ship that had been there was hit last night. They say they had a big air attack there last night. Around 1400 bogeys were reported way off. None came in.

2000 - Flash Red, Control Green.

2047 - Flash White. 2247 - Flash Red, Control Yellow. 2248 - G.Q. Bogeys within five miles. 2250 - Bogey flying low to water at 2 miles. All ships opened up on him. He crashed in the water. At 2317 there was a big explosion just ahead of us. Later found out that RINGNESS (APD 100) just missed by a suicider. At 2330 bogey passed at one mile on port quarter. All ships were opened up. Bogey crashed in ship in station Baker 34. At 2400 - we secured.

May 17, 1945.

At 0200 this morning had Flash Red. Lots of bogeys were in the area. They came from the west, so we were out of immediate danger or at least the Captain must have thought so, for we did not go to G.Q. 0410 - Flash White.

Today at noon, we had good news. We received orders to proceed to Kerama Rhetto for provisions and sonar repairs. We anchored in Kerama Rhetto around 1700. Mail boat came back with mail. These are the days I like - days we have mail. We know that although this seems as if we are never going to see the States again, we know that someone is thinking of us.

At 1900 - Flash Red - started making smoke. At 1930, we went to G.Q., for several planes were in the Rhetto. Destroyers all around us banged away. We just sat tight and hoped that no bombs would hit us. A large attack was going on over around Okinawa and Yonton Field. At 2140 - Secured from G.Q. 2315 - Flash Blue. 2330 - Flash Red, Control Green. Bogey in vicinity. But we were still in smoke and hidden. We did no firing.

May 18, 1945.

Stayed Flash Red until about 0200 this morning. 0500 - back at G.Q. Made smoke. Planes all around. 0810 - Flash White.

1900 - Flash Red. 1920 - Went to G.Q. Made smoke. Many bogeys over around Okinawa. Only one closed Kerama Rhetto. 2050 - Secured from G.Q.

2100 - All secured.

May 19, 1945.

At 0230 had Flash Red. Bogeys in area. We did not go to G.Q. We can't fire anyway in smoke. I was awakened though about 0400 this morning by the loud report of the guns on a destroyer next to us. I went right on topside. Even if the Captain does think it best if we get rest when there is nothing that we can do when we are up, I still don't like the idea of laying down there in my sack when there are planes in the area.

Around 0600 - White Flash.

The rest of today has been pretty calm. Laying around at anchor, taking on provisions and having our sound gear repaired.

2000 - All Secured.

May 20, 1945.

This morning at 0400, we got underway with USS LOY (APD 56) to rendezvous with a convoy approaching Okinawa. At 1450, we sighted convoy, changed course and resumed our stations around the Convoy. The Convoy consisted of Fleet Tugs, LST's, barrack ships, and APA's.

2000 - All is calm. Gosh, how I wish we had kept going the other way rather than going back to Okinawa.

May 21, 1945.

This morning the LOY destroyed a floating mine close aboard about 0800. This was just as we could see the end of Okinawa. A lot of mines are reported around here, and sometimes they are to be feared worse than zoomies. Lots of ships have been sunk as the result of running up on these mines.

We proceeded on into the Transport Area. Boat went off and brought back mail. Then about 1500, we received orders to take screening station Baker 30 again.

This is considered the hottest station around. Nearly every ship that takes that station is hit. We have had it before and came through all right. Baker 30 is right by Point Bolo and the enemy planes make Pt. Bolo their reference point.

At 1800 we went to G.Q. Big air attack followed. Saw four planes shot down and one ship hit. No planes came in at us. The ship about three miles on our port side shot down one of the planes. And for miles around there was plenty of ack-ack fire in the sky.

I suppose we are just darn lucky not having any more planes than we do come in at us. How long can it last though. Everyone on the ship is wondering that. Malandra still keeps his helmet on 24 hours a day. Sliwinski and Kwiatkowski still spend most of their night out on the boat deck ready to abandon ship at a minute's notice. The Captain is still the calmest man on the ship. Majka is still coming through the compartment at night at the first gong of the G.Q. bell. Several times as I was getting out of my sack lately, I have almost been knocked down by him. But in these days when bogeys come in at a minute's notice, and the way they come in - you know that a minute may make the difference.

A lot of our own planes have been shot down by our ships. This is because the gunners on the ships just do not stop and wonder. They know that if it is an enemy plane that they have to open up quick. For once a suicider is on you, there is not such a good chance.

1900 - All calm.

May 22, 1945.

It rained all night last night. Consequently we had a good night of rest - no bogeys. Around 0830 this morning we moved out further and took over station A-

33-A. All was calm today until around dusk. We went to G.Q. Flash Red, Control Yellow, around 1930. Many bogeys were all around. Lots of ack-ack firing. At 2050, we secured from G.Q.

2100 - All Secure.

May 23, 1945.

Last night at 2330 - Flash Red, Control Yellow. Stayed this way until around 0200. Bogeys were close but we didn't go to G.Q. Visibility was poor. Nearest approach to our ship was four miles. Around noon today mail ship (LCI 818) came alongside and sent over mail. How good that was. I had lots of letters. As usual the majority were from Kay. She is so good to write me so often.

At 1810 we were relieved on station A-33-A by USS BARRY (APD 29) and ordered to report back to Baker 30. Back to "suicide corner" as we have learned to call it. We had just arrived on Baker 30 when we had a Flash Red. But nothing came of this raid. Our CAP's are beginning to take care of most of the "bogeys" now. However, there are still plenty that get through. 2000 - All Secure.

May 24, 1945 & May 25, 1945.

Back to G.Q. around 1130 last night. Around 30 "bogeys" closed Okinawa. Red tracers filled the sky all around. Ship behind us hit by a bomb. One plane crashed in the water off our port bow. Secured around 0200 this morning. At 0345, Flash Red again. Another big air attack, but we saw little of this one.

We fueled this morning around 1000. Then we were ordered to take new station, Baker 14.

At 1922 back to G.Q. This was a hell of a raid. Two ships were hit as I know of. One ship in two stations from us. Ack-ack firing was going on for miles around. Saw no planes shot down, but we had lots of reports over the TBS that many were being shot down.

At 2030 - Secured. At 2050 - many more bogeys came in around Okinawa. Closest to our ship came about five miles. We did not go back to G.Q. Flash White at 2200. At 2330 - Flash Blue. At 2400 - Flash Red, Control Yellow. 0025, Bogey closed our ship to two miles. G.Q. - Just got to G.Q., opened up on plane which crashed into water by SIMS. SIMS was about two miles ahead of us in Baker 15.

About five minutes after this crash, saw two big explosions about four miles on our port bow. Later found out that two suicide planes had crashed into the BARRY (APD 29) in station A-33-A. This was our station that we left on the 23rd. Several other ships reported being hit. And several planes reported shot down. This was a very heavy raid.

0400 - Secured from G.Q., but bogeys still around in the distance. None closer than 20 or 30 miles. I don't suppose we can stay at G.Q. all the time. At 0500, we left station B-14 to take station in daylight A.A. screen. At 0850, we went back to G.Q., for bogeys were close around. Two shot down close to the water a few miles from this ship. At 1043 - Secured. 1126 - Flash Red, Control Green. Set Condition 2M. 1210 - Mail Ship came alongside and we had mail. No time to read it; for while this exchange was going on, the G.Q. bell clanged away. Stayed at G.Q. till 1500. No planes closed our ship. Closest came in about seven miles. Back at G.Q. at 1800. Firing going on all around. Saw no ships hit nor planes shot down.

2100 - All Secure.

May 26, 1945.

Was a calm night. No bogeys at all came in. But I should think we have had enough of them for a little while. The Captain read the results over the loud speaker this morning. Not such good news. We are destroying a lot of planes but a heck of a lot of ships are getting hit. It is a poor swap - one suicide plane for one U.S. ship. The FLEMINGS relieved us around 1200. We proceeded in to Hagushi Anchorage.

2000 - All Calm. Hope we get to stay in anchorage a couple of nights. It is really rugged duty out there on those screening stations now. Our luck has been too good. I can't figure it out. I suppose some ships are supposed to come through it all O.K. Maybe we are one of them.

FLASHBACKS

I was quite proud of my 16 men (boat crews). They became just a regular part of the ship's company, stood watches and had deck cleaning and other duties. When the UDT 13 team was aboard, my crews and I had no responsibilities for the boats. UDT 13 had its own boat crews. So we did not escort them on their duties - like blowing up the beaches at Iwo Jima and Okinawa.

C. Richard Keys, Lieutenant (jg)

*   *   *   *   *

Each day we wondered how long it could go on--and each night and morning the kamikazes came again. The papers reported at home that "a few planes came over Okinawa last night with negligible damage resulting."

Eugene L. Swearingen, Ensign
from his journal, "My Ramblings Aboard the Barr, APD39"

*   *   *   *   *

May 3 Left Boston six months ago today! Still screening on Northwestern part of island, Suicide Carnoi. Received news today that Hitler is dead and Germany surrendered Italy. Had fourteen raids today. Japs sure are raising hell--sank two destroyers and another sinking. Bombed airfield.

Joseph E. Purgatorio, Gunner's Mate   from his journal

*   *   *   *   *

James mentioned the many times the enemy had us in his sights, and then, for whatever reason, we were spared. Well, my little wife was praying, back home. Could that have been the reason, maybe?

Guy E. Farley, Radioman

*   *   *   *   *

I also remember when we saw the Japanese pilot in the water and we were all at the side of the stern looking over at him when someone yelled he has a bomb attached to him and everybody ran to the other side of the ship. I thought we were going to tip. It was then that the Captain decided to sink the body with 50 mm fire. What the pilot had attached to him was part of the plane because they would tie themselves in when they went to crash the plane.

Timothy P. J. Nolan, Electrician's Mate

I seem to have reached the point where I don't remember a whole lot about the scary or the heroic times on the Barr. I just remember the funny and embarrassing things. Like the time when we were in the protected (by mountainous islands in a circular pattern) anchorage near Okinawa, called Kerama Rhetto, taking on supplies, as were a number of other ships. Also that was where they took all the ships that were hit by kamikaze planes, so there were many ships anchored in fairly close quarters. We had a large kamikaze attack in the middle of the afternoon, and Capt. Dickie sent me and one of our boats equipped with a smoke making machine over the side to go around the ship making smoke - which we did. But all the ships, including the Barr, were also making smoke with larger smoke machines, and by the time we'd finished our second trip around the Barr, we couldn't see our hands in front of our eyes. So we had to just stop the whole thing. We just drifted with the tide or currents and had no idea where we were going. It was several hours later, and had grown dark, before we could see anything. We were afraid to get too close to any ship, because there were reports of possible suicide boats loaded with high explosives coming from the islands surrounding Kerama Rhetto and attempting to crash into ships, which had prompted all the skippers to have several men on watch armed with rifles. Finally the smoke cleared and we saw a destroyer within hailing distance, but far enough away that we weren't too good a target. They let us come aboard, gave us coffee, contacted our ship and gave us a course to get back. We had drifted several miles from the main part of the anchorage.

C. Richard Keys, Lieutenant (jg)

*   *   *   *   *

One night we were screening the island for aircraft and here comes a Japanese plane over. I looked up and it looked like a bomb, but it was a flare they were releasing to get us to respond by firing so we would give away our position or location; in other words, it was a suicide mission. Capt. Dickie said to hold fire because he knew what was happening. I give Dickie credit for saving our lives by knowing their plan. This was just one of the many incidents I remember. Our ship was the only one to return without any casualties. This was in large part due to Capt. Dickie.

W. Elwood Overstreet, Seaman

*   *   *   *   *

In my opinion, (and it is shared by others) the men of the Barr would not be here in the present numbers, nor would they have all survived the Pacific action if it had not been for the good judgement and command of Pete Dickie. He made many correct decisions, but two stand out in my mind, and both relate to Kamikazes. 1.) Do not steam at more than 5 knots after dark. If you do, your phosphorescent wake will be a target for Kamikazes. 2.) Hold your fire against kamikaze until you are sure you are his prime target. If you do not, he will likely turn and dive down your tracer bullet trail. The Barr had an incredulous record of not getting hit during all the patrols, and I believe this is why.

John W. Hubenthal, Lieutenant (jg)

*   *   *   *   *

On the night of the 13th (May), the Evans and the Hadley were out on picket duty. A raid of 50 planes attacked them, and the Evans shot down 18 planes while the Hadley was ringing up the amazing total of 19 (that figure includes the six that crashed her.) Both ships were hit badly, but both of them came in on their own power. Casualties, of course, were heavy.

Eugene L. Swearingen, Ensign
from his journal,"My Ramblings Aboard the Barr, APD39"

*   *   *   *   *

May 15 Pretty rough out. At 1400 we met the hospital ship and headed back for Okinawa. We are to stay 10 miles behind her by day and 3 miles by nite. We are just standing by in case there should be survivors if it gets hit. Can't trust those Japs.

Zenon C. Wolan, Electrician's Mate   from his journal

*   *   *   *   *

We took the tracers out of the 20 mm shells so the kamikazes couldn't follow the tracers to our ship at night. The tracers had phosphorus in them and would catch the plane on fire when it hit, so we could tell when we were hitting the plane. We took the tracers out of the 50 cal. ammunition, too.

Clarence I. Priest, Seaman

*   *   *   *   *

While we were aboard ship, and most of the time in harm's way, I don't remember thinking about the dangers we faced. Yes, there were times when things were rough and frightening, but I think the excitement took over most of the time, instead of fear. I was raised with strong Christian values, and I believed that if I had to meet my creator, I would be ready. However, there were two occasions when I thought I was going to die. And strangely, neither was due to the actions of the enemy. Even to this day, I still recall the fright that I felt.

One of these occurred on May 17, 1945 when we were at anchor in Kerama Rhetto in very close proximity with other ships. We on the Barr felt relatively safe after having been on screening duty for so many days, and being subjected to the Kamikaze suicide attacks. We were relaxed while in the harbor covered by a very thick smoke screen generated by the smoke pots of many ships in the harbor. We could hardly see parts of our own ship. The smoke was that thick. There were enemy planes in the area and overhead as well. Most ships were at general quarters (G.Q). We were on a limited watch as the captain wanted to give the crew as much rest as possible. They all deserved it too. Our watch consisted of an officer and lookout on the flying bridge with other personnel stationed on the bow, the fantail, and at midship, port and starboard. This action was designed to repel enemy suicide swimmers who in the past, had swam out to ships with explosives attached to their bodies to blow up the ships. That in itself wasn't very comforting.

I was watch officer on the 12 to 4 watch. The condition was Flash Red, Control Yellow, indicating optimum enemy action. Conditions were dark and very smokey, and I was relaxed. I spent time talking to the lookout on the bridge with me, and we both were anxious for our watch to end so that we could get some sleep.

Suddenly, it seemed that every ship in the harbor opened fire with the exception of the Barr. In the darkness and with the smoke screen, I could not imagine what they expected to hit. The noise was ear splitting. The tracers and other fire were so close to us, I truly thought we would be hit by our own friendly fire. I experienced no comfort when I recalled seeing two of our own planes shot down by our own fire in the heat of the battle a few days before. The lookout and I were crawling on the deck on our bellies. I reached the ship's phone and rang the captain. Very excitedly I yelled, "Captain, all hell has broken out up here." I'll never forget his very calm reply. "Well Jack, just sound the alarm for General Quarters." Looking back, I felt kind of stupid for getting so excited. But then again, I thought I was going to die, and at the hands of our own people. This after being so lucky in our encounters with the enemy.

John J. Reilly, Ensign

*   *   *   *   *

Another time, we were on patrol off Okinawa and my division officer - seemed like he was usually on watch the same time I was- and he quickly opened the door and stuck his head in and said "Ernie Pyle was killed out here in Ie Shima." I wasn't on the instrument at that time; I got out and went and looked. It seemed like it was only a mile or so away, but it was obviously more. He was like a member of the family to us, because he was the service man's hero. He told it like it was; he went where they were at. It was such a tragic loss to history and America to lose him.

Warren T. Pierce, Sonarman

The Bates was hit on May 25. She sank not too far from Ie Shima where Ernie Pyle was killed. This sister ship was one of the 4 B's who carried UDT's at Iwo - Barr, Bates, Bull, Blessman. Except for Blessman which was badly damaged by Betty bomber at Iwo, all 3, with others, started pre-invasion work 3/25/45 (Palm Sunday), week before the 4/1/45 main landing.

Philip P. Jones, Lieutenant

      *   *   *   *   *

May 25 . . . Jap bogeys and also friendlies all around us. The C.A.P. is really giving them hell. A tin can just knocked down a Jap 'Betty' off our starboard. A plane came near us right on our course so we and the APD in back of us fired on it. We came within a hair of shooting him down. It turned and hauled ass. It happened to be one of our own TBM's. The pilot then radioed back to his command and said, 'I have my identification radar on and I also have my running lights on but they're still firing on me. I'm going back to Okinawa. The Japs are much poorer shots than those ships are.'

Zenon C. Wolan, Electrician's Mate   from his journal

We had an ice cream machine, like those in fast food places where you put the mix in, let it mix, pull a lever and it comes out. It seemed like that was a perfect job. Every evening I would mix this ice cream, put it in little wax paper cups and put them in the freezer. You can imagine with a crew like that how much it would take. Well, I couldn't guess it exactly. Naturally, I knew all of the fellows in my compartment well. Our compartment was just outside the hatch and a hatch down, so I yelled down one time "Would you guys like some ice cream?" And there was just an uproar. I had practically a gallon left. It went over so good, I purposely from then on would always overmix an awful lot, because everybody liked fresh ice cream as well as I did. Then one time I had already handed down one gallon and was handing down another when the supply officer stepped out of the wardroom near where I was and said "What's going on?". I said "Sir, I mixed too much. Rather than flush it down the drain, I thought these guys would eat it." He said "That's a good idea. Anytime you have some left over, go ahead and give it to them." He wasn't aware that I had been doing this all along.

Warren T. Pierce, Sonarman

Sailors on the Fantail

CHAPTER 12

SAIPAN AND MANILA - R & R

Had recreation yesterday and also again today. I went this afternoon. And when I returned to the ship I had mail. More letters from my girl. O, she is sweet. Everything at home is fine and that helps out a lot.

<u>May 27, 1945.</u>

Gosh, what a wonderful day. This morning a message came over the TBS ordering us to report for Convoy Duty at 0700 this morning. A break at last.

This morning at 0731 - Flash Blue. Set Condition 2M. 0743 - G.Q. Flash Red. Big air raid. As soon as we got to G.Q., we heard that three ships out on the picket line had already been hit by suicide planes. But somehow no planes got in the anchorage, although there was a lot of firing just outside the anchorage. Lucky us to get off our station for the ship that relieved us was hit too. That has happened several times. I'll bet all the ships that know of that sure hate to relieve us. For several times ships that relieve us have been hit that same night. Yes - we are lucky - very much so.

0839 - Flash White - secured.

0900 - Underway with large convoy for Saipan.

0915 - Flash Red, Control Yellow. More enemy planes, so back to our stations. Four or five planes got in on the convoy. One was shot down by ship a couple miles from us.

So we left Okinawa this morning while there was an attack. And O, how thankful I am. We have been so lucky. I will never figure it out. It is true that we have broken all law of averages. I have prayed every night and during the day. There have been so many times when I was praying that it was like my last prayer, somehow you stop praying so much that God will spare us this battle. Seem to pray that all our sins are forgiven.

Newspaper article, author unknown, attached inside Yeoman Grenga's diary:

I WONDER, GOD...............

The following verses were found on the body of an American soldier who died somewhere in Italy. They were discovered by James Day of New York, and sent to the Globe by an Everett reader. The verses are printed today because of the vibrant note of faith that shines through the sincere, rugged lines.

Look, God, I have never spoken to You,
But now I want to say: "How do you do?"
You see, God, they told me You didn't exist,
And, like a fool, I believed all this.
Last night, from a foxhole, I saw Your sky;
I figured, right then, they had told me a lie.
Had I taken time to see things You made,
I'd have known they weren't calling a spade a spade,
I wonder, God, if you would shake my hand?
Somehow, I feel that You'll understand.
Funny, I had to come to the hellish place
Before I had time to see Your face.
Well, I guess there isn't much more to say,
But I'm sure glad, God, I met You today.
I guess the "Zero Hour" will soon be here,
But I'm not afraid since I know You're near.
"The signal." Well, God, I'll have to go;
I like You lots, this I want You to know.
Look, now, this will be a horrible sight,
Who knows, I may come to Your house tonight.
Though I wasn't friendly to You before,
I wonder, God, if You'd wait at Your door.
Look, I'm crying, I'm shedding tears----
I wish I had known You those many years.
Well, I'll have to go now, God, goodby;
Strange, since I met You I'm not afraid to die.

Maybe a lot of people feel like I do. So many ships have been hit - four or five thousand sailors killed. And you know that you can't always escape. But so far we have. And now we are so happy. So much relieved. Never do I want to see Okinawa again.

2000 - All is calm with us now, but have just heard that a big air attack is underway at Okinawa. Off to Saipan.

May 28, 1945.

This morning around 0100 we had a little scare. "Skunks" were reported about 18 miles away. Finally they were identified as the MISSOURI and escorts.

2000 - All Calm - And how nice it is.

May 29, 1945.

A very peaceful and restful night. But this afternoon at 1300, bong, bong, bong. We left station immediately to investigate sound contact. We made a couple of runs, but no results. We finally lost contact and returned to the convoy.

2000 - All Secure.

June 1, 1945.

The past two days have been calm. However, we were warned by radio to be on the alert for mines. Several have been sighted on this route.

This morning at 1000 we had target practice firing at balloons. I had some fun - and it is a lot better to be shooting at balloons than bogeys. They can't shoot back.

This afternoon around 1400, I saw the sky filled with Super-forts. I suppose they are off for Japan. I hope they give them plenty of hell.

June 2, 1945.

Land sighted at 0625 this morning. At 1130, we anchored at Saipan. Mail boat went over but didn't get any mail.

2000 - All secure.

June 4, 1945.

Had recreation yesterday and also again today. I went this afternoon. And when I returned to the ship I had mail. More letters from my girl. O, she is sweet. Everything at home is fine and that helps out a lot.

At 1741 - Underway with SIMS (APD 50) enroute to Leyte, P.I. O, boy, maybe we will hang around there for a while. Hope so.

June 8, 1945.

This morning at 1013, we dropped anchor in Berth 48, San Pedro Bay, Leyte, P.I. Had a very nice trip. The sea was calm. Had Gunnery Drills every day. Sent up balloons and saw how many we could hit. Haven't seen anything of the island yet. Maybe soon we will have a chance.

I should have started a new book before now. I see that I will not have enough space in this one for much more writing - that is, if I am going to put a lot of pictures in it.

After Officer's Club attitude adjustment
Front: Lt. Cdr. Gordon, Lt. Jones, Lt. Kaiser
Back: Lt. McKinlay, Ens. Huber

Beer party in Saipan, S1c Priest,
F1c Muha and EM2c DeSanto

June 9, 1945.

This afternoon I went over on the Recreation Party. More like taking a trip in a jungle. But Leyte Beach is pretty nice and I swam for a long while this afternoon.

The Filipinos came around in their little canoes to barter with us. We are not supposed to swap cigarettes with them but everyone does. I obtained a necklace made out of shells. Will send it to Kay. I know she will like it.

June 10, 1945.

Today, I attended church over on the beach. This is the first time I was in a church on land since I left the good old States. Enjoyed the services very much. I packed the necklace and sent it off this afternoon to Kay.

June 11, 1945.

Went for a swim off the fantail this afternoon. The water was nice. No mail down here as yet - but we should have some soon.

June 12, 1945.

Went over on liberty today. Or should I call it liberty. We just go over, take some beer with us. Sit around and talk mostly.

Watched some of the boys trading with the Natives this afternoon. The Natives had some grass skirts. But there was not much to them - and there was no top piece. Don't think my girl would wear it so I didn't purchase it. Suppose I will wait till I go back through Pearl Harbor and get a nice one.

June 13, 1945.

And today we had mail on board. And I sure did have plenty of letters. Gosh, but mail sure is a welcome thing out here. Wish I could have some every day.

June 17, 1945.

This morning at 0800 we pulled up the anchor and got underway for Manila.

We went alongside the SHANGRI LA and took aboard 55 passengers for transportation to Manila. This morning before we left Leyte, we also took on board more ammunition. It is rumored that we are again to go back to "Bogeyville." Oh, I hope not. Not so soon - we just left that place.

1700 - We left the harbor of Leyte. Underway for Manila. O, yes, I lost my yeoman, Stein, today. Sure hated to see him leave.

2000 - Dark as night - sailing along. Hope we get to stay in Manila for a while. That may be nice.

June 18, 1945.

This morning around 0900 we passed the ELMORE (DE 686); she was the Barr's old friend over in the Atlantic. At 1209, we entered San Bernardino Strait. At 1350, we entered Ticao Pass.

A large naval battle between the Japs and our Navy was fought at San Bernardino Strait. I have heard a lot about that.

1930 - Passed Sibunfan Island to port.

June 19, 1945.

At 0850 this morning we anchored in Manila Harbor.

Never in my life have I seen so many sunken ships. They say that was part of the Jap Fleet that was there when our Navy caught them. I just wish I had a camera and could take some pictures. I will never forgive myself for not bringing a camera and a lot of film along with me. Boy, what pictures I could get. Gosh, everywhere I looked today I could see sunken ships. And from what I could see of Manila, I could tell that she must have taken a beating.

Tough luck, we anchored at 0850, and got underway for Lingayen Gulf at 1200. What a break. - The first time since we left Pearl Harbor that we have had a chance for a little civilized liberty and look what happened. All the sailors were going ashore dressed in Whites. O, how it would feel to make a liberty in Whites again.

Around 1530, we passed through the harbor entrance. Corregidor on one side and Bataan on the other. Just small little islands, but there were some large battles fought there in the early days of the war.

2000 - Our speed has been decreased to 8 knots as there is a possibility of an air attack. The Japs are still fighting hard to hold Luzon; so I hear. All is calm with us.

June 20, 1945.

At 0853, this morning we anchored in Lingayen Gulf, Luzon, P.I. Around 0930, we went to G.Q. Flash Blue. Enemy planes were reported pretty close. We are pretty close to the fighting on Luzon. Just over a couple of mountains.

1000 - Secured.

1200 - We got underway with a convoy of LST's for Okinawa.

2000 - All is calm, but we are on the alert. We are passing right by Northern

Luzon. And the route we are taking will lead us within 150 miles of Formosa, and about the same distance from Saki Shima. It's not bad enough to be going back to Okinawa - we have to go the hard way. This is the first convoy to go this route. I suppose we are pioneers. They say that if this one works all right that all ships will take this route and save valuable time and fuel. But we can't help but know that a lot of the planes that attack Okinawa come from Formosa and Saki Shima. We will just have to pray that nothing attacks us. Only have four escorts with about a dozen LST's. My, what a small group of planes could do to us. One convoy lately who were going from China to the Philippines was caught by Jap planes. Almost all the ships were hit. But why should we worry. We are lucky - nothing can happen to us. Will go down and get some sleep.

June 21, 1945.

This afternoon about 1400, we had a bogey on our scope, but he never closed the convoy. All is calm now, and it seems strange. We have been expecting some trouble. We are right north of Luzon and not so far from Formosa. Maybe all will go well. I hope so. Gosh, if things are still hot around Okinawa it will be awful. Really, we have had enough for a while. Our good luck can't hold out always.

June 22, 1945.

This morning one of the screening ships had a sound contact. No reports. The rest of the day has been very calm. We are still pretty close to Formosa but still no attacks. O, how good that is. The sea is nice and all is calm.

June 23, 1945.

Again this morning one of the ships had a sound contact. They left station. Reported probable sub sinking. Everything is still calm. We are east of Saki Shima now - and passing it with a little nervousness. We heard this afternoon that enemy planes were still coming in at Okinawa. Here we go back to that hell hole.

FLASHBACKS

June 8 . . . No. 1 fire-room couldn't run its feed pump so everything had to be secured. No steam - no power - no nothing. Was it hot! 130 to 150 degrees in places. Six guys crapped out from heat exhaustion. John and I had to secure the gyro and was it hot. Finally got power back at 1130.

Zenon C. Wolan, Electrician's Mate   from his journal

*   *   *   *   *

The second day of liberty on one of the islands in the Philippines we were ordered to take aboard quite a few Philippine sailors that were stationed aboard some of the larger ships in the Philippines. These men had not been to their homeland since before the war and they were going to Manila for a short leave to their homes.

We sailed through the San Bernadino Straits through the islands to Manila on the East coast of the islands. When we entered Manila Harbor, all we could see was the number of ships that were sunk in the harbor. A lot of surface craft lying dead in the water.

Andrew C. Soucy, Water Tender
from his personal diary and album

*   *   *   *   *

I recall going to the Philippines - Manila Bay. It was such a sight to see. The sunken ships - I don't believe a one of them ever sunk on its side; every one of them went straight down, because - it seemed hundreds, but it probably wasn't, of masts sticking out of the harbor. And that was all Jap ships that had been sunk by the Americans, not the allies. It was such a sight to see.

Warren T. Pierce, Sonarman

*   *   *   *   *

June 19 . . . Had a talk with one of the old Philippine chiefs and was surprised to learn that he considered Boston his home town and that he had been in New Bedford a number of times, playing with a Hawaiian orchestra.

June 22 Had a bit of laugh today from San Francisco. Heard the news reports that the Navy had summed up its losses for Okinawa and had come up with a total of 25 ships sunk and 38 hit by suicides. Boy, what a lie that is. We know for sure that on May 16, 169 ships had been hit, of which 50 had been sunk and we know that at least 50 more ships have been hit since then. I guess the Navy is right not letting the Japs know how effective the suicide plane really is.

Manuel Verissimo, Water Tender
from his journal, "Manny's Excellent Adventures"

*   *   *   *   *

We then departed Manila Bay and proceeded up the coast to Lingayen Gulf where we escorted several L.S.T.'s back to Okinawa. This was kind of a harrowing experience as we sailed close to Formosa that was heavily fortified with jap troops and planes. We arrived Okinawa luckily without incident and then were ordered to continue screening the island.

Andrew C. Soucy, Water Tender
from his personal diary and album

*   *   *   *   *

Humor during the harrowing days on the Barr, while there, was in short supply. We always enjoyed a good laugh. War didn't change that. Most of it was generated right aboard the ship, but occasionally we got some from outside sources. One source was from the Japanese themselves, although I am sure they did not intend to supply it. On the contrary, their English language propaganda was designed to demoralize the American troops and sailors--to make us home sick, frighten us, and to just break our fighting spirit. In most cases, I am sure it had the opposite effect. I am referring to the infamous "Tokyo Rose" radio propaganda. Her exaggerated reports of Japanese victories were so ridiculous, that it didn't take a genius to see what she was trying to accomplish. She also tried to demoralize us with statements about those men who were 4F and not fighting the war, stating they were stealing our loved ones' affections, while we were foolishly fighting a losing war with Japan. After a while, you could just about predict what she would say, and it became a fun thing just to listen to her propaganda. We actually looked forward to hearing her broadcast, because they did give us a few much needed laughs. The only truth from her propaganda was the reports of ships being hit by suicide planes. But thankfully, not in the numbers she would report, but much worse than we would like.

John J. Reilly, Ensign

It got boring just standing watch and then doing nothing. I decided to help the baker so I could get a chance at all those goodies they make. The only thing I could help him do, or he would let me do, was mix bread, which was done by hand.. The weevils in the flour were so thick that all the bakers would strip down to their waists - trying to brush them off. The weevils were just so thick, the baked bread looked like whole wheat bread.

Warren T. Pierce, Sonarman

Capt. Dickie at Okinawa

We experienced everything this earth will send. We were on patrol one hundred and five days, not counting the times we went in for fuel or supplies. Out of these 105 days we probably had General Quarters 90% of the time - from 2 to 3 hours usually to 12 hours or more. We saw mines that had broken loose and were floating an average of at least 2 a week. Sometimes it was a five foot spherical buoy that had broken loose. The Captain didn't call General Quarters; he just called the gun crew to fire 40 mm. to sink them. Once in a while they would hit one of those horns on the mine and there would be a terrific explosion. But the good Lord looked out for the Barr with the help of a great Captain. I learned so much about life, about the Navy and everything from this captain. He was the most gentle and the most goodly commanding officer that I ever served under - and I wound up with nearly five and a half years in the Navy. He was great. At night he went slow and he didn't fire at the planes, because it would be a dead giveaway.

Warren T. Pierce, Sonarman

CHAPTER 13

OKINAWA - FINAL BATTLE AND TYPHOONS

We have had "K" rations all day - really been rolling. The wind has been very strong. Waves look like they are going to swallow up the ship. They really are high. And you can feel the bow of the ship plunging into them - and the whole ship just shivers and you think it is going to fall apart. Sometimes I think the bogeys are better.

June 24, 1945.

All hands had a good scare this morning. About 0700 an object appeared in the water, not too far away, and it looked just like a periscope. Later we found out that it was just a log in the water. At 1030 this morning we passed Mae Shima abeam at two miles.

This afternoon we refueled and upon reporting to Com Task Force 31, were assigned this dern station again - yes, Baker 30. But while we were in this afternoon, we received mail on board. And I had lots of mail. All my family is well, and so is my little girl. After reading her nice letters, I know now that I have someone back home thinking of me. At least, I hope so, for it changes the outlook on things sometimes. I know that I have the most wonderful folks in the world. But I wish they didn't worry so much about me. I suppose though that they know all about things out here.

2000 - All calm here.

June 25, 1945.

Ho. Who said "bogeys" had gone from Okinawa. They were on us again last night at 2145. Several of them were knocked down in our vicinity. One ship was hit about five miles from us by a suicider. This raid lasted until 2330. Then we secured.

Screened all day today. Around dusk, we formed dusk A.A. screen. And at 1930 we went to our battle stations. Stayed until just a few minutes ago. No "bogeys" came close to our formation, but saw some ack-ack at a distance.

2100 - All Calm. Yes, they are still here. How much longer will they keep coming in on us - and how much longer can we last? They are not as bad as they used to be - but still they come in.

June 26, 1945.

Up again last night at midnight. Several "bogeys" around. Plenty of ack-ack firing. One that came close to our screen was shot down finally by ship in adjoining station. Another shot down over around Hagushi Beaches. Was a full moon last night. And how we hate nights like that. Several planes flew over us. We could hear their motors very plainly, and one was sighted dead ahead of us. Around 0245 - Flash White - Control Green.

This afternoon about 1400 a floating mine was destroyed by ship in adjoining station.

At dusk we formed A.A. screen. Disjoined after dark and resumed our station.

2000 - all calm.

June 27, 1945.

Calm night last night. Around noon LCI 818 came alongside to transfer mail. More mail for me. How nice that was. This afternoon at 1600, bogeys came in. Flash Red. None came around our ship, and we had no trouble. At dusk we formed our deck screen. 2100 - All calm.

June 28, 1945.

Last night at 2345 - Flash Red, Control Yellow. Bogeys came in from the north. Two passed right over us. We didn't open up for we were pretty well hidden. But we sure did hear the motors plainly. Lots of firing went on around the transport area.

This morning real early we almost had a collision with the ship in the next station. That happens every once in a while. Screened all day and no bogeys. At 1800, we came in to anchor.

2000 - Anchored off Hagushi Beaches. Calm.

June 29, 1945.

At 0330, this morning we had orders to get underway immediately to take station to help hunt down a sub that was sighted visually just off the transport area. Sub was reported sunk by one of the ships.

We reported back at Hagushi Beaches and guess what, they gave us another screening station. We are now on Station Easy 29.

2000 - All Calm. Boy, they never give us any rest. We can't even get to stay in anchorage a whole night. And we are so sick of those screening stations. We have been on about all of them.

June 30, 1945.

This morning at 0030, bogey closed. Stayed Flash Red till about 0200. Three bogeys were shot down. About 0230 back again. Darn those bogeys. About 0300 one came over us. We didn't open up, but the destroyer next to us got him. At 0350 - Flash White.

This afternoon we came in to fuel. And after fueling were assigned Station E-4. just off the transport area. At dusk we formed A.A. screen.

2000 - All Calm.

July 1, 1945.

This morning, we were at it again. 0030 - Flash Red. Several bogeys came in the vicinity. The raid did not last long - about a half hour. A little ack-ack was seen at a distance. At 0400 - Flash Red. No bogeys came close to our ship. Must not have been but a couple as the raid only lasted about 15 minutes.

This morning we thought we were going in for a rest. Around noon we left E-4 and proceeded to transport area. No sooner had we arrived than we were ordered to take station E-35. And around 1800 tonight we were ordered to take station Charlie 3.

2000 - All Secure.

July 2, 1945.

At 0100 this morning we had G.Q. Flash Red, Control Yellow. Bogey closed us as soon as we got to our stations. But bogey turned from us and went in for the ship in the next station. It was reported by the ship in the next station that bogey dropped something in the water (presumably a torpedo). The bogey got away. Was surprised that he did not crash dive the way most of them have been doing. Maybe they are running out of planes and pilots. It sure is about time. They have certainly used a lot of them down here.

This morning at 1000 we went to G.Q. Secured about 1030. No trouble. About noon LCI 819 came alongside and transferred mail. More mail. Boy, this is nice.

2100 - All Secure. Gosh, but it would be nice to get to go in and lay around for a couple of days. The raids now are not as bad as they used to be. But it doesn't take but one plane to change an outlook on life.

July 3, 1945.

At 0330 back again. Won't those bogeys go away. And we had a close call this morning. A plane came in at us and the other ship with us, but he sure messed up the water. Hit pretty close to the other ship.

At 0900, we had to leave our station and patrol station north of Ie Shima while the ship there joined a killer group to attack a sub that was sighted a few miles away.

This afternoon at 1330, had another raid but none came close to our ship. Secured at 1410. And about 1500, LCI 818 was alongside with mail. Boy, we are getting good service. And so glad to get letters. They help out so much.

About 1700 we had a scare. A small native boat was sighted. But later found to be empty. Have to be careful around here with lookout constant for suicide boats.

1900 - All Secure.

July 4, 1945.

More mail this morning around 1100. That boat makes a trip around every day. I think that is wonderful. At 1700, Flash Red. No planes closed our station.

2000 - All Secure.

July 5, 1945.

Yesterday afternoon we were relieved around 1730. Went in and anchored for the night. But this morning at 1100, we got underway for a new station - Charlie 2. Back to our old job of screening.

2000 - Has been a nice calm day. We missed the mailboat somehow today.

July 6, 1945.

No bogeys last night. They are trying subs now. Ship in adjoining station had contact around 0330 this morning. She dropped depth charges on the contact. The sub got away. Then she was dispatched to join killer group to track it down. Then we had two stations to patrol - Charlie 2 and Charlie 1.

Mail again this afternoon. I sort of think that my girl loves me. Hope so.

2000 - All calm.

July 7, 1945.

Last night we went in to transport area and anchored for the night. This morning we took on board about 15 Army Generals of the Tenth Army and are now on a tour of the islands around Okinawa. We are in company with the PRICHETT (DD561). At 1400 we put the officers off at Kume and stood by.

2000 - All calm. Underway for Hama Shima.

July 8, 1945.

The day was spent going around to several small islands. Went by Hama Shima, Aguni Shima, Sheya Shima and others. At 1800, we returned to Kerama Rhetto and put off the officers. 2000 - All calm. We are now underway to take screening station Charlie 5.

Water on the fantail

Barr's *control room*

July 9, 1945.

This morning we were relieved on station about 0900. Proceeded to tanker which was underway just off the transport area. Took on fuel and provisions. It is a sight to see how the Navy takes on fuel and supplies while underway. After we fueled and provisioned we had orders to take another station. At 1100 we were on station Charlie 30. And this afternoon the LCI came by again. Yes, I had more mail. I don't like to brag, but I always have mail. Maybe I know somebody.

2000 - All Secure. Boy, it is nice these days. The bogeys are not coming in. We have been having a little bad weather for the past several days. But I hope that is not the reason for the slack.

July 10, 1945.

Calm night. More mail this morning. And I had some, too. I always do. Had a Flash Red about 1800 tonight. Saw very little ack-ack. Must not have been but a couple of planes.

2000 - All calm.

July 11, 1945.

Had small raid early this morning. Just a few planes. None closed our ship. More mail this afternoon came on board. I didn't get one letter. Can't understand that. Well, I have a tomorrow - I hope. Calm Day - nothing happened. Had a movie tonight in the mess hall. Sure did enjoy that.

July 12, 1945.

Bogeys closed last night, or rather this morning around 0300. About 12 explosions were observed on Ie Shima. We were patrolling about three miles north of where the bombs hit. One plane came right over us. We did not open up and he went on his way. Good thing it was a dark night and he could not see us. About 0400, all was secure. Bogeys left the area.

Mail again this afternoon. Eight sweet letters from my girl. Three from home and several others.

2000 - All calm.

July 13, 1945.

Had a calm night and all day today has been nice. Mail again this afternoon. Boy, that is what I call service.

2000 - All secure.

July 14, 1945.

This morning around 0400 - Flash Red. Several bogeys came in. None closed our ship. Around 0500 - all secure.

Mail boat LCI 1090 was by this afternoon. Picked up mail but had none for us.

1800 - All calm.

July 15, 1945.

Screening on station Charlie 4 now. This morning LCI 1090 came by with mail while we were having an air alert. Yes, they bring our mail through to us. About a half hour after we transferred mail we noticed that she was on fire. Ship in next station went to her aid.

Am glad we got our mail, but all the mail we put on her was lost. And I wrote a couple of very long letters to my girl last night. A lot of writing to go up in flames. And I also mailed several official letters that I will now have to type over.

2000 - All secure.

July 16, 1945.

Calm night. Screening all day. LCI 1208 brought our mail today. All is calm.

July 17, 1945.

This morning around 0500 a sub was sighted visually by a patrol plane. Sub reported submerged about ten miles from our station. We were all ready for an attack if one came. Nothing happened. LCI 818 brought more mail this afternoon. It is wonderful.

2000 - All calm.

July 18, 1945.

At 2200 last night we had Flash Red and yellow. Several planes came close to us, but none came in at us. The closest passed 3 miles. All ships around gave this one plenty of hell. He was shot down. 2245 - Flash White. Still screening on Charlie 4. We refueled this afternoon. Mail boat forgot us today. At 1600 we changed station to D-5A. At 2030, all hands went to G.Q. Several planes were in the area. Ship was hit about two or three miles behind us. Plenty of ack-ack, but I saw no planes go down. 2215 - secured. Flash White. 2230 - All secure.

July 19, 1945.

Around 0600 this morning, we got underway as a screening ship for a convoy retiring from Okinawa to evade a typhoon.

At 1300, all hands to battle stations. Several planes attacked the convoy. And what a bad day it has been all day. Even with us rolling way over, those darn planes still came in. I don't think any of our ships were hit this afternoon. Wind force all day has been from 20 to 30 knots, and we sure have been rolling and rocking. Sometimes we don't know whether the ship is going to straighten up again or not.

Tonight for supper we had "K" rations. No trays will stay on the tables. We all just sat around and ate what we could on the deck. What a life.

2000 - All calm - I mean so far as the "bogeys"; however, I can not really say that all is calm - not when I have to hold on to the desk to write.

July 20, 1945.

Last night, I just could not stay in my cot. I sleep in the office at night now. I can usually sleep all right at night when the ship is just rolling a little - but not when the legs come off the deck, and sling me against my safe or the other way against my desk. I just had little cat-naps all night. All the boys said they didn't sleep either.

We have had "K" rations all day - really been rolling. The wind has been very strong. Waves look like they are going to swallow up the ship. They really are high. And you can feel the bow of the ship plunging into them - and the whole ship just shivers and you think it is going to fall apart. Sometimes I think the bogeys are better.

July 21, 1945.

This morning we got back to Okinawa around 0900, and about 1100 they had us back on a screening station. We are now on Dog-2. Day has been calm.

July 22, 1945.

This morning at 0200 back on our battle stations - Flash Red, Control Yellow. Three "bogeys" were reported close by. Saw one plane go down. And about 0230, we felt an underwater explosion. At 0350 - we secured. The rest of the day has been calm. Screening and screening. How boresome it gets.

July 23, 1945.

At 0100 this morning we went to G.Q. About ten minutes after we got to our stations, a low flying bogey was sighted by Gladhill, who was port lookout. Right after he saw it, he pointed him out to me. I did not open up right then for we have been instructed not to open up at night unless given the word. We don't like to commit ourselves. However, it was a bright moon-lite, and we could see the bogey very well. Plane closed us about 300 or 400 yards and dropped torpedo in the water. It missed us quite a bit. We missed the plane, and it did not make another run on us. It went away. That must not have been a suicider - for he sure had a good chance of coming on in. So glad he didn't for we may not have gotten him.

The following poem was attached inside Yeoman Grenga's diary with note by him: "Composed by Borgeld SOM2/c in latter part of the Battle of Okinawa."

THE USS BARR

Better known as the old 39.
Though she is not a ship of first line
Her duties are many and perilous too.

So you lubbers may gather she has a tough crew
Who are ready to answer the loud battle call
Which usually occurs around nightfall.

When the Japs come in for their usual attack,
The crew are in gun pits instead of their sacks,
And the fortys, twentys, and fiftys doth spew
Red tracers at planes that come in from the blue,
Who never learn until it is too late
That messing with the BARR is a fast ending fate

Though we have no banners or ribbons to show
We of the old BARR would like for you to know
That we carry our load with a manner sublime,
And shall continue to do so until the time
When nations and people of the world shall sing
Peace to all mankind, let freedom ring

This dedication we BARR men are giving
To all men and women both dead and living

Remember when day is done and turns into night
The old 39 is still in the fight...

Those suicide planes are hard to knock out of the air. About 0215, we secured from G.Q. 0300 - Flash Red again, but no planes came close to us this time. 0340, Flash White.

At 1030 this morning bogeys were reported at 40 miles, but none came in. All calm the rest of the day.

July 24, 1945.

Today has been very quiet. Screened all day.

July 25, 1945.

Calm day. This afternoon we took a convoy of LST's around to Buckner Bay, and are staying here for the night. When we went in this morning to fuel at the transport area, we got mail on board.

July 26, 1945.

We got underway this morning for Hagushi Beaches. Only stayed in the beach area about an hour, and they put us on screening station Dog-1. No mail today.

1800 - All calm.

July 27, 1945.

At 0930 this morning, we had a Flash Blue. Several planes were approaching, but none came in. Our CAP got them. LCI 818 brought us mail today. Had Captain Inspection this afternoon. Will have a movie in the mess hall tonight.

July 28, 1945.

Last night at 2300, at it again. About twenty planes were reported in the area. One was shot down close to us. No ships were hit as far I could see. Saw lots of ack-ack. Today we have been on our station.

2100 - Anchored in Hagushi Anchorage - all calm.

July 29, 1945.

At 0015 this morning, bogeys came in again for an attack on us ships in the anchorage. We were covered in smoke and did no firing. Destroyers and cruisers all around us opened up by radar fire. Several planes were shot down during this attack. This Flash Red lasted till 0330. This morning about 1000, we got underway and escorted a convoy to Buckner Bay. 1800 - Anchored in Buckner Bay. All calm. Not as many attacks now. They can't get through our air screen during the day time, but they are still slipping through it at night.

July 30, 1945.

Quiet night. Been laying around in Buckner Bay all day taking on provisions, and working on the ship.

1800 - Will have a movie tonight - and on the fantail. That is somewhat hard to believe. But a heck of a lot of lights stay on over the beach all the time and on a lot of ships there which are unboarding. They stay on until an air attack comes and then they turn them all off.

July 31, 1945.

Had Flash Red this morning around 0300. All ships made smoke, and we only had a couple of bogeys in our vicinity.

Still laying around at anchor.

August 1, 1945.

Last night we were at the movies on the fantail and on came the bogeys. Was enjoying a good picture when the loud horn over on the beach blasted. About the same time our G.Q. bell clanged away. What a time we all had getting off the fantail and to our G.Q. Stations. And no sooner had we got there than two planes came in. One was shot down. The other got away, and left the anchorage. We started at once making smoke and were soon covered by it. About 2330 we secured.

And this morning the sea and wind started getting up. At 1700 we got underway on evasive maneuvers. We retired south of Okinawa. Winds were estimated at 40 knots. And boy, have we been rolling today. Sometimes, I think this little ship is going right on over. We are very much top heavy because of the boats and boat davits. Can't sit in my office; can't even stand on the deck. Can't lay in my sack. What a life is that of a sailor - especially when he has to put up with all of this.

Was out on the fantail a little while ago - that is - was at the hatch leading to the fantail - for the fantail stays under water most of the time. And that wind would blow one off the weather decks if they did not hold on to something.

1900 - Very rough - no bogeys.

August 2, 1945.

Same as yesterday - boy has she been rough. Half the crew is sick and the other half does not feel so well. The ship has looked vacant all day as practically everyone has been down trying to stay in their sacks.

FLASHBACKS

While at Okinawa we were given an assignment to pick up some high ranking army generals for an inspection tour of the surrounding islands. These generals were from General Joe Stilwell's staff. The Barr took these officers to the various islands for their inspection. We were escorted by the destroyer DD561, USS Prichett. The islands inspected were Tori, Theya, Kume and Iwo Shima.

Andrew C. Soucy, Water Tender
from his personal diary and album

* * * * *

James told about us carrying those high officers to visit those places at Okinawa. He made no mention how the Barr was shaking. We had run aground and bent one of our screws, or maybe it was a driveshaft. When the Barr was asked if we could make 29 knots, the engineer radioed back affirmative. When we opened her up, she shook pretty bad. But we were a proud bunch to be able to keep up with that destroyer. I'm sure every sailor was proud of his ship, but none could be more proud than we were of the Barr. One great little ship.

Guy E. Farley, Radioman

* * * * *

July 9 . . . Mailboat came alongside at 1300 and we got 66 bags of last Xmas packages.

Zenon C. Wolan, Electrician's Mate from his journal

* * * * *

For the life of me I cannot understand how he (James) could manage to get all that written - especially the times of day (or night). It, quite naturally, got me to thinking. Man! Those rough typhoons, not to mention the GQ's. Talking 'bout the rough weather: Sleep was hard to come by. One night I received an urgent message for the Captain. Going to his stateroom, I found him on the deck between his bed and wall - oops, bulkhead.

Guy E. Farley, Radioman

The next most frightening time I recall was the occasion recorded in the story of the Barr by the Leatherneck magazine, where the ship rolled to starboard 49 degrees. I was on 12 to 4 watch with Lt. Don McKinlay. As usual, we were on the flying bridge which is normal, especially in good weather. We were in the waters somewhere off Okinawa where we had been ordered to go to avoid one of the many typhoons that we had experienced in the past. The waters were extremely rough, and we were top heavy, because we were unable to leave the four landing craft, we carried, ashore before we disembarked. The weather being as bad as it was, made us decide to move to the wheelhouse just below the flying bridge. There were three of us in the wheelhouse, the helmsman, Don, and myself. The sea continued to get rougher and all the more frightening to me.

Suddenly the ship lurched and rolled to starboard. You could see the water on the deck rush to starboard further adding to our troubles. The instrument recording the roll registered 49 degrees. The ship shuddered and remained in the roll. I could almost touch the water it seemed. I thought we were all going into the water with the roll. I managed to grab the helmsman who had a hold of the wheel, and Don grabbed me. I think I was praying out loud. After what seemed like an eternity, the ship slowly came back to center or midship. What a feeling of relief I experienced. I can still hear the pots and pans rattling on the deck in the pantry. I was told that some of the crew had been rolled out of their bunks too.

John J. Reilly, Ensign

*   *   *   *   *

July 23 At 0100 a Jap torpedo bomber made a run on us at few feet altitude. Gun crews say he launched torpedo.

Zenon C. Wolan, Electrician's Mate   from his journal

*   *   *   *   *

Regarding the incident at sea when a Japanese plane dropped what might have been a torpedo. I was first lookout on the starboard side. I could see the Japanese pilots as clear as day. They were so close I swore I could feel their breath on my face. I had a 50-caliber machine gun to protect me, but it wasn't much help with the magazine lying on the deck.

Norman LeMere, Machinist's Mate

*   *   *   *   *

On July 23, Gordon Huber was the OOD and I was the JOOD. One of the lookouts spotted this plane a mile or more off our port side, about midships, flying parallel to our course. It was the middle of the night, so a little difficult to see. He was flying just a few feet above the water, and as I recall we were not picking him up at all on our radar. A few minutes later, he was flying directly toward us, head-on toward our bow and still very low. Of course, everyone on watch was paying close attention by that time, and I think most observers thought the plane was a Japanese "Betty", and some thought he dropped a torpedo, although I did not see that. The command "Right Full Rudder" went down the voice tube to the helmsman, just as the plane zoomed up and to port to avoid hitting the Barr. We continued straight ahead on the same course, and were in the process of going to GQ at the time. After we had secured from GQ a few hours later, I asked the man who was helmsman when the plane approached the bow, why we went straight ahead instead of right full. He was one of the valiant boat crewmen, affectionately known by the nickname "Big Stoop" because of his size and posture. He replied, "Well, Sir, it looked like he dropped a torpedo, and I just decided we were a lot safer going on course than exposing a whole side of the ship." By disobeying a direct order, the helmsman may have put the Barr at greater risk or he may have saved the Barr. We'll never know! But one thing for certain, the Barr was a well-run, even a great, ship; ignoring orders and lack of good judgment were most definitely not prevalent.

C. Richard Keys, Lieutenant (jg)

*   *   *   *   *

I was Officer of the Deck (O.D.), assisted by my Jr. O.D., Dick Keys, on July 23rd, 1945. The port look-out reported a low flying plane on our port quarter to me and I raised my glasses to look at the plane. I followed him all the way up our port side and he then turned across our bow still flying very low on the water. When he got to about 30 degrees on our starboard bow he turned toward the Barr and made a run at us. I rang the G.Q. alarm and continued to follow the plane with my glasses, and as the plane closed and his image in my glasses grew larger and larger I felt sure this was a kamikaze who intended to crash his plane on us. However, at the last moment he pulled up and veered to the left, missing us by a hundred yards or so.

As Jim's entries said, it was a very moon lit night and the Bogey was easy to see and follow with my binoculars. Jim mentioned some people reported a torpedo dropped, but if so I did not observe that happening.

Having read many action reports of kamikaze attacks on U.S. warships during the Okinawa invasion, I felt sure our turn had come and I must admit the incident gave me quite a fright.

Gordon F. Huber, Lieutenant (jg)

Day after day when we listened to the reports on the radio, we heard the news from the States giving the casualties as about half what they actually were. . . . Even the statement as given in Time *after the end of the war does not tell the terrible toll taken, because some of the 223 ships listed as "damaged" were literally blown to pieces. You would have to see a destroyer that had taken four kamikazes and a bomb hit to know what I mean, or see a ship come in with an enormous hole in her side and burned and charred corpses piled high on her fantail. These men were in the engine spaces when their ship was damaged and a 400 pound steam line broke.*

Eugene L. Swearingen, Ensign
from his journal, "My Ramblings Aboard the Barr, APD39"

*   *   *   *   *

About 10 o'clock at night one time, the Captain sounded General Quarters. Then immediately he said, "You'd better make it fast, men; bogey five miles and closing." By that time, I'm on my way up the ladder. I had three stairs to climb; and as I'm going up the last one, the ship astern of us is firing. You can hear the plane - anybody that ever heard one of those Jap planes recognized it. He dropped a bomb on that ship. He flew directly overhead and the ship ahead of us opened fire. He followed the tracers down. That was a General Quarters I remember so vividly. They abandoned ship and two destroyers that happened to be in the area went alongside, lashed their ships to that big ship and saved them. The damage control was excellent. They got every man out of the water. They saved that ship, but it was out of commission. As the night wore on and daylight came, a brand new Sumner class destroyer was on our port side. The sky was overcast and they opened fire with fire-controlled radar. That was amazing to us because we had never seen it work. We could see the tracers going from stern straight up overhead right along where the bow was, and about that time a twin-engined Betty came down through the overcast, trailing nothing but black smoke. Here was a fleet tug towing into port that ship that had been ahead of us (I don't recall the name). That Jap tried to dive into him, but they had lost control. The cheers that went up seeing that Jap bouncing off the water were deafening. That was about 11 o'clock in the morning so we had been at General Quarters for about 13 hours.

Warren T. Pierce, Sonarman

*   *   *   *   *

I can remember going to G.Q when it was just about dinnertime and the food in the oven would start to burn while we were at G.Q. They called and said, "Hey, cookie, you got a fire in the kitchen. And I used to tell someone to get a fire extinguisher and put it out, that we were going to eat K-rations for dinner. So, I'd have to come back to the kitchen and break out the K-rations.

During the time we had typhoons, we had K-rations, too, because the rolls were so bad you couldn't cook anything.

Clarence I. Priest, Seaman

*   *   *   *   *

The following poem, author unknown was attached to Y1c Grenga's Diary:

THE SAILOR'S PRAYER

Now I lay me down to sleep,
I pray the Lord my soul to keep,
Grant me that before I wake,
No other sailor my shoes and socks shall take.
Lord watch over me in my slumber,
And see that my hammock stays on its number.
See that no clues or lashing breaks
To let me fall before I wake.
Keep me safe within thy sight
And let's have no General Quarters tonight.
In the morning let me wake,
Breathing scents of sirloin steak.
God protect me in my dreams,
And make this better than it seems,
Grant the time may swiftly fly
When I shall rest on high
In a soft and snowy bed,
Where I long to rest my head.
Far away from all these scenes,
From the odor of half done beans.
Take me back to the land
Where they don't scrub down with sand.
Where no demon typhoon blows,
And the women wash the clothes.
Lord you know of all my woes
Feed me in my dying throes.
Take me back, I'll promise then
Never to leave home again.

PART IV

POST WAR SERVICE

Even before committing to capture Okinawa, the US Joint Chiefs of Staff had set November 1, 1945, as the date for the invasion of the Japanese home islands: Kyushu, to be followed by invasion of Honshu. General Douglas MacArthur had been appointed supreme commander for this invasion. To augment the forces already on hand in the Pacific, 155,000 soldiers had been sent directly from Europe and another half million were designated to follow.

To the great relief of *Barr* crewmen, the invasion did not occur. Instead, on August 6 a B29 dropped an atomic bomb on Hiroshima. Three days later, a second bomb over Nagasaki persuaded the Japanese government to surrender on August 14. The formal surrender took place on board USS *Missouri* on September 2. The transition from full-scale war to peace was dramatic. In just three months the *Barr* would be homeward bound, but other significant missions were yet to come.

On August 14 the *Barr* joined the US Third Fleet on its way to Tokyo Bay to accept the surrender. On August 20 she, and other APD's in company embarked contingents of Royal Marines from the British battleship HMS *King George V* and other Royal Navy ships who had joined the third fleet, for delivery to Japan's Naval Base at Yokosuka for occupation duty on behalf of the Allies. Weather delayed this occupation until August 30, allowing sufficient time for the crew of the *Barr* to bond with their Royal Marine passengers.

The *Barr* was then assigned to the task of retrieving prisoners of war from Japanese prisons in the Tokyo/Yokohama area and delivering them to a hospital ship for repatriation. These prisoners, including women and children, had endured great hardships, and many were in poor health. In carrying out that humanitarian task on September 1, the *Barr* became the second US ship to enter Tokyo's inner harbor after the war, and the first to moor to at a pier at the Japanese Naval Base at Yokosuka. The repatriation of prisoners was completed on September 19.

After a visit to a, by then, peaceful Iwo Jima, the *Barr* was assigned for six weeks as barracks ship for the US Strategic Bombing Survey of Nagasaki before sailing for the United States on December 1.

Introduction concluded, Capt. A. Manly Bowen

Years from now there will be debate about whether or not we should have used the bomb, but not one person on our ship thought Truman made the wrong decision. We all knew that except for the atomic bomb our ship would soon be carrying a UDT team into Japan--the most dangerous amphibious operation ever.

It was not a secret on our ship that Japan itself would be the next target. We had seen the kamikaze attacks, the fights to death at Iwo Jima and Okinawa, and we had no illusions that attacking the Japanese homeland would be without huge casualties. To us, the atomic bomb had saved many American lives, and possibly ours. We felt relief and no remorse. We would soon be going home.

Eugene L. Swearingen, Ensign
from his journal,"My Ramblings Aboard the Barr, APD39"

Divine Service, August 26, 1945

CHAPTER 14

RUMORS OF PEACE

**What a happy day this has been. This morning, we got underway at 0500
to join the Third Fleet off Tokyo. . . . We are now underway at full speed.
Like we are going to a fire. And we have just found out that we are going
into Tokyo to evacuate the POW's there.**

August 3, 1945.

Around 0900 this morning, we were back in Buckner Bay. Did not sleep at
all last night. Just little cat-naps. We are back now for the completion of our availability.
We have three more days. And we are hearing rumors that upon the completion
we are supposed to go on another operation. I have two battle stars now - that's all
I want. We are close to Japan now. The only thing I can figure out is an operation
against the homeland. The Third Fleet has been up there softening them up and
there is no telling what this crazy Navy will do. All I can say is that it will be
rougher than Okinawa. I am afraid to tell myself just how I feel. And yet, I can't
figure out how we have been so lucky thus far. Maybe God will take care of us as
He has in the past. For so long a time now, my life has been completely in His
hands.

August 4, 1945.

Anchored in Buckner Bay. Calm night last night and calm all day.

August 7, 1945.

Last night we had a Flash Red at 2000. Lots of ack-ack fire all around, but
no ships hit as far as I could see.

August 8, 1945.

We left out of Buckner Bay this morning and took screening station Dog-5.
Surprise, I thought we were going on another operation. The radio has been blasting
away with good - O, very good news all day. We heard that Russia has declared
war on Japan. And also that the second Atomic Bomb has been dropped on
Nagasaki. The first was dropped on Hiroshima on the 5th of this month. Gosh it

is unbelievable to imagine all the damage done by those bombs. That is something that I would have to see to believe. Why, if all that is true and with Russia now in the war, it should not last so very much longer. Even though Japan does say they will hold out to the last man, I don't think it will last over three or four months.

August 9, 1945.

This afternoon we had some fun. A drone was furnished us by an LCI, and we practiced firing on it. On the second run, it was knocked down. I sure let my .50 eat. We had mail on board this afternoon. Got a lot of sweet letters.

August 10, 1945.

I couldn't believe my ears last night when I heard over the phone in my office when the Captain on the bridge called down to the Wardroom and informed the officers that he had just heard that Japan has offered to surrender. It was about eleven o'clock at night. And I thought sure that it was the OOD calling the Captain telling him how the situation was on the "bogeys". I have a bad habit of listening in on conversations over the phone. Plenty of times I have been almost to my battle station by the time the G.Q. bell rang. Get lots of hot dope over the phones. I got right out of my cot and went up to the C.I.C. room to investigate. And sure enough the reports were coming in. And all day today, we have been hearing radio reports. Gosh, if this is true, thousands will be happy all over the world. I pray that it is.

Even with reports of the peace offer, that does not stop the bogeys. This morning we were at G.Q. at 0500. Several bogeys came in. Closest came three miles to us. Boy, and did he catch hell. This raid lasted only about twenty minutes. And then again at 0730, Flash Red. None came close to us.

This afternoon Captain Kennaday (our Division {105} Commander) came on board and held an inspection. He looks like a tough old bird, but appeared nice to me. And this afternoon we had more mail. 1800 - All calm.

August 11, 1945.

Nothing today. Now we know that the dope on the peace offer is true. We hear that Japan has sent her message through Switzerland. Later, we hear now that the U.S.A. is thinking it over, because Japan wants to keep their Emperor. I say give it to them - but let's get this thing over with.

August 12, 1945.

About 0400 this morning we left our station to investigate the crash of one of our patrol planes. Back on Station around 0700.

At 1700, we were relieved on station.

Proceeded into anchorage. About 1830, the USS PENNSYLVANIA was hit by a suicider - right out of nowhere. I was standing out on the boat deck talking with a fellow and was just before going to the movies when just a little piece in front of us - O, what an explosion. Then there was a lot of ack-ack fire at another plane. By the time we got to our stations, the attack was over.

O, why don't they hurry and declare peace. We know now that it is in the making - and O, how hard it is to sweat these last few days out. 1900 - Clear.

August 13, 1945.

Still hearing reports on the peace making. Now, we hear that Japan wants more time. To hell with that, for just a few minutes ago an APA a couple berths away was hit by a bomb and a suicide plane both. Sure did light up the sky. And then several other planes came in and attacked us ships in the anchorage. Two planes were shot down as far as I could see. Now it is 2200 and all is calm. And I just heard over the radio that U.S. is studying whether to accept the peace terms. I don't suppose I could pray any harder. I suppose a million more are praying along with me. We have certainly won the war. The Japs can't hurt us even if they do keep their emperor.

August 14, 1945.

What a happy day this has been. This morning, we got underway at 0500 to join the Third Fleet off Tokyo. This did not seem to be such a good thing at first, but this afternoon about 1430, we heard that the war was over. We are now underway at full speed. Like we are going to a fire. And we have just found out that we are going into Tokyo to evacuate the POW's there. The sea is very rough now. And we are hitting every wave full in the face. All APD's in our task force. The 50, 10, 85, 124, 125. Captain Kennaday in Sims (50).

August 15, 1945.

This morning our unit changed to T.U. 30.6. This afternoon, we had a sound contact. Investigated, but had negative results. Sea is still choppy. And we are close to the Third Fleet now. This afternoon, we had firing practice on balloon targets. We knocked down several. 1800 - All calm. 2000 - Orders from Third Fleet to lay off. Third Fleet a few miles away under air attack. We also just heard that some other ships down the coast had an attack this morning. I suppose these are the trying days. We hear that the war is over, but there seems to still be a little trouble. Suppose there will be for a few days even if the war is over.

August 16, 1945.

This morning, early, we went in and took a screening station in a 40 ship screen - around parts of the Third Fleet. This afternoon we pulled out of our station and went alongside a tanker and took on fuel. We are now riding out storms. Holding up our entrance into Tokyo.

August 20, 1945.

The 17th, 18th and 19th were spent riding out typhoons. Now the sea has calmed down. This morning we closed T.G. 30.5. We took on board around 180 men from HMS KING GEORGE V and HMS GAMBIA for a landing party. It seems now that we will be a part of a landing force, rather than do the job previously assigned to us. We are now making preparations to enter Tokyo.

HMS King George V

"Limeys coming aboard"

"Limey sailors coming aboard for Japan occupation"

<u>August 25, 1945.</u>

We did not proceed into Tokyo. Had to ride out typhoons. Boy, they are bad around these waters. We got as much as a 52 degree roll out of this little ship. Most everyone has been feeling badly the past few days. And especially our English comrades. They have been sailing on large ships and are not used to the rough sea. They are very nice. I have enjoyed talking and being with them.

<u>August 27, 1945.</u>

At 1700, we anchored in Sagami Wan. This is right outside of Tokyo Bay. Seems funny, tonight we had a movie on the fantail. And we see now that we may soon have one right in Tokyo Bay. When we were down at Okinawa, we used to talk about the day we would have a movie on the fantail in Tokyo Bay. It just doesn't seem possible. But maybe it is.

FLASHBACKS

The first news of the dropping of the atomic bomb on Hiroshima came as I was awakened for my 4 to 8 watch. There was a lot of excitement that morning as we all tried to listen to the radio. All the news was about the bomb and how powerful it was. The talking was from London to Washington, DC, and Australia via short wave. Someone would say this is London, come in Washington and then from Washington to Australia, etc. Needless to say, most of us didn't sleep much the next few days.

Andrew C. Soucy, Water Tender
from his personal diary and album

*   *   *   *   *

Another incident occurred when we were at anchor in Buckner Bay. A Japanese plane hit Pennsylvania--only seconds before another plane hit a supply ship on our port side, blowing the ship into bits, her parts piercing the sky like so many bits of confetti.

At the time, four of us crouched on deck. We had gotten our hands on a 10-pound can of ham and a loaf of bread and had made sandwiches. We kept eating.

Norman LeMere, Machinist's Mate

*   *   *   *   *

Then while at anchor on August 13 at dusk, an APA several berths away was bombed and suicided by planes without warning. The night before, the USS Pennsylvania had been blasted while at anchor, with peace terms practically signed. The sweat-out was easing up and almost over, after 140 days. Of the 140 days, the Barr had spent almost 100 days at Okinawa and most of them on the exposed screening stations.

Eugene L. Swearingen, Ensign
from his journal, "My Ramblings Aboard the Barr, APD39"

*   *   *   *   *

Back to the typhoons - yes, the Barr was top-heavy, and rolled a great deal. She could stand on her nose and tail, too. I remember once, while on duty, my typewriter's carriage returned on its own.

Guy E. Farley, Radioman

—————— *Surrender of Japan* ——————

On about August 13, we were called into Buckner Bay for further assignment. This call was quite anxious for us as we were wondering what was next. We all knew that something big was taking place as our boat crews explained the activity that took place during that night. They told us that many officers were being transferred and moved about during the nighttime. We then loaded on as much food as possible, and the stores consisted of lots of citrus fruit. We later learned why.

Noon that day we took out from Buckner Bay along with 5 other APD's. The Captain told us early that he had an important message to give to the crew when we got out to sea. We knew something was up because we sailed directly north for several hours. That afternoon the Captain announced that we would be with a task group to evacuate allied POW's along the coast of Japan.

We rendezvoused with a large task force of ships - the largest I had ever witnessed. During this trip with this large task force we encountered a severe typhoon. We had just taken aboard a group of British Marines from the HMS King George V and the HMS Gambia. These men were to be let off on a beach in Japan for preliminary occupation forces. Most of the Marines became a little seasick as they were not accustomed to being aboard a small ship. They were a real good bunch of sailors tho and we enjoyed their company.

Andrew C. Soucy, Water Tender
from his personal diary and album

*   *   *   *   *

August 14 . . . The Captain spoke over the mike. He said that news he received said that Japan had surrendered. It had not been officially announced by President Truman, but it was the straight dope. . . . He told us that among the supplies we had brought were a lot of vitamin pills and fresh fruit as they expected the prisoners to be in bad shape.

August 15 . . . This morning we received word that we were to use ingenuity in case our passengers were women and children. This morning, they rigged up a shower on the fantail so that they could take a shower and be deloused out there. This afternoon we had two shots given us. One was a typhus shot. The doctor asked all men to contribute a shirt and a pair of pants. Everyone did. We're all ready for them now.

August 16 ... We were going right into Japan as we had expected to, as we had orders to stay out of Japan's home waters until the surrender papers are signed. Last night part of the fleet had been attacked by 12 Jap planes. Admiral Halsey ordered them shot down kinda friendly like. Even if it is a trap, I would sure like to get in the beach party.

Manuel Verissimo, Water Tender
from his journal, "Manny's Excellent Adventures"

     *   *   *   *   *

One thing every DE/APD sailor will never forget as long as his noodles keep functioning OK is the way the ship bounced around like a cork.

Philip P. Jones, Lieutenant

     *   *   *   *   *

From Commander J.M. Kennaday's Ninth Cruise - The Last Battle and Occupation of Japan, (furnished by Lt. Philip P. Jones):

At 0800 the 15th (August) we learned by radio that Japan had accepted the surrender terms and shortly afterward we received AlNav 194 - "War with Japan is over."! I signaled the unit, "Recommend simple thanksgiving services on this great and hard won day" and I think all ships held them. Frank Donahue was a devout Catholic and Sunday services had been held regularly aboard the Sims when conditions permitted for Protestants as well as those of his own faith. A very meaningful and deeply meant service, in which I took part, too, was held. The last battle had been a long and savage one, and much had been endured before it - much more, I know, by many in the division than by me. I think we all felt, too, the poignancy of the fact that President Roosevelt, who had to a great extent prepared the nation for all this, and had led so courageously and energetically in spite of his physical handicap, had not lived to see either the defeat of Germany or that of Japan.

The following was probably held in response to Commander Kennaday's memo.

USS BARR
VICTORY SERVICES

P.T.DICKIE   W.H. GORDON
Commanding Officer   *Executive Officer*

DOXOLOGY *(Standing)*

> *Praise God from whom all blessings flow;*
> *Praise Him all Creatures here below;*
> *Praise Him above ye Heavenly Hosts;*
> *Praise Father, Son and Holy Ghost. A-Men.*

INVOCATION *(Standing):* Prayer offered by WHITE.

SONG   *(Sitting):*

> *Stand up, stand up for Jesus, ye soldiers of the cross;*
> *Lift high His royal banner. It must not suffer loss;*
> *From victory unto victory, His army shall He lead,*
> *Til every foe is vanquished, and Christ is Lord indeed.*
> *Stand up, stand up for Jesus, stand in His strength alone;*
> *The arm of flesh will fail you, ye dare not trust your own.*
> *Put on the Gospel armour, each piece put on with prayer;*
> *Where duty calls and danger, be never wanting there.*

SONG   *(Sitting):*

> *He leadeth me, O blessed thought;*
> *O words with Heavenly Comfort fraught;*
> *What e'er I do, where e'er I be,*
> *still 'tis God's hand that leadeth me.*
> *(Chorus)*
> *He leadeth me, He leadeth me, by His own hand He leadeth me;*
> *His faithful follower I would be for by His hand He leadeth me.*
> *Sometimes 'mid scenes of deepest gloom,*
> *sometimes where Eden's bowers bloom;*
> *By waters calm; o'er troubled sea,*
> *still 'tis God's hand that leadeth me.*

SCRIPTURE READING: MARSCH and ROSENGREN

SONG   *(Standing):* Battle Hymn of the Republic.

PRAYERS *(Standing or kneeling as preferred):*

> *Washington's Prayer for the Nation BOWMAN*
> *Prayer of Thanksgiving   GRENGA*
> *Sentence prayers, begun by Mr. SWEARINGEN*
> *Lord's Prayer in Unison*

SPECIAL MUSIC: CHOIR

ADDRESS: Captain DICKIE

CLOSING HYMN: God Be With You Til We Meet Again.

Memo from Captain Kennaday to his division (furnished by Lt. Philip P. Jones):

August 15, 1945

TO THE OFFICERS AND MEN OF TRANSPORT DIVISION 105

On this great day, for which so many have fought and worked and prayed so long and hard, I want you to know what a pleasure and privilege it has been to me to command you even these few months.

I was shore-bound for much of the war. I was delighted to be ordered, last March, to command a division of fast transports, for my heart has long been very much with and for destroyer-type ships.

But I have been more than delighted in the actual experiences of the command. It has been my unusual good fortune to fly my pennant in four of the ships of the division, and I have seen and heard enough of the rest of you to feel I know you very well indeed. I am very fond and very proud of you all. In this final operation, generally conceded to have been one of the war's toughest, you have conducted yourselves in the most creditable manner - a source of great satisfaction to me and of discomfiture to the enemy.

I thank and congratulate you for being what you are. Keep it up, in the Navy or out. The country needs you.

Best of luck, always!

J.M. Kennaday
Captain, U.S.N.
Commander Transport Division 105

British Royal Marines

We heard that the war was over and that the surrender of the Japanese Navy would be signed on board USS Missouri in the Yokosuka Navy Base and that the island of Azuma in the base, close to the position that Missouri would anchor, would be occupied by a British force from the Fleet, some two to three days prior to the surrender being signed, to prevent any last minute sabotage by fanatics from that particular area. The American Marines would occupy the mainland for the same reason.

I was sent for by the Admiral Sir Bernard Rawlings and in consultation with the Captain of K.G.V., told to take half my detachment, mostly from Y turret and some forty Marines from each of two cruisers, embark in three American A.P.D.'s, fast transports, USS Barr, Pavlic and Sims, who would land us on the selected day. The landing force had to be a bit of a compromise, as the R.M.'s on all three ships manned a large part of the ship's armament, and no Captain would willingly give up a large slice of his fire power, in case the Japs decided to have a final fling.

Some ten days later at sea, we were transferred in landing craft, from our ships to the three APD's, armed to the teeth!!! We were very well looked after, a little cramped, and I must say that after the stately roll of KGV the quick, jerky motion of the APD's tended to cause a slightly uneasy stomach!! Two days before the landing an American Liaison Officer and I were to be transferred to their H.Q. ship for a conference concerning the landing; the HQ ship carried the U.S. Marine force. Transfer was to be made while steaming at speed. A stout rope was made fast to our APD, passed to the H.Q. ship where it was passed through two blocks and backed up by 20 sailors who, should the ships heel towards each other, pull like mad and keep the rope taut; and if the ships heeled away, they kept it taut by being dragged along the deck. On this rope was attached a device with a small plank attached to a pulley on which one sat with a separate rope by which one was pulled across. The sea was pretty rough and we were steaming at about 15 knots. The American went first and when halfway over, the ships suddenly heeled towards each other; this took the twenty by surprise, the rope went slack, and I saw the unfortunate Liaison Officer drop like a stone into the water still attached to his plank and then as the ships heeled apart, he shot up into the air like a yo-yo. Luckily, he held on; he was not strapped in any way and was not wearing a lifebelt or jacket. I think he would have been lost if he hadn't held on. I suppose the distance between the two ships some twenty to thirty feet. When my turn came, the twenty sailors had been backed up by ten more and I had an uneventful journey, but I must admit I was scared stiff and during the conference I found my mind tending to wander from the subject of our landing to the thought of the return journey. In the event, uneventful for us both.

Major P.L. Norcock, O.C.
Royal Marines HMS King George V, British Pacific Fleet

      *   *   *   *   *

Our ship was a battleship in the Royal Navy, known as HMS King George V. Bill Kerry and I and a number of other close shipmates worked a 5.25" gun turret. We were pretty good at what we did and we lived and worked together for two and one-half years on the starboard mess deck, which we referred to as the Marine barracks.

We were really young, most of us less than 20 years of age and we belonged to a very famous corps called the Royal Marines, whose motto was "per mare per terram", or by sea and by land - a motto which they had for some 200-odd years and proudly wore the globe and a laurel with a crown surmounting the globe. Both the Royal Marines and the United States Marine Corps, wear the globe as a badge and they have similar slang names - the Royal Marines are known as Bootnecks and the United States Marines are known as Leathernecks, both names being from the same origin - the use of strips of leather sewn into the collar to deflect a bayonet - very sensible!

Our ship, the King George V, was probably best known for its part in the sinking of the Bismarck in 1941. The report by the Captain at that time mentioned favorably the accuracy and firepower by the 5.25 turrets. I inherited a pair of decrepit gloves which were situated behind the ramming lever of the right gun. I wore those gloves for two months through the Okinawa campaign; and oh, my gosh, how stupid you are when you are young. I left them where I found them two and a half years before. Bloody idiot! I can just imagine my grandson, Trent, who is convinced I went to sea with a cutlass; God love him! He would have loved them; I would have had them sprayed, mounted and captioned "These gloves helped to sink the Bismarck and assist the United States Marines at Okinawa." Wouldn't that be something?

We joined Admiral Halsey's fleet on the 14th of July, 1945, and from then on until the 29th, we spent a fairly good time with bombardments. The last big bombardment, I think, of the war was at Hamamatsu on the 29th of July. Thereafter, I've got no record until the 6th of August - that was the dropping of the first atomic bomb on Hiroshima. That was closely followed by the second bomb on the 9th of August on Nagasaki.

On the morning of the 16th of August, we were mustered on deck and addressed by our very revered commanding officer, Major Peter Norcock, whom we would have followed through thick and thin. He was a very fine officer. He informed us that we were going to form a landing party, probably one of several, and briefed us as to what to expect. It was, in the main, the known positions of Japanese infantry and, in particular, the positions of heavy caliber armament, which surrounded the hills about Tokyo Bay. One very interesting part of Major Norcock's briefing was his reference to the Japanese civilian police force, which he informed us wore white gloves and used a whistle for traffic control, and also carried a ceremonial sword on their left side. His instructions were "If you come across a civilian police force, don't harass them, let them go about their business, and above all, do not disarm them, let them retain their swords, because to disarm them would cause them loss of face and make their job of controlling the civilian population somewhat more difficult than it should be."

Although we expected to go ashore very quickly, it was not to be. The typhoon was a problem to the fleet in general; and probably for a number of reasons, we were not taken off the KGV until the morning of the 20th by landing craft. Even when the landing craft did appear, it was quite daunting to see the swell in the ocean, anything between three and six, seven meters. That's one hell of a swell, if you're, as we were, suspended over a ship's side on scrambling nets, hanging for all you're worth onto a rope netting and trying to judge the speed of the landing craft coming up and also going down, because once it reached the peak of the trough, you really had to judge very quickly when to drop. Well, none of us broke our legs, so we were obviously good. We'd done this drill, but not for some time. Mostly as recruits, you did the drill and you've got to remember it when it comes to the real thing.

After getting into the landing craft, we headed for the Barr, which was perhaps one-half to one mile away. We got there in choppy seas, but had a much easier time getting aboard the Barr. We got helped aboard by a few willing hands and shown to quarters with triple-tiered bunks. Not a whole lot of room, but adequate. We'd been used to hammocks, so bunks were a little bit of a novelty also. We hung our gear on the end of them and soon made ourselves at home.

John B. Holdforth, Marine
Royal Marine Fleet Commando, British Pacific Fleet

＊   ＊   ＊   ＊   ＊

Our Royal Marines were only aboard the Barr from the 20 Aug '45 until the 30 Aug '45 and much of this time attempting to avoid the worst of the hurricane or such prior to landing. . . . Being a member of the R.M. Fleet Commando and our small, but I guess important part, the gallant USS Barr DE576/APD39 allowed us to take part in the final leg. . . . I admire the whole crew of the Barr and her much respected Skipper, especially from now knowing her origin in relation to PFC W.W. Barr, Silver Star, U.S.M.C., reading the painstaking log of James B. Grenga Y1c and most things that made her great.

The Barr had an atmosphere of her own which I felt as I stepped aboard her. It was reflected by her crew and rightly so in the amount of action they had shared in the past, together. We were immediately made to feel at home, and everyone we met was friendly and helpful. The food was excellent.

William E. Kerry, Marine,
Royal Marine Fleet Commando, British Pacific Fleet

——————————— *Life Aboard the Barr with Marines* ———————————

About 1315 hours, the broadcaster came on with a big crackle and an American voice said "Now hear this; now hear this. Chow is down for all British troops. Chow is down for all British troops." We looked at each other and thought, "Well, my goodness, late lunch; this is a luxury." We were already supposed to have had our lunch and here we are having a late one. We headed for wherever the chow was down. Then we had quite a pleasant surprise. We were confronted with a very efficient looking cafeteria system and picked up a stainless steel tray, compartmented for a variety of portions. I recall vividly that lunch consisted of creamed turkey and asparagus, small boiled potatoes and, I think, what we call square-cut beans, French beans. We had a little portion of ice cream with a sauce. We had some very excellent coffee and a portion of butter with a bread roll, rather on the sweet side, but very, very impressive. It was a different style of messing altogether. There was a lot more efficiency in a cafeteria system where you could put your stainless steel tray back at the end of the meal and see it scalded through a washing machine. A crewman picked up the trays, brushed off the residue into a bin and the tray went straight into a scalding hot washing machine. Very hygienic and very efficient. The US Navy was light years ahead.

The lunch was excellent; the coffee was excellent, but at 1630 a cup of tea which was made with every good intention (and God bless you, boys, we still appreciated it), but it was foul - oh, it was foul! As best we could, we broached the subject to somebody and what happened thereafter really "made our day"! We were supplied with a suitable large teapot and dried tea and all the necessary milk and sugar, everything needed to make a scalding hot cup of tea, and that we did - later in the evening after dinner - and two or three of the American boys had a cup with us and they pronounced it very good, the same as we pronounced their coffee very good. It was great coffee - on tap 24 hours - marvelous. So we settled into a bit of a routine, and quite a number of American boys had their tea for a change. About 50-50 we were drinking coffee and they were drinking tea, and we settled down to a very agreeable few days.

John B. Holdforth, Marine,
Royal Marine Fleet Commando, British Pacific Fleet

August 21   They (British Marines) all expressed their version of our chow (which we think is lousy) as the best there is. They say that the chow we had for yesterday's dinner was like Xmas dinner to them. They hadn't eaten like that for 12 months. All we had was chicken, spinach, corn, cherry pie and mashed potatoes, bread and butter. For breakfast this morning all we had was some lousy cereal, one slice of toast with hash, a cinnamon bun with coffee, and yet, they said that it was the best breakfast and the most food they've had for breakfast in 3 months!

I wonder what they'll say when we have some good chow? They said that yesterday morning before they came over from the King George, that for breakfast, that they had one hard, moldy sausage with a piece of year old bread.

They also expressed their surprise at the cheapness of things they can buy at our ship's store. We can buy a carton of Luckies for 50 cents. It costs them on their ship 20 cents for a package of cigarettes.

Manuel Verissimo, Water Tender
from his journal,"Manny's Excellent Adventures"

*   *   *   *   *

August 24 . . . Took on food stores this morning at sea - less one crate of good, juicy hams. Why couldn't it be fish or liver that dropped into the drink

Zenon C. Wolan, Electrician's Mate   *from his journal*

*   *   *   *   *

Fresh water on a ship of that size was at a premium; you could never make enough through the evaporators to satisfy everybody. You have to use things like salt water soap - that's dreadful stuff, but you just have to make do as best we could.

Rather stupidly, several of us young bucks took to using a series of ropes hung over the stern into the very active wake of the USS Barr and we attached our gear to it - shorts, shirts, whatever; we didn't have much, but what we had, we had to wash. This seemed like a good idea, but having washed it thoroughly in the ocean and dried it out, it was naturally salt encrusted. That set up an inflammation that wasn't so painful, but very irritating - so much so that after two or three days, I had to report sick. The American Naval doctor on board liberally plastered almost all of my nether regions with a blue chemical. It was like being stung with needles. For the sake of the regiment you don't show any signs of discomfort; you just cry a little bit. Two days later my underpants fell apart, and I know it wasn't the salt water that did it.

John B. Holdforth, Marine
Royal Marine Fleet Commando, British Pacific Fleet

(Ed. note: In a later conversation, John mentioned that he has since found out that the blue chemical was probably Castellari's paint, an antifungal preparation which is no longer used.)

*   *   *   *   *

One aspect of ship life was that both US seamen and British Royal Marines had communal use of what's known as the heads or toilets. On a small ship, these cannot be segregated into individual units. One gets used to it and quite oblivious to the indelicacy of it. I recall that on about the third or fourth day I was in the heads when opposite me was a large chief petty officer and a few other Marines and seamen were around. One yankee seaman came in. I said "How are you this morning" and he said "Great." The old Barr was rising and falling at a rate of knots - slap, slap. slap, slap - on a pretty choppy typhoon sea, and the water was rushing through as seawater does, used to flush through the heads continually, and it was a bit noisy. So you don't talk all that much. Suddenly, this chief petty officer looks around and he says, "Look at you guys, only a few days ago, you were going to chuck any Limeys straight over the other side of the ship if he came aboard. Now look at you - using the heads together!"

Speaking of choppy seas, and given that Royal Marine Sergeants have a propensity for keeping the rank and file as busy as possible to keep them on the straight and narrow, it wasn't long before one or more sergeants had us parading on the fantail. There wasn't a lot of room but enough to get into formation and do a bit of rifle drill. We were used to a fairly big ship that didn't have the quicker movement of the Barr in a choppy sea. Boots on a timber deck aren't too bad, but boots on a steel deck are a little harder to handle. The Americans were a bit amused to see these Limeys doing rifle drill on the fantail on a pitching ship just to keep occupied. We were absolutely delighted to be taking several days instead of two days before we were put ashore, so we were as happy as pigs in straw.

John B. Holdforth, Marine
Royal Marine Fleet Commando, British Pacific Fleet

*   *   *   *   *

August 25 . . . One of the Marine sergeants let me look at the invasion plans this afternoon. They're going to carry out the plans as if it were a real invasion. Throughout the plan they kept saying that we shouldn't get any opposition and no troops should be in the area, but they still tell you what to do if there is any opposition, and they say it often enough to convince me that they are not too sure that we won't get any opposition.

August 26 . . . The Missouri joined us late last night. News from Frisco says that the signing of the surrender will take place aboard her.

Manuel Verissimo, Water Tender
from his journal, "Manny's Excellent Adventures"

      *   *   *   *   *

While waiting for our assignment, we transported a lot of officers from other ships to the USS Missouri. We knew that Adm. Halsey, Adm. Nimitz, Gen. Douglas MacArthur and a lot of ranking officers were present aboard the Missouri.

Andrew C. Soucy, Water Tender
from his personal diary and album

      *   *   *   *   *

One of our lads was a fellow called Lofty Poole from Hampshire. He was a long-term Marine, and he chummed up with two or three American seamen of like age. They took to gathering after the evening mess or meal and drinking interminable cups of tea and coffee and talking away for all they were worth about their hopes and aspirations of what they were going to do after the war - where they came from and what life was like and all sorts of things and they were fairly immersed in this exchange of ideas.

I want to put in a little segment which involved myself and a gentleman named Celestin. And he was black and a US crewman. I don't know what rank he was, but he was a congenial sort of bloke and, unlike Lofty Poole and his mates, we were somewhat younger and rather more raucous - noisy - and we were into discussions of jazz and also boogie, of which Celestin had a fair knowledge. I must confess so did I. I had learned my lesson from American servicemen in the U.K. I enjoyed the rhythm, and I was a fair exponent of the jitterbug. We bandied names backward and forward - names like Albert Ammons, Pete Johnson, Joe Turner and old Pinetops Smith came into it - all very good boogie pianists. There was no shortage of good music on the Barr's crew deck because it was relayed, I expect from one of the major United States services' radio stations and we had music all the time. There was something very suitable that came on the air and, spontaneously, Celestin and I did a reasonably energetic acrobatic jitterbug. You can't be too energetic on a small ship because you'll knock yourself to bits on the deck head. We got a fair hand of applause and thoroughly enjoyed it. It was maybe ten minutes later, going for another cup of coffee, one of our sergeants approached me very sneakily - moved up alongside me and said, " What you and that big bloke did, that was real good." I was surprised, I didn't think he would approve. Oh, happy days.

John B. Holdforth, Marine,
Royal Marine Fleet Commando, British Pacific Fleet

Entering Tokyo Bay
StM1c Williams in foreground

We're anchored in Tokyo Bay tonight with our lights all on and a movie on the fantail even.

Phil Jones, Lieutenant

We were the first ship to tie up to a pier in Tokyo. We were tied up to a pier right behind a hospital ship that was flying the Japanese flag.

Talmadge F. Grubbs, Seaman

Officers of the USS Barr *on deck in Japan: Lt. McKinlay, Ens. Hubenthal, Ens. Reilly, Lt. Jones, Lt. McEwen, Ens. Swearingen, Lt. Keys, Capt. Dickie, Lt. Unzicker, Lt. Cdr. Gordon, Ens. Huber, Lt. Aldinger, and Lt. Kaiser*

CHAPTER 15

TOKYO - MOVIES ON THE FANTAIL

Entered Tokyo Harbor around noon today with the REEVES leading. . . . BARR was first U.S. Vessel to tie up at the docks of South Tokyo - something that the whole U.S. Navy has been planning on for four years. . . . we are to have a movie on the fantail tonight. How about that. A dream come true - right here in Tokyo Bay.

August 30, 1945.

This is "Love" day as it is called. At 0500 this morning we pulled up the anchor. At 0800, set Condition Two Mike. All guns were manned; and we moved into Tokyo Bay. At 1000, British Marines away to Beach at the Yokosuka Naval Base. We tied up alongside a Jap oiler when we put the Marines ashore. And part of our personnel went over on the Oiler, and stripped it of all her guns.

"Limeys getting ready to go ashore at Yokosuka"

We noticed little white flags everywhere. The Japs have been ordered to put a white flag up wherever there was a gun emplacement. And there sure were a lot of them - everywhere. We hated to see the Marines get off. We had made very good friends with them. This morning when they disembarked, they were given three cheers by us; that was when we were pulling away, leaving them on the beach. And they also gave us three cheers - a swell bunch of fellows.

British Royal Marine Commandos
Marine Kerry-1st row, 2nd from right; Marine Crawford-2nd row, 3rd from right;
Marine Holdforth took the photo after landing at Yokosuka Naval Base, Japan

Also this morning, I saw Mt. Fujiyama, sticking way up over everything else. Was very pretty. Also I went over on one of the Jap ships, and got a flag (a pennant) that they use for signaling. I know Johnny will like it.

This afternoon at 1600 we went alongside the BENEVOLENCE (hospital ship) to take on POW's for further transfer. How nice it was to see the nurses on the ship. All the boys were excited. Just shows us that there are still such things in this old world. Just in our world, we didn't know.

We transferred the Repatriates on to another ship and are at anchor in northern Tokyo Bay. 2000 - All secure.

September 1, 1945.

Anchored in Yokohama anchorage overnight. At 0630 this morning, a group of War Correspondents and some high ranking Naval officers came on board from the SAN JUAN, and we got underway for Inner Harbor at Tokyo.

Entered Tokyo Harbor around noon today with the REEVES leading. REEVES first U.S. vessel to enter Tokyo Harbor in four years. BARR was second. BARR was first U.S. Vessel to tie up at the docks of South Tokyo - something that the whole U.S. Navy has been planning on for four years. At 1357, moored port side to docks. Officers disembarked to go and find repatriates.

No trouble with the Japs, but we were all standing by, ready. Instead, a disgusting show was put on by a little Jap girl. The Captain tried to keep her away, but she kept on coming back. She would do a strip-tease about every ten minutes. At least every time I was on the boat deck or out on the weather deck, I would see a gang watching. This was the most disgusting thing I believe I have ever seen. One of the boys gave her a piece of soap and motioned what it was for. She put the soap in her mouth-made suds and washed her hands. It makes me sick to even think about it.

Around 1730, we received around 30 Repatriates. Two were old women and also had three little kids. One of the women was a stretcher case. What a sight she was. And what stories some of these boys can tell. Hard to believe any people to be so cruel. Some of them have really had a tough time. Around 1830, we got underway. We took the POW's out to the BENEVOLENCE where we disembarked them. We are now anchored at Yokohama Harbor.

September 6, 1945.

For the past few days, we have been doing the same. Sometimes working all hours of the night getting all the POW's out of the Tokyo and Yokohama area. At 1915 we got underway for Hamamatsu, Japan. Going there to evacuate POW's. We have just come down from G.Q. Had to pass through mine fields and all had to be on the alert. Several ships have been hit by mines around this area.

2200 - All calm - Full speed ahead.

September 7, 1945.

At 0700 this morning, we anchored at Hamamatsu. Right after lunch we took on board POW's. This morning, there was a swimming party off the fantail. I didn't go and am glad. For it soon was secured as some sharks were sighted in the water nearby.

September 9, 1945.

At 0700 this morning, we left Hamamatsu, with over a hundred POW's. Boy, and have I worked today doing all the processing on them. At 2000 we arrived at Yokohama. We transferred the POW's to the BENEVOLENCE; and have anchored for the night right off of Yokohama. And we are to have a movie on the fantail tonight. How about that. A dream come true - right here in Tokyo Bay. And without the bogeys.

September 10, 1945.

We had been hoping that our job was done and we could go home. But this morning we got underway for Sendai. More Repatriates. Sea is pretty choppy and has been all day.

September 11, 1945.

Last night we had a movie on the fantail while underway. This is a peace-time Navy now. We still had to darken ship and the smoking lamp was out on the fantail. Still have to be a little careful.

Around 1300 - arrived at Sendai.

September 12, 1945.

Some Repatriates came on board this morning. This afternoon we had liberty - a sight-seeing trip into Shiogama. I got a couple of little Jap dolls. One for my girl and one for my other little sweetheart, my baby sis. Also got a man of war on a horse. And in a schoolhouse I got a trophy. It is gold and silver. Got that for mother.

Got several other little things including a Jap flag for Johnny. A couple of our boys got in trouble over on the beach today. They just think they can do as they please, but they are learning. They stole a truck and rode all over the place.

Will have a movie on the fantail tonight. Wonder if my girl thinks of me as much as I think of her. Sure would like to have mail again. I know that I will - in time.

September 14, 1945.

Underway around 1700 for Kamaishi, on the island of Honshu, Japan. Loaded with Repatriates.

September 15, 1945.

Around 0600 this morning we anchored at Kamaishi, Japan. Our boats took off the Repatriates we had. Put them on the SAN JUAN, and then went into the beach for more. Around 1600 we were loaded. But will stay at anchor for the night.

September 16, 1945.

At 0600, we got underway for Tokyo at full speed, loaded with POW's. Have been talking to a lot of the POW's today. Just can't ever find anyone from around home or who I know.

September 17, 1945.

At 0800 this morning, we were anchored in Tokyo Bay. Disembarked all the POW's by noon. This afternoon we fueled, and are now anchored in Yokohama anchorage.

September 18, 1945.

In the middle of the night, I was awakened by the boys on the fantail putting double lines on the buoy we were moored to behind. At about 0500, we had reveille, and set the Special Sea Detail. Got underway to get to a better spot for anchor. Our anchor was dragging when we got underway. The water is very rough here in the Bay. And that is hard to believe. And the wind is very strong - almost knocks you down on the weather decks.

2000 - At anchor again. We have reports that an awful typhoon has hit

Okinawa. Said lots of ships were beached. Well, I don't think one could hurt us too much here in the Bay. Or maybe it could, for we sure have been rocking today.

September 19, 1945.

This morning we had information that all the evacuation has been completed. We have certainly done our share. Now, we are sure ready to come home. Will have to sit tight for a few days and see what happens.

And this afternoon we had mail. O, it was wonderful. All home is well, and I think my girl still loves me.

September 20, 1945.

Had some terrible news this A.M. We are now assigned to a mail run from Tokyo to Iwo Jima and back. How can they do this to us. It's about time we start for the States. We have been out here longer than any other APD, and I know that they have plenty of APD's to do such crazy things. What a life!

F1c Muha and MM3c LeMere

September 24, 1945.

On the sea now with our bow toward Iwo Jima. We were going there one time before, but it is a different story now. We can't forget that place nor how many Marines gave their lives for that little rock in the water. Sea is calm, and we sure are hot about such a deal. We are supposed to be a mail ship, but this morning we left with no mail - no nothing - just going on a trip. Wonder when we will go home.

September 26, 1945.

This morning, we arrived at Iwo Jima. We anchored at 0700. I had liberty from 1215 to 1530. I went over with Sweatt, Haynes and Rushalk. We got a ride as soon as we hit the beach, and rode all over the place. We saw old Mt. Suribachi and where they raised the flag. Brought back some awful memories. Also saw the graves of the third, fourth and fifth Marines. I don't think that I have ever seen anything more beautiful - that is, in one sense. Thousands of little white crosses, row on row. I think it is a last tribute to the boys who gave all. The graves have little white fences around them. Also we walked along the beach where the Marines came ashore on Feb. 19, 1945. The whole beach was a mass of wreckage. They haven't cleaned it up. Maybe they will just leave it as it is. You sure could tell that there had been a battle there. Lots of landing barges and tanks were in the water just off the beach.

Coming back, we tried to get a ride on one of the B-29's there - but were unable for we didn't have enough time.

At 1800 - we got underway. Headed now back to Tokyo. Wonder where we will go from there. We have no mail on board. We do have about eight passengers. O, what a farce this is. Just like the Navy.

<u>September 28, 1945.</u>

This morning we moored back to our old buoy in Yokosuka Harbor. And this afternoon I went over on liberty. Can't remember when I have had a better time since I've been out here.

Over here, there is an old building that has been converted to an Enlisted Man's Club. It is nice. There are game rooms, movies, beer and famous bands. Today we heard the band from the NEW JERSEY. Was nice. But I forgot to tell about the rough weather we had coming back from Iwo. We had a storm and sure had a time for ourselves. O, I hate those storms.

Dance Hall in Japan

<u>September 30, 1945.</u>

Laying around at anchor. Boy, we are all praying now that the next thing we hear will be orders to return to the States. They've just got to come through. Had many more sweet letters today. Gosh, it is much harder to take now - (Navy stupidity) than while the war was on. Sometimes, I don't think they care about anything.

<u>October 10, 1945.</u>

Been laying around at anchor so far this month. And yesterday we got some orders. I feel like going over the hill. We are assigned now to go down to Nagasaki on a bomb survey.

So far this month we have been laying around mostly. Underway several

times around in the Bay. The water in the Bay has been very rough. Two typhoons came by. Have been having mail pretty regular and all the liberty we wanted to take.
<u>October 11, 1945.</u>

Got underway this morning. Went and tied up at the docks here at Tokyo. Tied up at 1100.

At 1300, I took off on liberty with a couple of the boys, and we took in the sights of what was left of Tokyo. Boy, the place sure is bombed out. Almost every place you look you can see where bombs hit. Tokyo really took a beating. We visited the grounds around Ye Imperial Palace. It was a beautiful piece of work and didn't appear to have been hurt by the bombs. And I have never seen any goldfish in all my life as large as I saw in the water that surrounded the Palace. They were at least a foot long. Sweatt went with me on liberty today.

SM2c Budak, Ensign Buller
and SK2c Haynes

Last night we had a movie over in a warehouse right here on the docks. Was nice and Decker didn't mess up once. Movie went right through without any trouble - a wonderful thing!!

All afternoon, the boys have been over on the docks selling cigarettes and candy to the Japs. After chow and before I went to the movies, I went over. We get from ten to twenty yen a pack. (15 yen equals one American dollar) Trying to get enough yen to buy my girl a kimono. I have seen some pretty ones that the boys have bought here in Japan.
<u>October 12, 1945.</u>

This morning we loaded jeeps, and U.S. Strategic Bomb Survey Group. Was all around the dock this morning getting yen. And this morning I got a red kimono

for my girl. Paid 900 yen for it. Sure looks like a good one. At least, it is pretty.
And this afternoon I got two more kimonos. I wanted one for my large sis and one
for my little sis. But can't find one small enough for my little sis, so I suppose I
will find one later. I think my girl needs this black one, too. It is also pretty. Don't
know which one I like the best.

2200 - Underway for Nagasaki.

The following list of movies seen on the Barr *came from almost daily letters
Ensign Hubenthal had written during 1945 to his wife, Gertrude. As
John said, "Since we could not write about where we were, or what was
happening, etc, movies became a topic of my letters, so these are probably
all the movies I saw--there were more."*

1/8/45	*None but the Lonely Hearts*
1/13/45	*Pearl of Death*
1/30/45	*Frenchman's Creek*
3/8/45	*My Kingdom for a Cook*
3/11/45	*The Man Who Came to Dinner*
4/7/45	*Lady in the Dark*
4/14/45	*Philadelphia Story*
4/18/45	*Mercy Island*
6/4/45	*The Fleet's In*
6/10/45	*A Tree Grows in Brooklyn*
6/13/45	*Hollywood Canteen*
6/16/45	*Practically Yours*
7/11/45	*Heavenly Body*
7/24/45	*The Amazing Mrs. Holiday*
7/28/45	*Desperately Dangerous*
8/4/45	*Having Wonderful Crime*
8/15/45	*Jane Eyre*
9/5/45	*Captains of the Clouds*
9/17/45	*Laura*
9/28/45	*The life of Edgar Allen Poe*
10/1/45	*The Princess and the Pirate*
10/3/45	*The Male Animal*
10/16/45	*Wilson*
10/28/45	*Royal Canadian Mounted*

*In addition, Bennie Rice recalls films of boxing matches, especially
those of Jack Dempsey, on the fantail.*

FLASHBACKS

───── *Arrival in Tokyo* ─────

We were landed by the USS Barr DE576/APD39 on 30 Aug '45. Thanks to the Skipper and men of this gallant APD we had arrived, with the possibility of the first to do so on the Jap mainland.

The Barr crew gave us three cheers as she pulled away, which we returned. I think twas an excellent parting gesture indeed and could not have been bested.

William E. Kerry, Marine
Royal Marine Fleet Commando, British Pacific Fleet

*   *   *   *   *

From letter dated August 31, 1945 from Phil Jones to his parents:

We landed British Marines yesterday at the Yokosuka Naval Ammunition Depot, 2 days before the main landings. I went ashore with a landing party from the Barr - it was our job to spike all the Jap guns in our area so the Japs couldn't use them against our transports when they start arriving tomorrow. No shots were fired and the Japs acted friendly - we took 15 prisoners, including one general. . . . We're anchored in Tokyo Bay tonight with our lights all on and a <u>movie on the fantail even.</u>

*   *   *   *   *

We were the first ship to tie up to a pier in Tokyo. We were tied up to a pier right behind a hospital ship that was flying the Japanese flag.

And right after that is when I started cooking - started striking for ship's cook. That was a nice job because I got most anything I wanted to eat. The food on the ship was fair, but when I started to cook, it was good to me. I could get anything I wanted to eat that was aboard ship. Then I made a few more friends than I had because they liked to eat with me. I did that until I left the ship in December and came back to the States.

Talmadge F. Grubbs, Seaman

From letter dated September 5, 1945 from Phil Jones to his parents:

We were to pull into inner Tokyo harbor alongside a dock and get some more ex-prisoners. . . . So for the first time since we left Frisco, we pulled alongside a dock - and it had to be in Tokyo. We were the first American ship to pull alongside a dock in Tokyo and there were correspondents all over us, so maybe they wrote up the story.

There were Jap soldiers on the dock and they took our lines and helped us berth. They were all over the place and fully armed and it seemed rather funny, especially knowing that we were all by ourselves, with our nearest troops on transports about 20 miles away.

We were no sooner tied up when two little old Japs came over, bowed a couple of times, saluted and told us that they were from the Tokyo Port Director's Office and they wanted to know if there was anything they could do for us. They had water facilities too, but we decided to continue to distill our own. . . .

While we were alongside the dock, we walked around a bit and looked the place over. There were Jap soldiers and civilians all over. They usually saluted us, seemed very polite and subdued. . . .

The Captain, 6 chiefs and one other man were transferred back to the States yesterday, so now Bill Gordon is Captain, Don is Exec. and I am Gunnery Officer. I'm OOD now and have John Hubenthal for my JOOD. . . .

We had Governor Stassen aboard the other day - he's a full Commander and is working on this POW business. He ate dinner with us and we really gave him our opinion of the Navy in no uncertain terms. He was surprised that none of us planned to stay in and join the Regulars. He's a huge man . . . he looks a little like General Eisenhower.

*   *   *   *   *

August 30 . . . We passed right by Yokohama. Pretty well bombed out. Saw a big sign in city which said 'Welcome U.S. Navy and Army'. It was made by American war prisoners in Jap prison camp in Yokohama.

September 2 . . . Took aboard Commander Harold Stassen, former governor of Minnesota and former Secretary of Navy. Passed right by as I was eating chow.
Zenon C. Wolan, Electrician's Mate   from his journal

*   *   *   *   *

I do remember his (Stassen's) visit fairly well. I had the gangway watch on 9/2, knew he was coming, and escorted him to Captain Dickie's cabin. When relieved from watch duty, I was happy to find that Stassen and the Captain had joined others in the wardroom and a lively conversation was going on that I thoroughly relished as I fed the inner man. I also remember him saying how he could catnap on even short political trips and so arrive at destinations relatively refreshed.

Philip P. Jones, Lieutenant

*   *   *   *   *

Pete Dickie was 32 years old in 1945, and I understand that he had been on continual sea duty since 1939. During most of this period he was skipper of smaller ships; then he became Executive Officer of DE 576 when she was commissioned. He was NROTC at the University of Washington and was called to active duty in 1939. At the end of the war when the point system came out, he had enough to be mustered out immediately. He asked for relief of command and left the ship heading for home without waiting for the official approval. Bill Gordon, our Exec. took over in the midst of a night trip from Tokyo Bay to Tokyo Harbor. We had never done it, and didn't know if anyone else had. In short, Pete said "enough, already - I'm outta here!" This sounds flamboyant and macho, but he was the exact opposite of this. I did not know him at all, except as a very polite, mild mannered guy who was in charge. Others undoubtedly knew him better.

John W. Hubenthal, Lieutenant (jg)

POW'S

We picked up about 1200 POW's - Americans from the Bataan Death March, Brits, even missionaries, and that was quite an experience. The procedure was they'd come aboard on the fantail, take off all their clothes and throw them overboard, take a salt water shower on the fantail, then go directly to the regular showers and get new clothes issued afterward. Some of them had been there for years, and I remember one man was the skipper of that famous submarine that was sunk or captured in Tokyo Bay. He had been subjected to a lot of unspeakable torture because they thought he had a lot of information. Most of the prisoners said they had gained 20 or 30 pounds in the last couple of months before we picked them up, because it had been obvious that we would win the war, so their jailers started treating and feeding them much better.

C. Richard Keys, Lieutenant (jg)

*   *   *   *   *

We on the Barr never suffered anything like the men who were in hand to hand combat or the people that were on the Bataan Death March. I had a friend in Texas (he was a country boy from Texas), who went into the Army before Pearl

Harbor. He was in the Philippines. they moved him to Corregidor and he said they were all sick. They had everything you could name and number one was diarrhea. He said "Those Japs started marching us and when nature would call these people went to the side of the road to relieve themselves and they were killed on the spot. The only other choice they had was to let nature work, but keep walking." And these many, many miles they had to walk - no food. Eventually they wound up in a coal mine close to Nagasaki.

Warren T. Pierce, Sonarman

*   *   *   *   *

To the great chagrin of the POW's, we made them throw everything away. They and their possessions were infested with lice and fleas. We made them take a saltwater bath, dispose of all clothes, get a very short haircut, and go through a quick medical scan. Some of the worst cases were sent immediately to a hospital ship.

As Supply Corps Officer it was my job to see that the POW's were clothed and fed. The main food they wanted was white bread and butter. My chief petty officer came to me and said, "The first 100 men have eaten 40 pounds of butter." Perhaps half of the butter was hidden for future consumption, but many of them became sick from eating too much fat.

Many of the POW's had been in Japanese prisons since 1942. Some were just skin and bones even though they had been eating well for the past two weeks. The stories they had to tell would make another book.

Eugene L. Swearingen, Ensign
from his journal "My Ramblings Aboard the Barr, APD39"

*   *   *   *   *

One thing I have not mentioned was the complete moral disintegration, as well as physical, that some of the prisoners had suffered. They had to steal even to exist, and for some it had become a very real part of their lives. When we were processing one bunch of POW's, a man came up with a carton of cigarettes, (which we were giving out freely to anyone who wanted them) telling us he had just seen them and stolen them by force of habit. I told him to keep them, but he would not do it. When stealing has become so ingrained in a man's life that he steals when necessity no longer exists, it may be difficult to adjust to life without stealing again if things get tough.

Eugene L. Swearingen, Ensign
from his journal, "My Ramblings Aboard the Barr, APD39"

The POW's asked thousands of questions such as how bad was San Francisco bombed and New York. Also, how many of our ships were lost. One interesting incident was meeting a man from my hometown who was on the Bataan Death March. He was several years older, but he knew me and I knew several of his classmates. When he returned home, he immediately visited my father to tell him that we had a long chat and that I was OK and well.

Andrew C. Soucy, Water Tender
from his personal diary and album

*   *   *   *   *

The POW's that were physically able were taken to a transport. The ones that were not able were taken to a hospital ship. One evening they were so late that the POW's had to be kept aboard that night - it wasn't a big batch of them, maybe thirty. Well, I was one of these smart-alec young servicemen who, if color sounded and I was by the door or a hatch, I would step inside real quick. That was just a habit with me - a terrible habit. So the next morning here are these POW's helping one another - it didn't matter if it was a general or an admiral and the sick guy was a lowly enlisted man, they helped - everybody was the same rank as those prisoners. They were out on the fantail and they fell in when the color sounded and they saluted the colors. Big tears flowed down their cheeks. That made me so ashamed of myself that from then on I was a rabid flag person. If I ever caught anybody that failed to salute the colors, I would tell them about it. I felt so ashamed of myself seeing those poor guys - so skinny, and they were only issued Navy dungarees, blue shirt, blue pants and black shoes. And here I was, I had been in the Navy all this time and I would salute the colors if I got caught outside, but I'd get out of it if I could. But, from then on I'd go out of my way to salute the colors. It was so terrible to see.

Warren T. Pierce, Sonarman

*   *   *   *   *

I remember going where the POW's were and going into the crematorium bringing back the ashes of the guys who had died up there at the copper mines at Hokkaido where they had been working. They were Americans and their dog tags were all on these vases. These were brought back to be returned to their families.

We had to cook special food for the women missionaries; their stomachs had shrunk and they weren't very well. We just cooked light for them for awhile. The children all wanted ice cream, but we'd give them just a little bit.

Clarence I. Priest, Seaman

——————— *Other Assignments* ———————

From letter, dated Sept. 17, 1945 from John W. Hubenthal, Lieutenant (jg) to his brother Karl:

Ever since we arrived here at Tokyo, we've been operating with the Hospital ships in the evacuation of Prisoners of War, and have been pretty busy keeping up with the bungled orders that we keep getting concerning them. We've been south to a place called Hamamatsu, and north to the Bay of Sendai, and further to a place called Kamaishi. Everywhere we've been, they've been completely bombed out, and the people look as though they could use some clothes and a little more food. It's been pretty interesting to go ashore in these places and wander around, and there's really a wealth of souvenirs to be had. . . . I've picked up a few things, none of which are particularly valuable or different, but some of the crew have really gotten some good stuff. This place up north of Kamaishi was a steel town that the 3rd Fleet had bombarded, and it was really flattened!!! Not enough left to see even. The local mayor had a bunch of beer stored away in a cellar, however, and we had a party on that. The beer over here is excellent, and this Saki is O.K., but just a little too potent to play around with.

    *   *   *   *   *

From there we started up the coast of Japan and picked up some POW's from Sendai which is about 300 miles from Tokyo and then to Kamaishi, about 600 miles north of Tokyo. Many of these men were pilots shot down, prisoners taken from different battle engagements. We then proceeded to discharge our POW's to the Benevolence Hospital ship.

        Andrew C. Soucy, Water Tender   from his personal diary and album

    *   *   *   *   *

We went on to the trading store where the articles had evidently been accumulated from the homes in town. They had one man who had learned English in a YMCA night school in Tokyo. He would tell us the price of different articles in terms of packages of cigarettes or bars of soap. I suppose there was some pilfering during the day, but most of the boys had brought things to trade and I laughed at how fast the Japs were learning to stay even with or even profit from the Americans. I dare say that many of them became rich during the occupation and hated to see us leave.

        Eugene L. Swearingen, Ensign
        from his journal, "My Ramblings Aboard the Barr, APD39"

Then there was the time when we were at anchor and showing a movie on the fantail. I don't recall just where we were, but a 50 foot motor whaleboat from some ship came alongside and requested to come aboard because they were lost. It was about 9:00 at night and it was finally decided they would spend the night and go back to their ship the next morning. So, inasmuch as one of our LCPR's was tied up behind the fantail, they tied their boat up behind it. Then about two in the morning, one of the men on watch came and woke me up and said I'd better get up on deck immediately. What I saw when I got up there was almost unbelievable. My LCPR was suspended completely under water with lines up to the fantail and to the whaleboat. LCPR's were made of plywood, and the whaleboat had a very heavy, solid and pointed bow. Apparently the ocean currents had caused the whale boat to crash into the LCPR, and it took on water until it sank. We were unable to save the boat, so we had to write a letter to the Navy Dept. explaining how we lost it. I believe that happened just after the war ended and Bill Gordon was skipper. I recall that he had us rig up a marker buoy to identify the spot in case the Navy wanted to try to salvage the boat.

C. Richard Keys, Lieutenant (jg)

*   *   *   *   *

From letter, dated September 15, 1945 from Erik Rosengren to his wife:

Here it is early morning and as I have nothing to do I thought I would start my letter. Last night just before sunset we left Sendai and proceeded to this place that we are anchored at now. The name of the place is Kamaishi. When we were enroute it was a pretty sight to see. We were all in column formation with all lights on. It's really swell to have lights on after all the darkness. We arrived at this place just at sunset. We are in a cove with high hills all around us. The clouds are low and are laying on top of these almost mountainous hills. We are anchored very close to the shore as the cove is a bit small for all the ships in here. There are nine ships which are assigned to the work we are doing of which two are hospital ships. Before us in a valley is a small village. To the left of the village are factories which take up twice the space the town does. No doubt that is where the Jap bastards had the prisoners working. I might go over there this afternoon.

It is now exactly eight thirty in the evening. I have just finished getting cleaned up and am sitting in the mess hall writing. There is a movie going on but I don't care to see it. I went over to the beach this afternoon just for a look around. What a mess. Ninety percent of the place is flattened. Our battleships had been shelling it. The factories were smelting refineries of copper and iron. I was able to pick up a few souvenirs. There isn't much to be had at any of these places.

This is more important. There are twenty-three of us out of a crew of a hundred and eighty that are eligible for discharge. We were asked if we wanted immediate discharge from the ship or wait and go back with the ship which should be soon. The majority of us chose the former. I would not mind going back with the ship if they knew exactly when it would be going back, but they don't. Therefore, I'll take my chances on transfer from the ship as soon as transportation is available. It might mean getting kicked around here and there, but at least I'll be on my way. Six o'clock tomorrow morning we are leaving here for Tokyo. We, as well as the other ships, have our load of repatriates to take back. These boys are Canadian, American and Javanese. We will arrive in Tokyo about six o'clock the following morning. Chances are we will be getting transportation for the states there. I have my fingers crossed. Goodnight my darling! I'll be with you soon. --

Here it is Sunday morning. We are underway at full speed for Tokyo. It's a little over 360 miles away. We will be there in the morning. I have just finished packing my bag with all the things I won't be needing. Now if I get the word it will only take me five minutes to get ready. Chow will be down in a little while so I'll write more later.--

It is now late afternoon. A lot of the guys are kidding me about going home. Calling me civilian and mister and so forth. Some of them want to know why I don't stay aboard and wait to see if the bureau rates me chief. There isn't a rate in the Navy that would make me stay in it any longer than I have to. Coming home to you means more to me than any rate. They are getting the mail ready now so I'm going to finish this up. So long and it won't be long now. Give my love to Mom and Pop and say hello to everyone for me.

    *   *   *   *   *

While we were in Japan, our authorities started a program of hiring Japanese men, and they were available to do maintenance work on ships. I think they paid them about 15 cents a day, but it beat starving. We had liberated a quantity of Japanese paint, which contained a lot of fish oil of some kind. So, every day a couple of our bosun's mates, packing 45's, would go down and march a large work party of Japanese men back to the ship. They worked like beavers, hardly ever even looked up, and in a very short time they chipped and repainted the entire exterior of the Barr with the paint we had liberated from one of their big caves. I wouldn't be surprised if some of those men didn't get rich a few years later, selling us Hondas and Sonys.

C. Richard Keys, Lieutenant (jg)

    *   *   *   *   *

After Iwo Jima was secured, some of us took the PR boat and went to the top of Mount Suribachi, where the Marines raised the U.S. flag.

Norman LeMere, Machinist's Mate

September 20 . . . Capt. Kennaday came over this noon and told us we can officially record our return to the states within two months. He is also going to see commander of 5th fleet and find out why we're getting these dirty deals. Will also try to get us back sooner. I hope so.

Zenon C. Wolan, Electrician's Mate   from his journal

*   *   *   *   *

Captain Kennaday arrived at Okinawa after we had and was our commander probably until we left for Nagasaki. He flew his flag on 3 APD's. On Navy Day, 1945 somewhere in Japan he formally inspected us - exact details a memory loss, but not our feeling of resentment that we were going through such nonsense "there" when we should have been one of the ships sent back.

Philip P. Jones, Lieutenant

*   *   *   *   *

Our next assignment was a trip to Iwo Jima. While at Iwo Jima we were allowed liberty and Jim Vertes and I went to the top of Mt. Suribachi. The Marines were building a monument there for the men that had the famous flag raising. Jim and I took several pictures and I have them in my album. We visited the Marine cemeteries on Iwo, and the marine detachment was doing a wonderful job of dressing up the area. There were many headstones and plaques placed on the graves of their fallen comrades. The island was quite different from several months earlier.

Andrew C. Soucy, Water Tender
from his personal diary and album

Fishing Boats at Nagasaki

By the time we got there, all the bodies and human wreckage had been cleaned up, but the physical wreckage was undisturbed. It was awesome! At the center of the bomb blast, there was nothing larger than a saucer--just rubble. As you moved away, there would be an occasional pressure tank that remained whole, and on the fringes you could see pushed over remains of buildings. Sheet metal siding was welded to the steel columns by the heat.

John W. Hubenthal, Lieutenant (jg) from his autobiography

Ruins at Nagasaki

Atomic Area at Nagasaki

CHAPTER 16

NAGASAKI - STRATEGIC BOMB SURVEY

This afternoon I saw - and I still can't believe it - I saw destruction and death at its worst. I am sure that there has never been anything like this in the history of the world. It is almost impossible to conceive that one little bomb did all of what my eyes saw this afternoon.
...Then the loud speaker barked - the Captain said - "We are going home."

October 13, 1945.

Been underway at full speed all day. Sea is pretty calm, but ship is shaking for going at high speed. The Captain said this morning that we had to be on the alert for floating mines - said that there were a lot of them reported where we are going.

October 14, 1945.

Enroute to Nagasaki, Japan. Calm day.

October 15, 1945.

At 0900 this morning, we arrived at Nagasaki, Japan. And O, what a sight and what a smell. Smells like everything here is dead. All you can see is ruins. How did these people hold out as long as they did - that I will never quite understand.

We hear that all liberty is restricted. Just because one sailor went wrong, the whole Navy has to suffer, but that is the way it has always been. Over on the beach the other week, a sailor raped one of the Jap girls and killed her father. We have all kinds of men in this great Navy, but it doesn't seem right that we all have to suffer the little enjoyment that we could have out of life just because one of us goes wrong. Things like that happen every day back in civilian life. Well, that's the Navy. I don't think, anyway, that I would care for much liberty over here, but boy, somehow, I've got to see where the Atomic Bomb hit. I could shoot myself for not having a camera and plenty of film with me. Gosh, I could get some pretty nice pictures.

At 1610 this afternoon, we tied up starboard side of USS Kingman (APB-47). Having movie on fantail tonight.

October 18, 1945.

This afternoon I saw - and I still can't believe it - I saw destruction and death at its worst. I am sure that there has never been anything like this in the history of the world. It is almost impossible to conceive that one little bomb did all of what my eyes saw this afternoon. I am sure that I would not believe it if I had not seen it with my eyes. And yet it is too hard to believe.

The radio reports said - "Wiped out - flattened out" - how right they are. Never have I seen such a thing. A whole side of a mountain torn away. Trees for miles around were bent almost to the ground from the impact. For at least two miles around the center where the bomb was dropped - well, there was just nothing but little pieces of debris that may have one time been something. And the damage could be noticed for miles away. Lots of houses and buildings were damaged.

I heard that around 80,000 were killed by the bomb - and that is not hard to believe. There were three or four buildings that were still partly standing. These were light colored buildings. I heard that white buildings sort of withstood the Atomic Power. I also heard that the bomb exploded up in the air some hundred feet.

Private Residence, Nagasaki

Ruins at Nagasaki

Boy and this whole place stinks. Dead bodies are still being dug out of this city.

November 24, 1945.

Dreams do come true - O, yes they do. When the news was received on board that the war was over - well, we just felt, more or less, relieved. For the strain was getting bad on everyone. I think I forgot, but we did have one fellow to go crazy back in the closing days of the Okinawa Campaign. And I have often heard it said since then that it was a good thing that we did not have three more months like April, May and June, for there would have been more to go off a little.

Back where I was talking in comparison to the news of the end of the war and the news that we had just a little while ago. Yes, we're coming home. We have a radio message that orders us to report to Tokyo, to load to capacity with East Coast passengers - to proceed to Pearl Harbor, T.H., then to San Diego, California, then on to the East Coast.

We do not know yet what port we will pull in on the East Coast - but that is no worry. We are going to the East Coast and that is all that is important - we are coming home. Back to all we love.

I heard the news soon after the Radioman got it. While he took it in to the Captain, I went down and told some of the boys. They thought I was joking. Then the loud speaker barked - the Captain said - "We are going home." Then he read the message over the speaker. What a yell there was then all over the ship. Makes the one we heard when we found out the war was over sound weak. O, it was such good news.

I am so excited that I can hardly write - and for the past couple of hours, the whole crew has been in a daze. You could ask one a question and he won't even hear you.

I have skipped a few days in my writing. Most of the days here at Nagasaki were just routine. I will now try to sum up some of the things that have happened and things I have seen since we came here.

I could just say that all I have seen was awful and that would summarize it good. I did take another trip to the Atomic Bomb area about a week after we got here. This time I had a camera and 24 rolls of good American film. I got the film from the Supply Officer and used Hohlts' camera. We sure got some nice shots. Hope they all come out well.

I have also been able to procure a string of pearls, a pearl ring and pearl earrings. Wonder if Kay will like them!!

Liberty has been good. About a week after we arrived here, we were free men. They have an enlisted men's club here that I have enjoyed immensely. It is an old building that the Navy took over, and they really have a nice place over there now. Free movies. Have table-tennis tables, pool tables. Serve all the beer you care for. And some swell music all the time donated by different ships' bands. The best band was from the JERSEY.

Everything else here has been restricted since we've been here; but still some of the boys have been out drinking Jap whisky and fooling around with the Jap girls. And here we are about to leave here, and have only had a few boys to get out of the Marine Brig.

Y1c Grenga at Atomic Field

*SM2c Budak,Y1c Grenga
and SK3c Peoples*

November 25, 1945.

At 0700 this morning, we got underway for Tokyo. The sea has been pretty calm all day, and we are rolling right along. This morning I had a radio installed here in my office. Sure is nice. Pretty music most all the time. Nice to have music while I am writing Kay. Maybe my letters will be more sentimental.

Crewman at Bar built by Sailors

Basketball Court built by sailors

November 26, 1945.

Sea got up last night and O, what a rough day we have had. No work done in the office today - could hardly sit in my office. Due to arrive in Tokyo tomorrow morning.

All afternoon I have been reading over some of my letters from Kay, sitting around listening to pretty music over the radio.

O, yes, this morning I took a few shots of the ship with the bow under the water. Hope that they will come out all right.

November 27, 1945.

This morning we arrived at Tokyo. A big fog was laying over the bay. Couldn't see far ahead. We finally anchored just off South Tokyo dock by the ANCON. Went to the movies tonight.

Thinking of home and my girl now - all the time. The longing seems intensified now since I know that I am on my way.

The following poem, author unknown,was attached inside Yeoman Grenga's diary:

LOVING A SAILOR

Loving a sailor is not all play;
In fact, there's very little of it gay
It's mostly having but not to hold
It's being young and feeling old.
Loving a sailor is all milk and no cream;
It's being in love with a misty dream.
It's getting a valentine from a southern camp,
And sending a letter with an up-side down stamp.
It's hoping for leaves you know won't come;
It's wondering if he'll ever get home.
And when he does come, it's laughter together,
Unconscious of people, of time and the weather.
It's hearing him whisper his love for you;
And your answering whisper that you love him too,
And then comes the ring, and the promise of love
And knowing you're watched by the Father above.
And loving a sailor's goodbye at the train;
And wondering if you'll ever see him again.
And reluctantly, painfully letting him go;
When inside you're crying for wanting him so.

Loving a Sailor, cont'd.

Then you watch for word that he's well;
And wait for a long dragged-out-letter spell.
And your feet are planted in sand, not sod;
And your source of strength comes solely from God.
Loving a sailor is undefined fears;
And crying until there are no more tears.
And hating yourself, and the world, and the war;
And stamping and kicking 'til you can't fight anymore.
And then giving up and kneeling and praying;
And really meaning the prayers you are saying.
And when the mail comes you bubble with joy;
And you act like a baby with a shining new toy.
And now you know he's an ocean away;
And you must keep on loving him more each day.
And you're proud of the job he's helping get done;
And you don't care any more if loving's not fun.
No, loving a sailor is bitterness and tears;
It's loneliness, sadness, and undefined fears.
It's sweating and fretting and living;
It's nothing to take for a darn lot of giving.
No, Loving a sailor is really not fun------
But, It's sure worth the price when the battle is won.

Tomorrow morning we are to go over to Yokosuka, and provision, fuel, and take on passengers - getting ready to sail for God's Country.

Was sorry that I did not get to go into Tokyo today. I did want to - very much. Now that I have a camera and some film. O, it made me angry. For I know I will never have the chance again.

November 28, 1945.

At 1200 we got underway for Yokosuka. At 1500, we tied up alongside RUNELS (APD 85) in Yokosuka Harbor. Will have movie on the fantail tonight. Guess I will go.

November 29, 1945.

Dern all the luck anyway. They tell us we will not be able to sail until the first. The SIMS (APD 50) came in yesterday morning, loaded and passed us when we were coming in. They sent us a visual - "See you in Pearl." Now, here we get held up. Did not have liberty today - because a couple of dopes broke into the sick-bay and stole some rubbing alcohol. Boy, some people will drink anything. And as the result, the whole ship loses liberty.

November 30, 1945.

Passengers started coming on board late yesterday afternoon. All of them are on board and we are all ready to sail.

This afternoon, I took off and went on liberty with Hohlt. Took the camera and some film. Was cloudy when we left, and it did not get any better.

Chief Hohlt at Atomic Blast Epicenter

Y1c Grenga with Children in Nagasaki

I only took about four shots of the Enlisted Men's Club over on the beach. Hohlt and myself spent the afternoon at the club. About an hour before time to return to the ship we went shopping. I had about 60 yen left and wanted to get rid of it. Bought some pictures and a little box for you know who. And we shook hands with all the Nips and told them good-bye. We will sail in the morning. Can't believe it - but it's true.

Nagasaki Scene

Atomic Field in Nagasaki

Nagasaki Street Scene

Two-man submarines at
Nagasaki Boat Works

Scenes at Nagasaki

Scenes at Nagasaki, continued

Scenes at Nagasaki, continued

Scenes at Nagasaki, continued

FLASHBACKS

We arrived at Nagasaki on October 15, and of course, we wanted to see the effects of the bomb. I stood directly under the place the bomb exploded, and there was nothing on the ground over one-inch high. No rubble, no twisted iron, no concrete--nothing. All had been vaporized.

Eugene L. Swearingen, Ensign
from his journal, "My Ramblings Aboard the Barr, APD39"

*   *   *   *   *

We tied up to the dock in Nagasaki, and the ship was used extensively by many officers of several nations that came to survey the bomb area. The US Strategic Bomb Survey Group with many dignitaries from Washington, DC. were in charge. We also transported about 10 jeeps from Tokyo for transportation of these officers. We all got to drive a jeep occasionally to assist the Army major in charge of transportation.

Andrew C. Soucy, Water Tender
from his personal diary and album

*   *   *   *   *

By the time we got there, all the bodies and human wreckage had been cleaned up, but the physical wreckage was undisturbed. It was awesome! At the center of the bomb blast, there was nothing larger than a saucer--just rubble. As you moved away, there would be an occasional pressure tank that remained whole, and on the fringes you could see pushed over remains of buildings. Sheet metal siding was welded to the steel columns by the heat.

We were the only Navy presence in Nagasaki, and this was fortunate. . . . On one of our "liberties", most of the officers of the Barr went to a small fishing village north of Nagasaki, where I acquired a ceremonial drum, and all of us inhaled too much saki. On the way home in our borrowed Marine jeep, we were picked up by the Marines and held for being in an illegal area, drunk and disorderly, and in possession of a stolen Marine jeep.

Bill Gordon, our new skipper, had been under the weather and did not accompany us; this allowed him, as the senior Naval Officer in the theater, to take over disciplinary action on behalf of the Navy. We were confined to the ship for 10 days.

John W. Hubenthal, Lieutenant (jg) from his autobiography

Nothing but debris and total destruction in the center of the blast area. One of the fascinating things that I witnessed were the shadows cast by the telephone poles as a result of the blast. Actually, the shadows were the unburned areas shielded from the intense heat by the poles while all the surrounding areas were burned black.

Andrew C. Soucy, Water Tender
from his personal diary and album

*   *   *   *   *

James and I talked a lot as we were both in the area of the ship which put us close. He being a yeoman and me a signalman put us in the super structure (the upper part). We also both drove jeeps for the atomic bomb group in Nagasaki.

George Budak, Signalman

*   *   *   *   *

Many jeeps were assigned to the USBSG and with only 8 ship officers we would have one day on Officer of the Deck (O.D.) duty and seven off. On off days a group would take off in a jeep or two to explore the area. We found the quaint little town of Mogi on the inland sea and went there several times. At that time the rate of exchange was 15Y to $1 and for 10Y (65 cents) we could buy a plateful of fresh shrimp, sit on the veranda of a small hotel and watch Japanese harvesting the shrimp from the nearby sea.

Ship's company also built a basketball court near where the Barr was tied up and subsequently played several games there against other ships' companies. The downtown section of Nagasaki was off limits and after being in the area for a few days it was obvious as to why. In the other areas of Japan we had been in (Tokyo - Sendai) the natives were solicitous and friendly (at least to our faces), but in Nagasaki there was much hatred shown in facial expressions for they had suffered greatly from the A-bomb explosion. About 1/3 - 1/2 of Japanese we saw had been hurt and scars and bandages were plentiful.

It was interesting in the evening at chow time to hear the civilian engineers discuss their findings and make their assessments relative to the bomb and the destruction it had brought to the Nagasaki community.

Gordon F. Huber, Lieutenant (jg)

We were assigned to Nagasaki to do bomb surveying. Only first class crew and officers were assigned to this task. I was assigned to measure all the buildings. We were never told that we were standing on highly radioactive ground. I only learned after working for GE through KAPL how significant radiation is. Luckily I was never affected.

Armand J. Marion, Machinist's Mate

        *   *   *   *   *

If I had been expected to come home with clear ideas about world affairs, I would have disappointed people. Seldom before in my life have I had such varied feelings about a race of people or about problems concerning them. Some days you heard stories coming out of the prison camps, and you hated them, one and all. Then you saw the destruction that we had caused them, and you wondered if we were free from blame. Then you thought that they brought it on themselves and had it coming.

Eugene L. Swearingen, Ensign
from his journal, "My Ramblings Aboard the Barr, APD39"

Homeward bound pennant on the Barr

When we tied up, I saluted the quarter deck for the last time and left the USS Barr with some mixed feelings. She had been a good and sea-worthy ship having logged thousands of miles in the South pacific through good weather and foul weather (including 4 typhoons) while being heavily involved in Iwo Jima and Okinawa invasions and part of the occupation forces in Japan proper.

Gordon F. Huber, Lieutenant (jg)

SM2c Budak checking the "kills"
of USS Barr *APD39*

CHAPTER 17

HOMEWARD BOUND

Gosh, what a big ocean this is. . . . We go so slow. . . . Yes, a victorious ship is coming back with all its men. But we can't forget those ships and those men that will never come back. . . . It is so hard to believe that in the morning when I awake that I will see "God's country" in the distance. A dream comes true . . . God has been with us and I will forever be thankful.

December 1, 1945.

Underway at 0800 this morning. Enroute Yokosuka, Japan to Pearl Harbor, T.H. O, how I enjoy putting that down.

Last night, I worked till around midnight getting out sailing reports and passenger reports. The Exec. took the reports over to the Port Director after midnight so that we could sail without any delay.

At 1000 we tied up to a tanker and took on fuel. We are traveling alone. Sea is choppy and seems to be getting rough. But we'll ride 'er out. I'd ride anything to get home again.

December 2, 1945.

Very rough night, and same all day today. What a life. Slept most of the morning - or rather laid in my sack. Too rough to be up. And re-read some of Kay's letters all afternoon. Headed home now. Yes, it is just like you said it would be. But it still is hard to believe.

Some of the boys are telling me that I won't last long after I get home. So good to be going back to such a wonderful family - and, I believe about the best little girl I could ever hope to find.

Clocks put ahead one hour at 1600.

1900 - All secure - but sea is O, so rough.

December 6, 1945.

Sea has finally calmed down. We have been in one storm after another since we left Tokyo. Have taken a few shots of the ship - some with the fantail missing, under the water; and some with the bow digging up the sea.

For the past few days, I have just been laying around - reading over letters from Kay - which is always a treat - in any kind of weather. Am still very happy over coming home. It is a wonderful feeling.

December 7, 1945.

How lonesome I have been today. All day long I have not known what to do with myself. We will pass the International Date Line tonight at 2000. That will make tomorrow the seventh of December too. - No work tomorrow - no pay. I suppose we will be in Pearl Harbor on the tenth. And then on to that last stretch. Gosh, what a big ocean this is. I just sit out on the boat deck and watch our wake. It is bad - for that just shows me how slow we are going - and it is such a large ocean. We go so slow. But only as the days go by, we know we are getting back, back to all we love. Will go to the movie on the fantail tonight.

December 11, 1945.

At 0800 this morning we passed through the sub nets, and around 0900 was anchored in Pearl Harbor.

I went over on business with the Captain soon after we anchored and finally got away from him about 1400.

Then I went into Honolulu, and got myself the largest steak I could find with all that went with it. It was nice to sit around in a civilized world again.

After I ate, I went out shopping. I was alone all day after I left the Captain. Probably good that I was, or maybe I would have gone out to Waikiki Beach with some of the boys. I purchased a heck of a lot of souvenirs of Hawaii - spent all my money. But am glad that I had it with me to spend. Got lots of pretty things. Will wait and see what Kay says about them.

Will have a movie tonight, so I suppose I will go.

December 12, 1945.

No liberty today for at 1500 we said aloha to Hawaii. We got away faster than we had expected - well and good. Now, we are on that last long stretch to San Diego - which is in God's country. We expect to arrive in San Diego on the 19th.

I forgot to say yesterday - but we had lots of mail waiting for us at Pearl. And how nice it was. But I find that all my family and my girl are praying that I will be home for Christmas. That makes me a little sad - for O, how I would like that. Would give anything to be home for Xmas.

December 15, 1945.

Another long day at sea - and, O, how long the days seem now. We are just going along at 13 and 14 knots now. And it is such a big ocean.

But we know where we are going and we can wait. Yes, a victorious ship is coming back with all its men. But we can't forget those ships and those men that will never come back.

Just four more days to pass by and I hope that I will be able to talk to my folks and my girl. That will be wonderful - a long, long time has passed.

The sea is calm and I am sleepy - so rock-a-bye baby - a nodding I will go.
<u>December 18, 1945.</u>

Am very happy today. Not only am I going to call my mother and girl tomorrow
night, but I may be on my way to Georgia. The Captain has said I could leave the
ship as soon as I could get some business taken care of.

It's a long way home--

Out on the foc's'le just a few minutes ago, I was looking forward and thinking.
Nice moonlite night and a very calm sea. Ship is plowing up the water and the
strike sure looks pretty - going home.

It is so hard to believe that in the morning when I awake that I will see "God's
country" in the distance. A dream comes true. I sure did not know last time I left
that someday I would sail right back. God has been with us and I will forever be
thankful.

I have all my gear packed and ready just in case I get off tomorrow. I will not
get my full 30 days, as I will have to meet the ship in New York. But if I can only
get home for Christmas - who cares. I know that it will be a happy one.

Arriving in San Diego, 1945

SoM3c Borgeld, WT3c Sonntag and WT1c Verissimo relaxing at the Continental Room, Hotel San Diego, December 9,1945

A frozen Barr *enters New York Harbor after the war.*

A poem (author unknown) attached to Yeoman Grenga's Diary:

THE OLD 39

She has sailed an ocean or two,
She's one scow that's really fouled,
Listen and I shall tell you,
She fought at Iwo Jima,
Like a good little APD,
She got in a good lick at OKINAWA,
And that is all that she did see.
She screened from Able TWENTY,
To CHARLIE FORTY FOUR,
And from the looks we thought
She'd screen forever more,
Then she played water taxi
For the Army's three star ginks,
For Kennaday she was 4.0
For her crew she was jinks,
Back once more to ABLE SIX,
She screened for a Nippon Sub
She shot a dead Jap.......Hooray,
Paint a flag upon that tub.
Came the big day in August,
She was off for Zambi Bay,
She carried the bloody Limeys
To Yokosuka in Tokyo Bay.
From there she carried everything,
From beans to bandoliers,
North and South and even East,
With time out for a few short beers,
They say she will return some day
To the shores of the U.S.A.
But she ain't doing much
To start upon her way.
'46 or '47 or maybe '48,
She'll sail without a hitch,
She isn't much for liberty,
But she is a screening ....

FLASHBACKS

I had enough points to be transferred to a Victory ship that was returning to the States. About a dozen of us were transferred to this Victory ship. We were all asked to stay with the Barr as all rated men were leaving including the officers. Of course, most of us refused as we had no indication of when the Barr would be allowed to go home. We boarded the Victory ship, and it pulled out and anchored in the harbor at Nagasaki. The very next morning the Barr sent a signal to this ship that they had just received orders to return home. As the Barr steamed by us at anchor, all we could do was wave goodbye. We finally arrived in Seattle on December 26, long after the Barr had reached the States. About 300 sailors boarded a train for Ledo Beach for discharge. I stayed in Seattle waiting for transportation at the separation center. We traveled all the way across Canada to Ottawa and then to New York. The ironic thing about this was that if we had stayed aboard the Barr we would have advanced to the next rate. But no way! We wanted to go home. I was discharged January 11, 1946.

Andrew C. Soucy, Water Tender
from his personal diary and album

*　　　*　　　*　　　*　　　*

I left the ship the first of December, 1945. At that time you didn't get out of the Navy unless you had enough points. I had been in the Navy only a little over 2 years, and so I didn't have any points built up. The morning I found out I was leaving the ship, they reported that anyone married with children could go. I was married with three children, so that's why I got out. They put us on a big transport ship and we left Tokyo and went the north route in the Pacific. We came into San Pedro, CA, five days after we left Tokyo.

Talmadge F. Grubbs, Seaman

*　　　*　　　*　　　*　　　*

My oldest son was born in September before I boarded the Barr. He was almost 1 1/2 years old when I first saw him in Jan. 1946. I left the Barr at Nagasaki. I believe the 20th of November. How strange things happen. I believe now that I would have gotten home sooner had I stayed with the Barr. I arrived Seattle, Washington on the 26th of December, and finally discharged at New Orleans Jan. 12th 1946.

Guy E. Farley, Radioman

In late November we received "homeward bound" orders, and left for Tokyo to pick up a convoy. By this time, everyone was getting out on "points", and our crew had been cut almost in half. . . . The people who had been discharged were the senior and most experienced people; consequently we who remained were not the most expert at our jobs. We had a new skipper who had just been assigned, and he decided we could not wait for a convoy to Pearl Harbor, but should proceed on our own. He consulted with me (the Chief Engineer) about the cruising radius of the ship, and our ability to get there. I, in turn, consulted the book, and told him confidently that it was within our capability. What I didn't take into account was that the book I had was for the original Destroyer Escort, not the heavier converted APD. The cruise was 5000 miles, and the "book" said our maximum was 5300 miles with a new, clean bottom, and a lighter ship. Also, neither of us took into account that we did not have any officers who had experience in celestial navigation. The first day at sea, we realized all we could do with any degree of confidence was take a sun line, which only gave us an approximate position. Fortunately, the gods were with us, and we arrived in Pearl Harbor with no fuel, having sailed for several days on a dead calm sea. We were short of fresh water because one of my men screwed up the principal evaporator system aboard, and there were other similar problems, but we made it just fine.

John W. Hubenthal, Lieutenant (jg) from his autobiography

*   *   *   *   *

A ship makes its own fresh water by taking the salty sea water and running it through an evaporator. Many times fresh water is not available except for cooking. This is when the evaporator has to be cleaned. It is then necessary to wash and shower in salt water with salt water soap. The salt clings to your body until fresh water is available.

Erik L. Rosengren, Signalman

*   *   *   *   *

Starting with the Naval Academy, I became disillusioned with the regular Navy people, and this was reinforced later. Nonetheless, I will forever be impressed with the Navy's ability to teach basic operational skills. I was Chief Engineer of a very complex piece of machinery, staffed with partially trained people, and we made it work even though none of us knew what we were doing. All we knew was what valve to turn, and how to shut it down in an emergency, but we had THE BOOK, and it worked.

John W. Hubenthal, Lieutenant (jg)

After our time was served at Nagasaki we had orders to return to Tokyo area after which we were to return to San Diego, California via Honolulu. By this time we had lost sufficient number of officers that G. Huber as a Lt. was second in command on the Barr and as Executive Officer had navigational duties among others. Although it had been some time since I had been in the Bowditch navigational charts, through perseverance and some luck we managed to find Honolulu and while there I checked to see if my point total (based upon service time and duty) qualified me to be discharged. As I recall one needed 45 points and I had 43, but the officer I talked with gave me permission to leave the ship when we docked in San Diego. An uneventful cruise from Honolulu to San Diego followed.

Gordon F. Huber, Lieutenant (jg)

* * * * *

I never was close to Jim Grenga because he slept in a different part of the ship and my work wasn't anywhere close or similar to his work. But he was a very good yeoman, because there was never anybody who complained about getting records mixed or anything. He did a great job.

Warren T. Pierce, Sonarman

* * * * *

On our way back after the war, we came into San Diego. They knew we were going to be there at Christmas and the officers asked one of the cooks to make plum pudding. So about six weeks before Christmas, they made the plum pudding and put it in a drawer in the galley. One of the officers would come down and put brandy over it every night. He wanted to make sure it was good and strong plum pudding. By Christmas it was pretty good - even the aroma would get you drunk. We had a couple of young boys that had gone to study to be ministers. They were on board at Christmas, and after dinner we started serving plum pudding. We had made hard sauce with butter and confectionery sugar and put three or four fifths of brandy in it. These two young boys wouldn't take a drink with us when we were out on the beach. So they got into that plum pudding and that sauce and you should have seen them tie it on. They got so drunk they were sick.

In San Diego we cooked Christmas dinner and the exec went over to an orphanage and got a bunch of kids to come over to eat Christmas dinner because we had cooked so much and we wanted to do something for kids. So we had a lot of fun. We had a bunch of kids from the orphanage and it was like having your brothers and sisters. Went through Panama Canal to Brooklyn Navy Yard, got rid of ammunition and then to Florida. Took troop train home from Jacksonville. Didn't stay long enough for decommissioning.

Clarence I. Priest, Seaman

EPILOGUE

Captain P.T.Dickie at the 1995 Barr *Reunion in Seattle*

Fifty years after the fact, there is universal agreement amongst the surviving crew and officers that the 250 man crew and 12 officers of the Barr owe their lives to our skipper's two decisions: (1.) to steam slowly at night, and (2.) do not fire at enemy planes unless they had already committed themselves to dive into us. We were very lucky! .
. . . At our reunion in 1995, he (Capt. Dickie) was surprised and flattered that we admired him, and his personality was just the same.
John W. Hubenthal, Lieutenant (jg) from his autobiography

EPILOGUE

The "Wonder *Barr*", as she was called in a 1946 article by Leonard Riblett and Karl Hubenthal (The Leatherneck, Magazine of the Marines, Volume 31, Number 6, June, 1948, pp.2-5) came through the war in the Pacific miraculously unscathed. She had taken her hit in the Atlantic as a DE. None of the *Barr* crew or UDT 13 were lost during the intense fighting at Iwo Jima and Okinawa. Unfortunately, this was not true for a large number of the other small craft, primarily in the outer screening stations, which suffered 95% of the approximately 5000 Navy casualties at Okinawa. At least seven ships that relieved the *Barr* on screening duty were hit by kamikazes within minutes or hours after relieving her.

Yet the *Barr* managed to rack up an impressive number of firsts during the Pacific war. *Barr* Lieutenant John W. Hubenthal cited some of these firsts in a letter dated September 17, 1945, to his brother Karl Hubenthal, co-author of The Leatherneck article:

* First ship to land troops (UDT 13) at Iwo Jima.
* First ship to receive fire from shore batteries at Iwo Jima.
* First ship to land troops (UDT 13) at Okinawa (this one shared with three other APD's also landing UDT's within minutes of each other).
* One of the first ships in Okinawa area to come under zoomie or suicide attacks.
* One of the first ships to enter Tokyo Bay.
* First ship to tie up at Yokosuka Naval Base and in the entire Bay of Tokyo.
* First ship into the inner harbor at the city of Tokyo and also first to tie up there.

Additional firsts cited in the Leatherneck article include:

* Probably landed first Marine Corps Personnel (two advance intelligence men) at Iwo Jima.
* First to land occupational forces at Yokosuka Naval Base (British Royal Marines.)
* Evacuated first women (three missionaries) from Jap prison camps.

The valiant men of this little indestructible ship were rightly proud of their ship and her war record.

From the time the *Barr* was commissioned on February 15, 1944 until she was decommissioned on July 12, 1946, a period of only 29 months, she was commanded by six different captains. Lt. Cdr. Henry H. Love was the first Commanding Officer, serving from the time the *Barr* was commissioned until after she was torpedoed in the Atlantic. Lt. Cdr. Porter T. Dickie, who was Executive Officer during the Atlantic operations, commanded the *Barr* throughout the war in the Pacific until he completed his military service and left on September 1945, after she had safely anchored in Tokyo Bay. The Executive Officer, Lt. Cdr. William Gordon, became the Commanding Officer until he, too, completed his service in November 1945.

Lt. George Rowan, who had been skipper of a PC in the Caribbean, became the Commanding Officer who brought the *Barr* back to the United States. The *Barr* arrived at San Diego on December 19, at which time Yeoman Grenga left the *Barr* ending his logs. After undergoing some repairs, the *Barr* left San Diego, passed through the Panama Canal once again, and proceeded up the east coast, docking at Brooklyn Naval Yard in New York on January 17, 1946. (On his honeymoon in New York, Yeoman Grenga rejoined the *Barr* for her brief stay there.) While in New York, the *Barr* underwent repairs and a pre-inactivation overhaul. During this period Lieutenant C. Richard Keys, Executive Officer, became the Commanding Officer.

Captain Keys set sail in early February for the *Barr*'s final voyage to join the "Mothball Fleet" at Green Cove Springs, Florida, where they arrived later that month. (Meanwhile, Yeoman Grenga had returned with his bride to Georgia and then rejoined the *Barr* upon her arrival in Florida.) The *Barr* was prepared for decommissioning, while many of her remaining men completed their service and were detached from the Navy. Yeoman Grenga was detached from service on March 8, 1946. Captain Keys also completed his service and was detached from the Navy before the *Barr* was decommissioned.

Ensign Frank Whaley, who had joined the *Barr* after it arrived in Florida, became the final Commanding Officer of the *Barr*. Captain Whaley decommissioned the *Barr* on July 12, 1946, sending the ship's ensign and flag to the mother of PFC Woodrow Wilson Barr, Mrs. Cora Dell Barr. The *Barr* remained in the reserve fleet until she was removed from the Navy list on June 1, 1960.

The *Barr* had earned three battle stars in World War II -- one in the Atlantic, where she lost 17 men, and two in the Pacific where no men were lost due to enemy action. As a somewhat ironic end to a valiant little ship, her final service to her country was as a defenseless target -- the "sitting duck" the men so frequently feared during the war. She was towed to the waters off Vieques Island, Puerto Rico and sunk by "friendly fire" in Naval exercises.

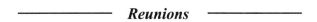

Reunions

Some men of the *Barr* participate in one or more of several associations. Among these are The Block Island Association and the Black Cat Association. The Block Island Association includes men from the USS *Block Island*, which was sunk in the Atlantic, as well as men from the accompanying ships, including the USS *Barr*. The Block Island Association has an annual reunion for several days around the date of the *Block Island* sinking, May 29. The Black Cat Association includes the UDT 13 men as well as crew from the USS *Barr*, from which UDT 13 operated during the battles of Iwo Jima and Okinawa. Their reunions have been held annually, usually in November, since 1991.

Some of the *Barr* crew also organized a special 50th anniversary reunion in 1995, the star attraction being Captain Dickie. Dick Keys began trying to find the *Barr* men (using his PC with an address search program) in early 1995 with the idea of having a reunion. (Interestingly, Phil Jones and Andy Soucy had discussed a possible reunion when they met by chance in June 1994, as they just happened to visit on the same day the USS *Barr* Collection at the Mary F. Shipper Library in Keyser, West Virginia. According to Jones, he later contacted Keys "before Keys had to wrestle with 20,000 or so New Jersey P. Jones".)

Keys located some of the *Barr* men, including Captain Dickie. The captain was then 83 years old, had recently lost his wife, and was in poor health. Since he was living in Oregon and one of the reasons for the reunion was to express their appreciation to him, they decided to have the reunion in Seattle, Washington, so that he would not have far to travel. John Hubenthal played a major role in the planning for the reunion.

The reunion was held in Seattle on August 18-20, 1995. Attendees included Stan Buller, Captain Dickie, Maxine Michaelson (accompanying Dickie), Charles and Peggy Hamman, John and Gert Hubenthal, Gordon and Betty Huber, Phil and Alice Jones, Dick and Caroline Keys, Ned Marrow, Bill O'Donnel, Joe Purgatorio, Jack and Barbara Reilly, Andy and Lorraine Soucy, Jim and Gloria Vertes and Gene Swearingen.

Photographs of the ship, the crew and Nagasaki, at least two different histories of the *Barr* and a mailing list of about 60 crew members were made available to the attendees. On Saturday night they enjoyed a boat ride and dinner at Tillicum Village. However, mostly they just enjoyed being together and talking about old times, especially with the Skipper.

1995 Seattle Reunion; Standing: W. O'Donnell, G. Huber, S. Buller, J. Reilly, G. Swearingen, R. Keys, J. Vertes; Seated: A. Soucy, M. Michaelson, P. Dickie, P. Jones, J. Hubenthal, and N. Marrow

About These Men of the Barr

Forty-seven men (and/or their families) who were on the *Barr* (officers, crew of the *Barr*, UDT 13 members and British Royal Marines) have generously contributed their thoughts and recollections to enrich this book. Information about these men follows the biosketch of James Grenga, which was written with the help of his family and friends.

James Benjamin Grenga, like millions of others in his generation, had a typical American boyhood in a small town, weathered the Great Depression with his family, and began his young manhood with dreams and aspirations that did not include risking his life under enemy fire on a small ship in the South Pacific.

James was born on January 18, 1922, in Newnan, Georgia. His father Angelo, as a boy of about sixteen had immigrated to America around 1904 from Sonnino, Latina, Italy. He returned to Europe in the 82nd Rainbow Division of the American Expeditionary Force in the Great War to make the world safe for democracy.

Eva and Angelo Grenga

Angelo Grenga owned and managed a restaurant in Newnan, and in 1920 married Eva Jane Kelley of Scottish-Irish descent. James' maternal grandfather, John Wesley Kelley, fought in the Civil War, and his great-great-great grandfather, William Kelley, fought under "Lighthorse Harry" Lee in the American Revolutionary War.

James was the oldest of 7 children (Louise, Angelo, Kelly, Robert, John, and Helen). As a young boy during the depression years, James worked at the restaurant and at many odd jobs to help the family: delivering newspapers, distributing circulars for a store in exchange for eggs, selling and delivering eggs from his family's flock of chickens, and taking responsibility for leading the family cow to pasture each morning and bringing her home for milking in the evening.

In the freedom to play and explore in a small community, James' love of water and flying showed up at an early age. As a small boy, he had young Angelo and Louise time him while holding his breath under water in the old claw-footed bathtub. He would go swimming in various ponds and lakes. In high school, he and his friends especially enjoyed family friend Joe Carrasco's Lake Raymond, a few miles from Newnan. Armond Brooks, James' closest friend in high school, remembers that they each paid Joe 25 cents for a ride around the lake in a Garwood speed boat.

James as a Boy Scout

James and Armond built and flew model airplanes out the loft of the barn/garage in his backyard at 66 Spring Street. When the planes ran out of fuel and crashed, he and Armond spent hours patching them up before they flew again--only to crash again and repeat the cycle. Armond also recalls when they filled balloons with hydrogen released from mixing aluminum with acid, tied them with strings, lit the ends of the strings, and released them to explode in the air. James was a Boy Scout, proud of his Boy Scout uniform when he and Armond went to Camp Thunder at Thomaston, Georgia.

He grew into a tall, robust football player at Newnan High where, during his first year, they didn't have a football uniform that fit him. Playing in his swim suit with protective pads taped onto his body put him in the news in Ripley's "Believe It or Not."

During one summer before he finished high school, James served, like so many other young men in the Depression years, in the Civilian Conservation Corps at Fort McClellan, Alabama. There his visiting brothers and parents found him in uniform living in a military type camp. James also attended a flying school at Cochran Field, Georgia, where he obtained his pilot's license.

After high school, James attended North Georgia Military College in Dahlonega (majoring in Business) from the fall of 1940 until December 1941, when the United States declared war on Japan. According to Louise, James begged his parents to let him join the Naval Air Force and they finally agreed. Although he was not accepted into the Air Force, like previous generations of his family he entered active service in the Navy on March 9, 1942, the eightieth anniversary of the first battle of the ironclads at Hampton Roads, Virginia, in 1862.

His diary relates his continued efforts to enter the Naval Air Force while serving on the *Barr*.

*Helen and Johnny
in uniform*

Back home, his "baby sis", Helen, played "Here Comes the Navy" frequently in their father's restaurant and also enjoyed wearing a sailor outfit her mother had given her.

James' diary and the reminiscences of his ship-mates record their longing for home and loved ones. When James left the *Barr* on leave at San Diego in December 1945, he returned home to marry Mildred Kathleen (Kay) Mann, whom he had dated in high school. For their honeymoon, they went to New York for James to meet the returning USS *Barr*. After the *Barr* left New York for Florida, James completed his leave in New York and Georgia, and then rejoined the *Barr* where she was to be decommissioned and moth balled at Green Cove Springs. He was honorably discharged from the Navy on March 8, 1946, a twenty-three-year-old with two battle stars who was eager to enjoy civilian life.

After rejoining Kay in her hometown LaGrange, Georgia, he pursued a sales career (insurance, cars, and jewelry) They had one child, Celesta Kay. James' former brother in-law, Lester Mann, says that James had a marvelous personality; he loved people, accepting them as they were, regardless of their background or station in life. James and Kay, like so many couples in the post-war years, eventually separated and divorced.

*James in Mobile,
Summer, 1967
Photo by Kelly Grenga*

James moved to Mobile, Alabama, where he continued in sales. James also worked at Brookley Field in Mobile, where he met Betty Joyce Owens, whom he married in 1954; they had three children, Joyce Rene, James Larry, and David Anthony. James loved being near the sea again and deep-sea fishing. As he settled into life in peacetime, his brothers, sisters and their families joined him and his family for summer vacations and deep-sea fishing at Dolphin Island off Mobile. They all remember James as a caring, generous, and fun-loving person.

Always a good salesman, James made his last sale (a house) while under sedation in the hospital a short time before his death. His brother, Kelly, remembers having to explain to the buyer why James had difficulty speaking so that she wouldn't hang up on him.

After a brief battle with cancer, James died on July 18, 1979.

His diary and the recollections of his shipmates seem a fitting tribute to the men who gave a part of their youth doing extraordinary work so that the rest of us may live peaceful, ordinary lives.

E. Lewis Bartlett served on a DE during the war in the Pacific. He joined the *Barr* APD39 in New York, where he was assigned to be part of the crew to take her to Green Cove Springs, Florida, to be put in mothballs.

George Budak was born of Romanian parents in Cleveland, Ohio. He talked his parents into letting him join the Navy at age seventeen, which was no easy task since they already had two sons in the military. George went to Boot Camp at Great Lakes and then joined the *Barr* in February 1944, and remained with her until April 1946. After leaving the Navy, George went to work for General Motors as a welder in Armor Plate Welding. After six months, he was promoted to foreman of a welding department, building tanks until 1967. Then he went to the Terex Division, building heavy earth moving equipment until 1973 when he moved to Detroit to help develop the XMI Abram as the new tank of the future. After contracts were awarded to Chrysler, he was transferred to the GM Allison Division at Indianapolis to build the transmission for the XMI Tank. He retired in 1983 and moved with his wife Mary to South Carolina where he works in his yard and plays golf year round.

Fred A. Carver grew up in Tallulah, Louisiana, where he participated in football and boxing as a high school student. He entered the Navy in 1940, and was serving at Pearl Harbor aboard the *Tennessee* at the time of the Japanese attack in December 1941. He also served on the *Indiana* for a brief time before joining the *Barr* DE576. He was on the *Barr* at the time she was torpedoed in the Atlantic, and he may be the only sailor in the Navy who was at Pearl Harbor when it was attacked and was then also torpedoed in the Atlantic. After the war, Fred went to college and then to law school on the GI Bill. He worked as a claims adjuster for five years and then practiced law in Beaumont, Texas, for forty years before retiring.

Edwin I. Cleveland graduated from the University of Pittsburgh in 1943 with his degree in Pharmacy. During the war, he was a platoon leader in UDT 13. After the war, he went to Jefferson Medical College of Philadelphia for his M.D. degree. He practiced medicine in Bronxville, New York, until his retirement thirty years later. In 1989 he moved to Texas where his two sons live.

Marvin Cooper was born in 1924 and grew up on an Iowa farm during the Great Depression. He graduated from Moville, Iowa, High School in 1942 and married his high school sweetheart Wynola Hansen in 1943. Marvin joined the Navy in 1943 and served in Navy Combat Demolition and Underwater Demolition until he left the Navy in January 1946. After the war, he farmed a 160 acre farm until 1952, when he, his wife and two children moved to California, where he worked as a machinist, tool and die maker, and a machine shop foreman. After receiving his Bachelor of Science Degree from California State University at Long Beach in 1966, Marvin started teaching at Millikan High School, where he taught courses in electronics, U.S. History, and mathematics until his retirement in 1984. His wife died in 1970, and he married his present wife Helen Taylor in 1975. Since 1990, Marvin has been researching and writing about World War II Underwater Demolition Teams. His 268 page manuscript, "The Men from Fort Pierce" is being published in serial form in the quarterly magazine of the UDT/Seal Association. Marvin began a search for UDT 13 members in 1990 and, with others joining his efforts, they formed the Black Cat Team Association with its first reunion in 1991.

Joseph G. Dalesandry served on the USS *Barr* DE576 during the Atlantic actions. After the *Barr* was torpedoed, he spent the rest of the war on duty in Guam and was discharged from the Navy in January 1946. After three and one-half years of war, he was still only twenty years old.

Edward N. Deringer was born in Miami, Florida, on November 10, 1926. He enlisted in the Navy on October 25, 1943, served with UDT 13 from its inception in June 1944, until it was disbanded in September 1945, and was then discharged from the Navy on January 18, 1946. After the war, Ed worked on aircraft propellers at Miami International Airport for thirty years. He and his wife, whom he married in 1946, have two sons, one daughter and four grandchildren.

Daniel L. DiBono left his Philadelphia home for Navy Boot Camp in Sampson, New York, at 8:30 PM, May 29, 1943, exactly one year before the *Barr* was torpedoed in the Atlantic. He was with the *Barr* when she was commissioned in February 1944. After the *Barr* was torpedoed in the Atlantic, he went to a hospital for treatment and then served his remaining Navy time on a Net Tender and other vessels. After the war, Dan returned home, finished high school, and then went to a teacher's college to study geography and history. He worked for awhile in Washington in geography, taught for two years in a one-room school house on a Pacific Island, and then returned to the states to a map making job in Philadelphia. Dan married, had two children and eventually became a high school teacher. He retired from teaching in 1991, but keeps busy working at the school teachers' union office and acting as a Blue and Gold Officer at the Naval Academy. He is an active member of DESA and the Block Island Association and enjoys seeing and visiting some of the old crew.

John A. Earle was drafted by the Navy when he finished high school. After attending boot camp and two fire control schools in San Diego, he joined the *Barr* as part of the skeleton crew that put her into commission. He was transferred from the *Barr* in Casablanca in June 1944. After attending school in Washington, D.C., he was sent to San Francisco to serve on the *Crescent City* APA 21, went to Okinawa on June 6, 1945, and remained there until the end of the war, being discharged on March 6, 1946. Then, on March 12, he and a high school friend double dated, tossing a coin to see who would get the blind date. John lost the toss (getting the blind date), but actually won because he and Margie were married a few months later and have enjoyed fifty-three wonderful years together. After they were married, John attended college, and his graduation present from Margie was their son Carey. After teaching and coaching for one year, John went to work for General Dynamics for the summer and stayed thirty-three years, retiring in 1983 as a Contract Administrator. Margie and John have traveled a lot -- to all 50 states and 21 foreign countries. They now have a two-year-old granddaughter Karen, whom they dearly love and enjoy.

Guy E. Farley was born on a small farm in Louisiana. He lived with his married sisters from age eight, when his mother died, until he was twelve years old, at which time he returned to his father who had remarried. He attended seven different schools over a few years' time and left school in the ninth grade. He enlisted in the old CCC at seventeen and married at eighteen. He was drafted into the Navy in 1943, and attended boot camp at San Louis Obispo and Radio School at Boulder, Colorado. He volunteered for and served with the 593rd Joint Assault Signal Group until he joined the *Barr* on December 25, 1944. After the war, he completed his education by night school and home study courses, finishing with an engineering degree. The completion of his education was rewarded by promotion to supervisor in the paper mill where he worked from age eighteen to fifty-five with time off for naval service. Problems with his back led to his early retirement in 1978.

Harry E. Gardner attended SMU on a football scholarship from 1940 to 1943, at which time he was called to active duty by the Navy, for which he had volunteered in 1942. He attended the TCU V-12 Program and the Northwestern Midshipmen School, was commissioned as an Ensign, and joined UDT Class Seven at Fort Pierce. Harry was awarded the Silver Star for "gallantry in action and for bravery, above and beyond the call of duty" for his work at Iwo Jima. After the war, Harry and his brother went into business together, raising and selling 20,000 broiler chickens every ten weeks, while Harry also attended Baylor University where he received his BBA degree in 1947. Harry's business career of more than forty years also included working with a major paint company, managing his own Purina Feed Store, managing Terrell Milling and Seed Store, co-owning Brazos Feed and Supply Company, owning and operating a filling station, and owning and operating a greenhouse with his wife Jerry, whom he had married in 1947. They had two daughters, both of whom are teachers, and prior to Jerry's death in 1990, had eight grandchildren. At a mini-reunion of his high school class in 1992, Harry became reacquainted with a former classmate, Helen Latimer, whom he later married and with whom he is now enjoying life again.

Max Glaser was born and grew up in Boston. As a young boy, he worked as a soda jerk. Max was initially turned down by the Navy due to a punctured eardrum; but later, as the manpower needs for the war increased, he was able to join the Navy. After the war, he attended school under the GI Bill to become a watchmaker. He owned a watchmaking business in Boston until his retirement about eight years ago. Max enjoys model trains, sports and traveling. He and his wife Ruth have six children and stepchildren (four boys, two girls) and seven grandchildren ranging in age from five months to sixteen years.

Robert E. Gleason was born and grew up in East Cleveland, Ohio. After graduating from Shaw High School, he attended and graduated from Purdue University with a degree in chemical engineering. For his leadership in clearing the beaches at Okinawa and Iwo Jima during WWII, he was awarded the Silver Star. After the war, Bob worked as a chemical engineer for Reilly Whiteman Walton Industrial Lubricants in Conshohocken for more than thirty years until his retirement in 1974. Bob was very active in his community. He and his first wife Isabelle, who passed away in February 1997, owned and operated a travel agency after his retirement and were also co-founders of a local YMCA. They had four children, nine grandchildren and one great grandchild at the time of Bob's death in September 1999. Bob's wife Frances, whom he married in 1998, contributed information for this book on his behalf.

George Gregory was born in Universal, Pennsylvania on November 6, 1922. He joined the Navy at age nineteen, went to boot camp at Newport, Rhode Island, and was on leave when Pearl Harbor was attacked. After attending diesel school, George was sent to Fort Caswell in Southport, North Carolina in 1942. His wife Joy was a hostess at the USO in Southport, where George met her. They were married on February 7, 1943, after which George was transferred to Solomon Island, Maryland, where he volunteered for UDT training. After the war, George worked at the Union Railroad in Universal, and then returned to Southport to work on his father-in-law's charter boat. After George obtained his charter boat captain's license in 1949, he acquired his own boat. Later he worked as a tug boat mate at Sunny Point Military Ocean Terminal near Southport, from which he retired in 1973. After retiring, George worked as a truck driver for a wholesale building business until 1987. George and Joy have two daughters, four grandchildren, and three great grandchildren.

Talmadge F. Grubbs grew up in Columbia, South Carolina, where he attended school through the tenth grade. He later worked for several years at Fort Jackson Army Base in Columbia before leaving there to attend school to learn welding. He became a good welder and then moved to a job in Panama City, Florida. Three months later, at the age of twenty-six, he was drafted into the Navy. Talmadge went to boot camp for about four weeks at Camp Perry, Virginia, and then spent three months aboard the battleship *Wyoming*, a gunner training ship. Finally, he was transferred to the *Barr* after its conversion to an APD. After the war, Talmadge returned to Columbia and worked for a Mack dealership welding truck bodies for about five years. Then he went to work for South Carolina Electric and Gas Company, from which he retired with disability after twenty-six years. Talmadge and his wife had seven children, three boys and four girls, and many grandchildren.

John B. Holdforth served in the British Royal Marines during World War II for two and one-half years aboard HMS *King George V*. As part of the British Royal Marine Fleet Commando, he was aboard the *Barr* from August 20 to August 30, 1945, when they were part of the first occupational forces to land in Japan. After the war, John left the Marines and attended Hotel School for six months during 1946 and 1947. After a very short period of working in a major hotel facing the ocean, he left the hotel business, became a merchant steward in the Royal Mail Shipping Company, and went back to sea. In 1951 he married, moved to Australia, and embarked on a very successful catering career. He was a catering controller for the Australian Parliament and also did work for the New Guinea (Papua) Parliament. He helped design the facilities for the Darwin Legislative Assembly and for the new parliament building in Canberra, Australia. John taught part time for several years at the technical college--mostly eighteen-year-olds who were looking for an entrance into junior management. He especially enjoys hearing from former students who have done well.

John W. Hubenthal graduated in 1943 from the University of Washington, where he majored in chemical engineering. He then entered the Naval Academy in January 1944 as a member of the second class of "90 day wonders" (a four month intensive program designed to train naval officers for wartime service) and was commissioned as an Ensign in the U.S. Naval Reserve on April 26, 1944. A few months later, John was assigned to the *Barr* which was being converted to an APD. He had gotten married while on a two-week leave after finishing the Naval Academy, and his wife Gert joined him in Boston until the *Barr* left in November. John was discharged from active duty on January 26, 1946, and then served in the Naval Reserve for a brief period. John worked in sales for seventeen years for the Fluor Corporation, then briefly with two smaller product companies before becoming Executive Vice President for the Ceramic Cooling Tower Company, a division of Justin Industries in Fort Worth, Texas. His work over the years has taken him to most of the U.S. and several foreign countries. John retired as Chairman of the Board of Ceramics in 1983.

Gordon F. Huber graduated in 1943 from Monmouth College in Monmouth, Illinois, where he majored in economics and business administration. In February 1944, he married his high school sweetheart Betty. Gordon reported to the *Barr* in the fall of 1944 as radar and sonar officer and left the *Barr* in San Diego in December 1945. After the war, Gordon worked five years in telephone company management, and in 1952 entered the franchised food industry with Dairy Queen. He was responsible for establishing its international division in 1968 and served as operations chief in the 1970's and 80's. In 1995 Gordon was inducted into the Monmouth College Hall of Achievement. Gordon and his wife Betty recently celebrated their 55th wedding anniversary. They have three children.

Marvin A. Johnston enlisted in the Navy on July 20, 1941. He initially served aboard the USS *Enterprise*, where he was injured during the Battle of Santa Cruz in October 1942. Then he attended Turbo Electric school in New York and received further training in Florida before joining the *Barr* in February 1944. For injuries received at Santa Cruz, Marvin received the Purple Heart from Captain Love in ceremonies aboard the *Barr* DE576 at Bethlehem-Hingham Shipyard. Marvin left the *Barr* later that year after she was torpedoed in the Atlantic and served on two different hospital ships before leaving the Navy on January 27, 1947. After the war, Marvin had a successful business career while he also earned several degrees, including his Ph.D. degree in Business Administration from Texas Tech University. He was a Professor of Accounting and Computer Science at Southwest Texas State University from 1971 until his retirement in 1990. Marvin married his childhood sweetheart Gurty on July 26, 1943; they have one son and two grandsons.

Philip P. Jones graduated from Hamilton College in 1942 and then attended Northwestern Midshipmen School. He served on two other ships before joining the *Barr* in August 1944. After the war, he had a thirty-five year career in business machine and systems sales, primarily in the New York City area. Phil's parents were school teachers in New York City. He and his wife Alice have two children, a son who is a teacher and a daughter who is a minister.

William E. Kerry M.M. was born on May 8, 1924, in Stroud, Gloucestershire, England. His father and his father's four brothers served in the British Forces during World War I. Bill volunteered, from a reserved occupation, to join the British Royal Marines, with which he served for four years. In World War II, he was a 5.25 inch GunLayer aboard the HMS *King George V* in the Pacific Fleet. The Royal Marine Fleet Commando was formed and commanded by Major P.L. Norcock. After the war, Bill joined The Black Watch (Scottish Regiment), in which he served from 1946 to 1958. In 1952 his Regiment (1st Battalion, The Black Watch, Royal Highland Regiment) took over the "Hook" position in Korea from the U.S.M.C., which had received heavy casualties in winning this position. On November 18, his regiment was attacked, but repelled the enemy forces and held the "Hook" position. For his patrol action, Bill was awarded the Military Medal by Her Majesty The Queen at her Investiture, Buckingham Palace, on July 21, 1953. After The Black Watch, Bill joined the Royal New Zealand Infantry Regiment, in which he served from 1958 to 1970. He served five years in Waiouru Military Camp (at the Regular Force Depot and the School of Infantry), and the remaining years in Papakura Camp, after which he retired as a Warrant Officer 1st Class.

C. Richard Keys remained in the active Naval Reserves after the war until he had twenty-one years of service. He made Lt. Cdr. in 1954 and was in NRSD(L) (Naval Reserve Surface Division - Large)11-46 in Santa Monica, California from about 1950 until 1960, serving as Commanding Officer for the last three years. The NRSD(L) was composed of about a dozen officers and 250 enlisted men, most of whom were UCLA students.

Norman LeMere joined the Navy at age eighteen and went to boot camp at Sampson, New York. He joined the *Barr* just before she was converted to an APD. After the war, Norman married and had two daughters. He worked for research and development in the atomic electricity industry and later worked on welding reactors for the Navy's atomic submarines.

Harold E. MacNeill was born in 1923 and grew up in Ilion, a small town on the Mohawk River in central New York. He enlisted in the Navy in 1943, attended Boot Camp at Sampson, New York, and Torpedo School in Newport, Rhode Island, and was then assigned to the *Barr* DE576 as part of the original crew. After the Atlantic action, he served on other ships until the war ended. After the war, Harold completed college on the GI Bill and went to work in manufacturing engineering at General Electric in New York. He was later transferred to Phoenix, Arizona, and worked there until retirement in 1981. Harold married in 1959. In retirement, he enjoys following various sports and is an avid golfer.

Arthur W. Magee was born in Hartford, Connecticut, and lived there until his father, an insurance executive, retired and moved to Florida. When Pearl Harbor occurred, Art tried unsuccessfully to enlist in the Navy at the age of fifteen. He attended Bolles Academy, a military school, and in 1943 at the age of seventeen, he enlisted in the Navy. After attending Boot Camp and Signalman School, he was assigned to a beach battalion. Later he joined UDT Class Seven at Fort Pierce. After UDT 13 operations at Okinawa, Art involuntarily rejoined the beach battalion and was injured shortly thereafter. He was discharged in September 1945 from the Navy Hospital in San Diego. He worked as a sports reporter and later as a radio sports announcer at the University of Florida at Gainesville while attending college. He then pursued a career in sports broadcasting, working in many different cities, including Houston, where he was partnered with Dan Rather. Art and his wife Rima moved to California in 1967 where they operated a messenger service business. Their office was at the Warner Bros. studios, and they had many well-known movie stars as clients. Later, they sold the business, did some traveling, and returned to live in Southern California a few years ago. Art passed away in August 2000.

Armand J. Marion was born in St. Matthew, Quebec, Canada on December 2, 1918. At the age of six he moved with his family to Cohoes, New York, where he grew up, went to high school, and later returned to live. After high school, Armand went to work for General Electric Company in Schenectady, where he worked as a toolmaker for forty years -- with time out for the Navy. He and Nataline Caputo of Mechanicsville, New York, were married on August 8, 1942. In the fall of 1943, Armand was drafted by the Navy. After Boot Camp at Sampson, New York, he was assigned to the USS *Barr* on which he served both in the Atlantic and the Pacific. He left the *Barr* at Nagasaki and was discharged in December 1945 as a first class petty officer. After the war, Armand returned to General Electric as a toolmaker in experimental work on atomic reactors for submarines at the Knolls Atomic Power Laboratory. Armand and Nataline recently celebrated their 57th wedding anniversary. They have two children, a daughter who has her doctorate in education and a son who has an MBA in finance; they also have four grandchildren.

Ned J. Marrow was born in Galeton, Pennsylvania, on March 14, 1923. He attended Naval Training School at Sampson and Norfolk, after which he was assigned to the *Barr* DE576. He left the *Barr* after the Atlantic action but continued to serve in the Navy until March 25, 1946. After the war, Ned was employed by the New York City Railroad working as a train man for PC and Conrail until retirement forty years later. Ned and his wife Evelyn, whom he married in Chicago in 1948, have one daughter.

Donald H. Murray received his architectural engineering degree from Washington State in Pullman in 1943, after which he joined the Navy and was assigned the rank of ensign. Don attended Officers Training School for three months at Cornell University, completing the program in March 1944. He had orders to join a destroyer after graduation, but on his last day at Cornell, a Navy Commander convinced him and several of his classmates to join the underwater demolition class being formed at Fort Pierce. Don served with UDT 13 until October 1945, when he was assigned to the *Admiral Rodman*, a fast troop transport where he became First Division officer. Don made three trips to the Orient, two to Japan and one to the Philippines, bringing back troops. In March 1946, he received the Silver Star for UDT extra hazardous duty and operations in Okinawa. Don married Dorothy Elliott in Ft. Pierce; they have two children and two grandchildren. Don became an architect and eventually had his own firm. He sailed and raced sailboats for thirty years. He currently enjoys his 36 foot Catalina sailboat.

Timothy P.J. Nolan, after graduating from high school and while working as a stock boy at Mark Cross on 5th Avenue in 1944, went to Staten Island to see his "90 Day Wonder brother" off to the Pacific aboard a freighter which carried him and his PT boat to war. Shortly thereafter, he got permission from his father to join the Navy at the age of seventeen. He attended boot camp in Sampson, New York, and electricians' school at Newport, Rhode Island, completing his training in Gulfport, Mississippi, where the latter school had moved during his studies. Tim was then assigned to the *Barr* APD39 until she was decommissioned in Florida.

Colonel Peter L. Norcock, O.B.E. was born in the Royal Marines Depot, Deal, England, in 1911. He was Acting Major when he commanded a British Royal Marine Landing Party, British Pacific Fleet, from H.M.S. *King George V* and two cruisers, who were among the first to occupy Japan after the surrender was signed. Although he was aboard the USS *Sims* because of additional duties in Tokyo, part of his marines were aboard the USS *Barr* for the journey to Yokosuka Naval Base, where they disembarked. After the war, Colonel Norcock was a member of the British Royal Marine Commando's in the United Kingdom for about ten years, serving in Palestine, Canal Zone, Port Said and other trouble spots around the world. He retired in 1961. His grandfather, also a Royal Marine, had previously landed in Japan on military duties around 1856.

W. Elwood Overstreet grew up in Alma, Alabama. After the war on January 11, 1945, he returned home, and went into the paperwooding and logging business with his father. In 1948 he went to work for the land owners of 22,000 acres as the overseer and game warden. He retired in 1989, but found that he didn't like retirement, so he returned to work for the landowners and continues to work for them. Elwood married Louise McDonald and they have four children, nine grandchildren and seven great grandchildren.

Austin J. Page entered the Navy on August 23, 1943, at the age of seventeen. After training at Newport, Rhode Island, his first ship was the *Barr* DE576. After the *Barr* was torpedoed in the Atlantic, Austin had a thirty day survivor's leave, then reported to Miami and was sent to Manitowoc, Wisconsin, to join the ATR-89. While in Manitowoc, he also met his future wife, whom he married when he returned to the States. Austin enlisted in the USAF in 1951 and served in the Strategic Air Command. He was stationed at Nouasseur A.F.B., Morocco, and at Warren A.F.B. in Cheyenne, Wyoming. He retired with the rank of Master Sergeant in 1965. Austin and his wife had three sons. They lost one son, Lt. Rex Page VF 101, in 1977. Their oldest son is a Lt. Colonel; the youngest works for the Post Office and, as Austin proudly says, "is also in uniform."

Warren T. Pierce, who was born in 1921, grew up on a farm near Russell, Iowa. When Warren was drafted into the Navy in 1944, he had a wife, a daughter two and one-half years old, and a son one and one-half years old. After the war ended, Warren returned home for a brief period and then reenlisted in the Navy for another four years, during which time he was on a ship that made an around-the-world Good Will cruise. After his separation from the Navy, Warren was employed at the Navy Electronic Lab in San Diego for twenty-seven years until his retirement in 1976. During these years, Warren traveled all over the country. In the 1960's he helped build what was at that time the world's largest transmitting antenna in Arizona. Later he helped locate and build a transmitter on a mountain in San Diego County, where there was minimum electrical interference so that signals could be bounced off the moon to transmit messages from California to

Washington, DC. Warren and his wife Frances live on a small ranch in Young County, Texas, while his two children and six grandsons live in Iowa and his granddaughter lives in Honolulu.

Clarence I. Priest grew up on a farm in Stow, Massachusetts. He enlisted in the Navy at age seventeen and went to boot camp in Rhode Island. He served on the *Barr* both in the Atlantic and in the Pacific and helped take her to join the mothball fleet in Florida. After the war, Clarence completed his high school education. He worked on a farm in New Hampshire with his grandfather and uncles and also attended agricultural school. He married in 1951. Clarence then worked in construction, building roads with bulldozers and other heavy equipment. Later Clarence moved to Georgia for awhile and then to Enid, Oklahoma, where he worked as a brick layer before getting a job at Vance Air Force Base. He worked at the base for about fifteen years until he retired in 1993. Clarence has seven children, including an adopted son from Korea, thirteen grandchildren and one great grandchild. Three sons went into the Navy and two of these served in the Vietnam conflict.

Joseph E. Purgatorio served on the *Barr* both in the Atlantic and the Pacific. He had earlier been in both the CCC and the Coast & Geodetic Service. After the war, Joe was a civilian for a short period and then reenlisted to serve on the *Huntington*. On one of his ships he enjoyed an around the world cruise. After leaving the Navy, Joe was a crane operator for General Metals of Tacoma for fifteen years. He was also a member of North Shore Golf and Country Club for twenty-five years before his death. Joe and his wife, who was a Navy nurse he met at Great Lakes Hospital, had three children and three granddaughters. Joe's daughter, Lisa Schaffert, provided information for this book on his behalf.

Warren G. Quinn was aboard the *Barr* when she was commissioned -- just three days after his 20th birthday. Shortly thereafter, he left the *Barr* to serve on LST 552 until the end of the war. After the war he returned home to North Carolina, attended college for awhile, and after about a year decided to return to the Navy. Warren served three tours in Vietnam attached to units of the Marines and Army. As a Chief Petty Officer in 1975, he retired in the Philippines, where he met and married his wife. Later he, along with his wife and six-month-old daughter, again returned to North Carolina. Warren is a member of the American Legion, VFW, the Fleet Reserve Club, and the World War II Last Man's Club. He enjoys following baseball -- the American Legion Team, the high school teams and the Charlotte professional team, but he most especially enjoys babysitting with his two grandsons.

John J. Reilly graduated from midshipman school at Columbia University on October 27, 1944, and served on the *Barr* from December 1944 until July 1946 when he helped put the *Barr* in mothballs. He then attended college, graduated in June 1947, and went to work for Old Mission Portland Cement Company (later sold to the Ideal Basic Industries) in November 1947. He held various positions with the company that produced Portland cement and potash, starting as a control chemist and retiring as a Terminal Superintendent in July of 1983. Jack, as he is known to his friends, and his wife Barbara raised five daughters, who in turn have given them fifteen grandchildren and two great grandchildren.

Bennie M. Rice, born in 1925 in Mohall, North Dakota, joined the Navy in August 1943. He went to boot Camp at Farragut Camp in Northern Idaho. Bennie went to Naval Diesel School at the University of Illinois at Champaign, and then to Camp Bradford, Virginia. He volunteered for hazardous duty and went to Fort Pierce, Florida, in the spring of 1944, where he and other regular Navy men joined the CB's in training for UDT. Bennie was one of the first group of regular Navy personnel to join UDT, who were all CB's until then. He went through all the training in Florida and went to Maui with Team 13 where he was put on a boat crew as a Motor Machinist. He says he was not a good enough swimmer, but did do work in the water at Okinawa. He was on the boat crew Baker (USS *Barr*) 39-2 with crew members H.J. ("Honest John") Rice and Charles Rudy.

Bennie was released from the Navy in April 1946 at Bremerton, Washington. He was married in September 1946 to Lois Stewart, with whom he had seven children - four girls and three boys. They now have twenty-two grandchildren and five great grandchildren with one more of each expected soon. Bennie started farming in the fall of 1947 and is still farming to a smaller degree; according to Bennie, "Some guys don't know when to quit."

Erik L. Rosengren enlisted in the Navy in 1942, leaving behind his fiancee. They were both twenty years old at the time, and Erik had been working in a bank in New York and attending college at night. Erik went to boot camp in Newport, Rhode Island, and then to Chicago for training as a signalman. Afterward, Erik had several assignments, including amphibious training at Little Creek, Virginia, with a group known as the Alligators, who later made a landing with General Patton's division on Fedala, French Morocco. Erik joined the *Barr* DE576 in February 1944. After the *Barr* was torpedoed in the Atlantic, Erik had a thirty day leave, during which time he and his fiancee married. Erik underwent additional amphibious training in Florida and then rejoined the *Barr*, serving on her throughout the remainder of the war until mid-September 1945.

George P. Sark was born on April 10, 1917, and grew up on a farm in Ohio. As a young man, George worked on the farm for his father. After George and Wavolene were married on July 28, 1940, George continued farming with his father for awhile, but later left the farm to work in town. He had tried to join the Navy years before he was married, but was unsuccessful. Shortly after he left the farm in 1943, however, he was drafted into the Navy. At that time, he had two young sons, one two and one-half years old and the other only eight months old. While in the States, George was able to get week-end passes to be with his family every three months. George returned home after the war ended in 1945. He and Wavolene had six children, one of whom enlisted in the Navy. George died on March 27, 1986. His wife, Wavolene, contributed information for this book on his behalf.

Francis J. Skotko was married with one child and worked as a printer before the war. He served on the *Barr* both as a DE in the Atlantic and as an APD in the Pacific. After the war Frank returned to his job as a printer, retiring in 1981. He and his wife Frances, to whom he has been married for fifty-nine years, have three children and seven grandchildren. One of his grandsons is a 2nd Lieutenant in the Air Force and should get his 2nd Lieutenant wings very soon.

Andrew C. Soucy was born in Leominster, Massachusetts. His parents had three sons, all of whom served in the military, one Army and two Navy. Andy joined the Navy in 1943, attended Machinist Steam Engineering school at Ford Motor Company in Dearborn and advanced school at Norfolk, before joining the *Barr* in February 1945. He was with the *Barr* from the time she was commissioned until November 1945. After the war, Andy worked with the General Electric Company until his retirement in 1984. His department at General Electric had manufactured turbine generator sets for Destroyer Escorts during the war. Andy and his wife Patricia have two sons and one daughter. Andy has been very active in recent reunions with the *Barr* and other Destroyer Escorts.

Eugene L. Swearingen attended Navy boot camp at San Diego, emerging as an ensign in the U.S.N.R. He then attended Naval Supply Corps School at Harvard College in Boston. His first ship was the *Fiske* DE 143, which was sunk in the Atlantic, where Gene spent about five hours in the cold North Atlantic waters before being rescued. He was assigned to the *Barr* in Fall 1944 until she returned to the States in December 1945. After the war, Gene completed his education on the G.I. Bill with a Ph.D. in economics at Stanford University. He served as Professor, Dean, and Vice President at Oklahoma State University until 1967, when he became the President of the University of Tulsa. In 1968 he became the President of the Bank of Oklahoma, where he also served as Chairman of the Board and Chief Executive Officer until retirement in 1980. Since his "retirement" he has taught and served as Dean of the School of Business at Oral Roberts University in Tulsa and is currently the holder of the Chair of Free Enterprise. He is the author of *Success and Beyond - 50 Keys*, which was originally published in 1987 and revised in 1996.

Manuel Verissimo, Jr., who was born on January 12, 1925, was the son of Emilia Pereira and Manuel Verissimo, Sr., who had emigrated from Lisbon, Portugal. He attended New Bedford, Massachusetts, Vocational High School and enlisted in the Navy on May 21, 1943. After boot camp at Newport Naval Station, Manny took additional training at Wentworth Institute in Boston and was then stationed at Norfolk for awhile before joining the *Barr*. He served on the *Barr* in both the Atlantic and Pacific actions and was honorably discharged from the Navy on April 20, 1946. After the war, Manny had several jobs before joining Goodyear Tire and Rubber Co. in 1947, where he remained until his retirement as Foreman of Production in 1987. For his significant contributions to Goodyear, he received the "Award of Excellence" and the "Mildred V. and Edwin J. Thomas Goodyear Spirit Award". Manny married Margaret Marie Morrow in 1948 and they had three children, JoAnn, Ed, and Scott. Manny devoted his adult life to his family and his career with Goodyear. He passed away quietly on June 10, 1994, while watching a ballgame on TV. His wife and his son Ed provided Manny's stories for this book on his behalf.

Donald M. Walker volunteered and was accepted for bomb disposal training after being commissioned in the US Navy on July 1, 1943. Later that year he volunteered and was accepted for Naval Combat Demolition Unit (NCDU) in the 2nd class at Ft. Pierce. In May 1944, Don's NCDU unit-13 was initially assigned for temporary duty with UDT 4 for landings in Saipan, Guam, and Tinian. In August 1944, Don's unit became part of UDT-Able for the invasion of Peleliu, but their ship USS *Noa* was rammed and sunk by another US destroyer prior to the invasion. All of the men were rescued, but were out of action for the remainder of the Peleliu operation. UDT Able was returning to the states for survivors leave, but was ordered to disembark at Hawaii where they were dispersed among other UDT's, at which time Don became Executive Officer of UDT 13. After the war, Don resumed his career as a registered pharmacist and practiced this profession until his recent retirement. He now enjoys just being with his family.

Frank B. Whaley was born and reared in Corpus Christi, Texas. Frank was a high school tennis star, winning seven state doubles championships from 1938 to 1941. He entered Naval Flight Training in 1943, graduated from midshipmen school in 1945, and was assigned to the *Barr* in 1946. After leaving the Navy in August 1946, he taught and coached tennis in high school until 1960 when he launched a very successful career in the Scenic and Advertising Post Card business. He and his wife Golda have three children.

Zenon C. Wolan grew up in Elizabeth, New Jersey. After finishing high school in 1943, Zeke enlisted in the Navy and, before retiring in 1968, he had attained the rank of Master Chief Petty Officer (E-9). Zeke is a veteran of World War II, the Korean War, and the Vietnam War. After leaving the Navy, he was employed by the Naval Ship Engineering Center and Naval Sea Support Center as an equipment specialist in electronics. He retired from federal service in 1983. Since then Zeke has enjoyed golfing, gardening, and spending winters in South Florida. Zeke and his wife Betty recently celebrated their 50th wedding anniversary. They have a son and a daughter (an MD), two granddaughters, and one great granddaughter.

FLASHBACKS

It turns out that the Leatherneck had advance information that the Barr would be going to the Brooklyn Navy Yard. My brother decided to surprise me and meet me when we came in, but he couldn't afford the trip from Wash., D.C. On the other hand if he were to go there while covering a story, he could go on expenses. So, he and Riblett cooked up the excuse to go by selling their editor on doing a story about the Barr, and their "hook", besides the fact that she was named after a Marine, was all the "firsts". Karl would be a "leg man," and Riblett would write the story. He met the ship, had dinner aboard, and interviewed some of the officers. He reviewed the log books (probably provided by Jas. Grenga), sat down at a type-writer on the Barr and wrote the story in rough for Riblett. After that we went out for a damn good week end on the town. . . . As an aside, Karl became a nationally syndicated Editorial Cartoonist for the Hearst syndicate. He died in August, 1998 at 81 years. Friends have published a 53 page website about his life and work at: http://www.bobstaake/karl/hubenthal.html.

                                        John W. Hubenthal, Lieutenant (jg)

*   *   *   *   *

 *I served on a DE during the war in the Pacific and after the war we came back to Oakland and got it ready for decommissioning. When the ship was no longer livable, I was given a 30 day leave and was told to report to the 3rd Naval District (NY) for assignment. The assignment was the Barr and I helped take it to Green Cove Springs, Florida for putting it up in mothballs. All this took place in a span of three months and mostly consisted of berthing with a bunch of ships and many a trip ashore to the officers' club.*

                                        E. Lewis Bartlett, Ensign

*   *   *   *   *

The one thing I did have the pleasure of doing as the last Commanding Officer of the Barr and the one in charge of her decommissioning was to send the ship's ensign and flag to the mother of PFC Woodrow Wilson Barr, Mrs. Cora Dell Barr. I felt that these items would be far more meaningful to Mrs. Barr than to some Navy official in Washington. My thinking proved to be correct. I received a very sweet letter of thanks from Mrs. Barr.

                                        Frank B. Whaley, Ensign

The USS Barr DE576-APD39 now rests in her watery grave in the Caribbean, where the Navy used her as a target ship. She was a gallant little ship; she will always be remembered by her crews as we all know we did a little part during World War II.

Andrew C. Soucy, Water Tender   from his personal diary and album

*   *   *   *   *

I didn't write anything like that [diary] myself. I guess I was too busy writing letters to a young lady in Rhode Island, who has now been my wife for 53 years. She saved all my letters and I saved all of hers. They were tied up in a nice bundle, and one day when our kids were little, they and some of the 80 or so other kids on the block, decided to play postman. They delivered our letters all over the neighborhood, and we got precious few back. So other people's diaries come in real handy.

C. Richard Keys, Lieutenant (jg)

*   *   *   *   *

The only man in our Royal Marine occupation group that I have met since the war was Jack Crawford, a good shipmate to both myself and Johny Holdforth. The meeting took place on the 18 Oct., 1973 in the "Schooner" pub, which is a stone's throw across the road from Auckland Harbour, New Zealand. There were not many folk there, and so enabled a seaman and myself to lean on the bar counter and have a yarn over our beer. I heard my name spoken, and on turning round came face to face with Jack. I recognized him almost immediately; his face wearing his broad grin, had changed little, causing the years from the war's end in Japan to our again shaking hands in the "Schooner" to appear so much shorter than the twenty eight years in time. Jack told me he had heard my voice, the accent of which seemed familiar, and moved to a spot where he recognized me from. After leaving the Royals, Jack had stayed at sea, and in doing so, made a trip out to New Zealand and came ashore to live. He remained at sea, but only on boats that stayed in New Zealand waters. We kept in touch from there on, and between Jack's trips and shoretime met up and had a few tots of Jack's favorite tipple, "Grouse Scotch Whiskey." A few years passed when suddenly Jack was hit by cancer. We had our last tot together, and when Jack died, I attended and saw him laid to rest, his coffin covered by his National Flag of his loved birthplace of dear old Ireland. Both John and I have great respect for Jack. He was a fine figure of a man in all respects. A good Marine to have alongside you, if the occasion required it. This, together with his broad smile, which was never far away, and his quiet, but unmistakable Irish brogue made Jack a credit to Old Ireland. "Time and tide waits for no man."

William E. Kerry, Marine,
Royal Marine Fleet Commando, British Pacific Fleet

I think of the Skipper [Dickie] again so many times. He was such a good skipper that every Sunday he would hold Catholic mass and Protestant services. I don't know how many captains would have done that, because I never experienced it before or after. He was a very, very kind-hearted man.

Warren T. Pierce, Sonarman

*   *   *   *   *

In 1991 someone wrote and told me about the UDT reunions. I answered the letter and have been an interested member since. For years, Marvin Cooper and Art Magee have held our team together.

Edwin I. Cleveland, Ensign, UDT 13

*   *   *   *   *

As questions arose at our first reunion (47 years later), it seemed apparent that some of the crew still had doubts about the safety of the tons of explosives that were aboard. I feel that, as of now, they are quite certain that we were up front with the information provided.

The officers and crew bonded well with our UDT group, thus enabling us to successfully complete the jobs that we were trained for and we were able to return safely from two very crucial invasions. Remembering and renewing friendships after these many years speaks for itself.

Donald M. Walker, Lieutenant (jg), UDT 13

*   *   *   *   *

John Hubenthal lives a few miles from us here in Southern California. We get together once in a while. He remarked at lunch one day, when I complimented him on his duty as Engineering Officer, "Hell, I didn't know anything about running a ship. But I had a damn good Machinist's Mate." "John, I replied, had I known about that, I would have jumped ship in the middle of the ocean." You know what? He still was a damned good Engineering Officer.

Arthur W. Magee, Signalman, UDT 13

*   *   *   *   *

In recent years there have been several reunions. . . . It has been very enjoyable for me to attend these reunion meetings and to get reacquainted with some of my friends from the Barr.

Gordon F. Huber, Lieutenant (jg)

From a letter to Phil Jones from George Budak, Signalman to be read at the 1995 Reunion:

I only know of a few things that may bring some humor and laughs back to the guys:

1. When H. Love (Capt.) went into the sub base (I think it was Portland or New London) and got fooled by the current in the river and almost cut the dock in half. His buddy was commander of the sub base at the time.

2. When we (signalmen) sewed together a pirate's flag skull and crossbones for H. Love to fly when we went across the bow of the Elmore. Love wanted to have some fun with his buddy, Harris (Capt.). In return Harris flew the question mark flag back at Love.

3. When we met Love in Hawaii and he told Dickie that 4 of his 6 ship flotilla had run aground during practice maneuvers. He asked Dickie for some of his crew and got a negative from Dickie.

4. When Love came to a stop in the Atlantic and called for a swimming party because it was too damned hot to continue to sail. Stop was for about 2 hours so both port and starboard could swim.

5. When the stops on the 5" guns had to be reset as it allowed the 5" to almost blow the port and starboard 20 mm to the rear of the 5" off their mounts.

6. How about all the raisin jack that was in the water kegs on the life rafts. Dickie should remember this as it took place in the Pacific.

7. Last one - When J. Meehan was running through a yard in Nagasaki and fell into a hole to his waist filled with human waste (Jap fertilizer). We had to throw him into the bay to get him clean.

. . . P.S. Forgot about the San Diego hotel which said they hoped the Barr's crew never came back as they were the wildest - toughest - meanest crew they ever had in their hotel - a real bunch of scrappers.

*   *   *   *   *

The following was in a letter to Bill Kerry from John W. Hubenthal, Lieutenant (jg): We had a fine get together, even though there were only a few of us. Capt. Pete Dickie was there and received much attention from all of us. To a man, we told him we felt we owed our lives to him because of the decisions he made at Iwo Jima and Okinawa. Of course there were many stories that one remembered and another had forgotten. Phil Jones reminded us of one that involves you. . . . Jonesy remembered that the Japanese were supposed to put yellow flags on all of their guns so the allied forces could identify them. We could see a few flags when we anchored prior to your landing, and that night, you guys started singing "Waltzing Matilda" at the top of your lungs. The next morning the hillsides were covered with yellow flags. Obviously the Japanese had a great respect for you!

John Hubenthal, bless him, informed me of Phil Jones' remembering the increased number of "yellow flags" the Japs had displayed, by first light, after possibly hearing us singing the night before. Would like to use a Kiwi saying "Good on ya Jonesy" although the Australians (Aussies) reckon they own that "Waltzing Matilda" piece. She'll be right mate.

William E. Kerry, Marine,
Royal Marine Fleet Commando, British Pacific Fleet

*   *   *   *   *

The following poem was written by Rima Magee (wife of UDT13 member, Art Magee) in 1993, originally dedicated to Gil Reimer, a member of UDT13 who had passed away on April 1 of that year, and then rededicated in 1999 to all Frogmen, their shipmates and First Mates.

In Memoriam

Some rode the wind,
Some trod the earth,
Some prowled the restless seas -
To ride the waves,
To dance with sharks.
And they were some of these.

No greater love
Can bond the men
Who swim beneath the seas;
Who must share trust
In calm or storm.
And they were some of these.

We needs must say
Farewell to them
Who've crossed to unknown seas;
Our hearts will keep
The love we shared.
And they are some of these!

Copyright 1993, 1999 by Rima Magee
Published with her permission

APPENDICES

A. History of the USS *Barr*

B. Officers and Crew of the USS *Barr*

C. History of Underwater Demolition Team #13

D. Officers and Enlisted Men of UDT #13

E. Navy Rating Structure

F. The *Barr* Rag

The Appendices are designed both for the younger reader coming new to World War II and for the Old Salt who wants more details.

APPENDIX A

HISTORY OF THE USS *BARR*

(The following histories were attached inside James Grenga's diary with no identification of the author(s). According to Gordon Huber, the first of these was written by the ship's medical officer, Dr. Thomas Kaiser; the author of the second, a chronological history, is unknown.)

HISTORY OF THE USS BARR
DE(576) - APD(39)

FOREWORD

This is the story of the USS BARR. As such it is, too, the story of the reserve Navy, the civilian Navy. So as such, it needs telling, now especially.

Few of you aboard, know the whole story. All of us have forgotten or will forget many of the incidents, deeds, and dates without a record of this sort. Because of censorship restrictions much of the BARR's activities never got back to the wife, mother, father or children at home until months later when the story was staled by newer movements and the writers engrossed in new excitements, new fears, new hopes (and old); plus the same old longings--intensified.

Every story needs an accent, a pattern. So with the BARR. And the accent, the pattern, is emergency. Here was no beautiful, carefully loved and labored-over piece of mechanical perfection. Rather here was utility, hauled, yanked and buffeted together with the urgency of need; commissioned hastily, prematurely; manned suddenly with a crew adequately, but hastily trained, green--oh how often that word was heard--sent to sea crowded with uncertainty of minds and awash with uncertain stomachs; kept at sea with all the initiative, ingenuity, and hard work born of the incentive, nourished by the necessity.

From shakedown's triumph over fears, hurriedly into Anti-Submarine Killer operations, ship and men were at each turn engaging in something novel, something not quite fathomed. No time to solidify, to vegetate in a fat routine. The need was there, the job had to be managed and was.

After the blast and shock, the hollowness and hurt of the torpedoing of the BARR, the transfer of so many who had come to mean so much to each other, there came more newness and more urgencies: APD--what is it? What's it do? When? Where? Pearl, Maui, Ulithi (what in hell is that?) UDT's (an insect powder? a hangover symptom?). Iwo, Okinawa, (these departure rumors can't be true. We just got back from Iwo.) Kamikaze, zoomies, Baka, Pt. Bolo, Hot Rocks, green beach, yellow beach, Higashi, Hagushi, Kerama Rhetto, Buckner Bay, Sagami, Yokosuka, Hamamatsu, Kamaishi, Nagasaki (we had heard of that one).

Changes were constantly taking place; new equipment, new men, new specialist ratings assigned. As a DE the emphasis was on Sonar gear; hedgehogs, K-guns, speed drills, attack teams, interpretation. As an APD it became boats, LCVP's, PR's, winches, Welin Davits. From Ulithi on it was guns, A.A. guns. Get more, any size, in every blind spot.

Through it all, ship, officers, and men learned, did, made do, got, because of the need--a war to be won, a mad people to be beaten, put down and made without power to hurt. And the job was done, and well.

There this story should rightly end--with the ship gently laid away, crew returned to homes, jobs and personal interests again first. A weapon wielded roughly in haste and fury, used for the emergency, motivated by the need, knit by circumstance into a Naval vessel of the U.S. Navy.

But one last paragraph about the BARR and her war. About her nonentity, the wonderful, ridiculous nonentity of so many of the "lighter vessels", "smaller craft", "support ships"----Amphibs. In time even the less violent opinioned among the sailors of such ships felt a bitterness about a system that, perhaps necessarily, reduced so many fine accomplishments, so much fear, so many "firsts" and "longests" to a notation of "and lighter units". So this history is a good thing. It needs telling. It should intimate why with those aboard, now that the urgency is gone, the ship, this ship, is everything. It is still a ship in the U.S. Navy--but the stimulus, the impetus that makes of a ship a Naval vessel, in the very meaning of the term, is gone. And that is as it should be.

HISTORY OF THE USS BARR
DE 576--APD 39
20 OCTOBER, 1945

On November 5, 1943, at Hingham, Mass., the Bethlehem-Hingham Shipyards laid the keel of another destroyer escort, to be named after Pfc. W. W. Barr, a marine hero who was killed at Tulagi. She was launched December 28, 1943. On February 16, 1944, a windy, bitter, blear New England day, she was commissioned as the USS BARR (DE576) and turned over to the men and officers, fresh from Norfolk pre-commissioning training, who were to man her; these men had been chosen and trained to man a DE. About the Navy and the sea, few knew little else. The mother of the boy for whom the ship was named attended the ceremonies.

A destroyer escort is a junior member of the DD Navy, a product of World War II, designed as an "expendable", mass-production ship, to carry on many of the essential destroyer functions in convoying, shipping and smashing the U-Boat menace in the Atlantic; 306 feet long, 39 wide at her widest, the BARR was no fortress. With her ribs visible creases beneath the skin of the hull, with her deck plating billowing and bulging, few thought her a sleek and slashing greyhound of the deep as the blurbs have it. However, an amazing amount of fighting gear had been incorporated in her hull. Topside were three 3"/50 caliber guns, a 1.1" A.A. quad. and ten 20 mm. Oerlikons, plus the (shshsh) hedgehog, K-guns, D.C. racks,--and torpedo tubes, yes torpedo tubes. And there were range finders, directors, sonar gear, fathometer, radar, radio, and indicators of a hundred sorts. To churn her through the water at a top speed of 26 knots, she was equipped with a twin screw, turbo-electric propulsion unit, built by G.E. at Syracuse, N.Y.; her steam lines carried superheated steam at a pressure of 400 pounds; her engines were rated at 12000 HP. Thus, with two engine rooms, two fire rooms, cafeteria style mess in the crowded but adequate berthing spaces on the second deck, a 26 foot motor whaleboat, and tons of stores, ammunition, and fresh clean logs, the BARR moved away from the chaos of the Hingham Yards to the maelstrom of Charlestown Navy Yard, Boston.

A ride high and dry up the Marine Railway at Chelsea for deperming and a bottom coat, return to Charlestown Yard for prettying up, trial runs for calibration, test firings, and acquaintance sake, then through Cape Cod canal to New London for more calibration, and finally on March 9, the BARR really put out to sea, underway for shakedown exercises at Bermuda.
There followed six weeks of trials, inspections, drills, inspections, speed runs, tests and inspections, training with tame submarines, damage control problems, A.A. and surface firing at targets, and --inspections. Here and there, briefly,--a liberty. When the BARR left Bermuda in company with her sister ship, the Ahrens (DE575), and a DE known for TBS reasons as Rover Over Out, the crew was wiser, many of the bugs were ironed out and by emergency standards she was RFS, ready for sea.

After a week of post shakedown availability at Boston, the BARR reported to Norfolk, Va. for duty, and was assigned as one of four screening vessels to operate as a killer group with the USS BLOCK ISLAND (CVE 21). The DE's AHRENS, ELMORE, and BUCKLEY were the others. The group, operating as TU21.11, departed Norfolk on 22 April for anti-submarine duty in the South Atlantic.

During the next month, on glassy seas, the group chased down reports and contacts of submarines in an area off the Cape Verde Islands. Maneuvers of the escorts about the carrier were generally at full speed. On dark nights with radar, a new and sometimes confusing instrument, near collisions were frequent. G.Q. clamored out three or four times a day as one escort pinged off fish, fowl and what not. The carrier maintained a constant air patrol. Eventually her planes caught a sub on the surface and attacked. The USS BUCKLEY was dispatched to assist. Approaching to short range undetected, the BUCKLEY shot out her ready boxes and rammed the sub. Near hand to hand battle ensued with the sub sinking and captives taken. Those on voice radio circuits listened to the entire action. A week later the ELMORE in a less dramatic action, was credited with a probable sinking.

About the 22nd of April the group worked north and made the port of Casablanca and there for a few days rested, beered and played ball. Liberty meant brandy, wine, dirty Arabs, the Place de Paris, the Bushbeer.

Back to sea after a few days, the group was to swing in a lazy arc and head for the states at the end of two weeks. Everyone felt confident, light-hearted. Going home. The subs were almost to be pitied. Between the escorts and the air-craft they were badly outclassed. Besides, wasn't it often said that they didn't fire torpedoes at escorts! Something about their shallow draft was the touted reason.

May 29 was much the same as any other day. Sea calm, weather balmy. Early that day we had fueled from the BLOCK ISLAND. They sent over maple walnut ice cream and the ship's newspaper. At 2014, after a short sunset, the OOD noticed two puffs of smoke on the carrier's side. She seemed to be dead in the water. He rang G.Q. All hands tumbled to their stations. A third puff blasted the carrier. Sound and visual contacts began coming to the bridge. The BARR maneuvered toward a possible contact when suddenly she was struck astern. Amidships the vessel seemed to lurch violently. The alidade flew off the gyro repeater. Further aft men and depth charges were blown upward and forward. About twenty feet of the stern was blown off completely, the shafts bent upward at 45 degree angle, the decking forced up and forward to curve into the aft 3" gun mount. The AHRENS, taking on survivors of the BLOCK ISLAND, and dead in the water near her, picked up a sub contact by sonar and directed the ELMORE to it. The ELMORE fired several patterns of hedgehog and at length jubilantly reported definite under-water explosions, and was confident that the sub had been sunk. The BLOCK ISLAND sank after staying afloat an hour and a half. Shortly violent underwater explosions occurred, either from her depth charges or boilers, rocking the *Barr* heavily in her unstable condition. That night with the escorts loaded with BLOCK ISLAND survivors so heavily that some dared not use more than 10 degrees rud-der, the lay to while the PAINE patrolled about her. Next morning with the seas increasing for the first time in six weeks, patients and most of the crew were trans-ferred to the ELMORE. The BARR had five dead, twelve missing and eleven injured. The BLOCK ISLAND suffered five casualties from the explosions, and four of six pilots in the air at the time were lost making for land. At that time, few DE's had suffered as much structural damage and remained afloat.

For six days through strong seas the BARR was towed into Casablanca, first by the ELMORE, and finally by a fleet tug. In drydock the damaged stern was burned off, spaces cleared of oil and wreckage and a transom welded on for the trip home under tow.

During this period Lt. Cdr. H.H. Love USNR was relieved by Lt. Cdr. P.T. Dickie as commanding officer, and all but four officers and 80 men were transferred to the United States. Most of the crew remaining lived in barracks ashore. Watches were light, liberty frequent, and the BARR ball club began its string of victories, sustaining its only loss when a pick up team was defeated by an Armed Guard outfit. The game is still referred to as the one in which Borgeld walked 14 men in one inning.

In tow by the USS CHEROKEE the BARR on July 3rd began the trip back to Boston. Because of the hurricane weather, the ships put into Bermuda at St. George, one of the most delightful foreign liberties had by the ship. On July 25th she arrived at Boston. Her new stern was waiting for her on the dock. Word came fast that she was to be converted to an APD, a high speed destroyer type transport. Until the end of October the BARR was in South Boston Navy Yard. All gear and supplies were in storage, the crew in barracks, chow lousy and not much better at Crowley's, but the weather good and Boston gay and friendly. And thirty days leave all hands. In late October new crew members and officers put in appearance. Soon the horde of workers, welders, electricians, shipfitters and sundry thinned out. The compressed air hammers stopped banging; it became safe to lean against a bulkhead without fear of a welding torch searing through; the spaghetti mass of wiring, welding hose slithered over the side to the dock; stores and spares were brought back; the APD 39 was about ready for sea.

But many changes had taken place. A new stern, the boat deck extended aft covering the main deck to where the 1.1" AA mount had been. The sides were extended to the boat deck providing main deck berthing for 150 passengers.

A towering tripod mast with two booms and heavy winches was installed at the break of the boat deck aft. Welin davits with their heavy crossbar cradles were installed on either side with accommodations for four landing craft, each 36 feet long. For guns there was a five inch dual purpose main battery, twin 40 MM mounts and six 20 MM. The boat deck was pretty well cluttered with winches, stack uptakes, spud lockers and gun shields.

After an inclining test that didn't seem to decide much about the top heavy appearing ship, and short sea trials, the BARR put out for Norfolk and a short shakedown cruise mainly to smooth out operations with the boats.

A few days availability at Norfolk followed training in the Solomon Islands of the Chesapeake, and on November 15th, 1944, escorting the USS TETON (AGC14), the BARR with 75 passengers for Pearl Harbor, set forth for Panama.

Liberty in Panama was brief and alcoholic. On 22 Nov. the canal was passed through and that night, course was laid for San Francisco. Here more supplies came aboard and mail for delivery to Pearl Harbor. On 3 December, escorting the USS CECIL (APA96), the BARR put out from the Golden Gate, skies clear, seas strong, but not uncomfortable. Pearl Harbor was reached on the 9th December, 1944.

In Hawaii the BARR shuttled between Maui and Pearl several times, but most of the stay was at Maui, the gay isle, with UDT teams aboard for training in handling of boats and explosives. Practice demolitions and bombardments of the shore were held. The perfect climate, fine swimming and startling scenery of the towering volcanoes rising sheerly from the sea were the un-Naval features of the stay.

In Pearl for Christmas Day, the ship's cooks put out the dinner of the year, ham, turkey and two desserts. That evening the officers served a buffet to the crew on the fantail. Local talent, songs and a movie closed out the day.

With LCP(R)'s replacing the more cumbersome LCVP's, the BARR returned to Maui, took aboard UDT#13 and trained with them for several days before returning to Pearl where full provisioning was done. On 10th January 1945 in a large Task Group of BB's, cruisers, destroyers and sundry amphibs, all under command of Admiral Blandy, the BARR was enroute for Ulithi. The trip was taken up with drills, inter and intra ship. Truk was passed abeam at 75 miles with some nervousness, but otherwise the trip was routine. Still there was no ignoring the fact that among the UDT gear carried aboard there were 90,000 pounds of a powerful explosive called Tetrytol. The optimistic outlook was that the ship rode much better with all that weight aft.

Ulithi was anything but routine. It was the BARR's first acquaintance with Pacific Atolls, formed by low coral-ringed and palm-covered islands. The anchorage within covered some 200 square miles. Never had such a mass of shipping been assembled, particularly of naval vessels; carriers by the dozen, BB's the oldest and newest, cruisers and destroyers a dime a dozen, supply ships, communications ships, reevers, oilers, ammunition vessels. All this, here, and no one aboard had heard of Ulithi a month previously, except once when it was announced that a place called Ulithi had been taken by our forces along with several better known groups.

While the BARR lay in the Southern anchorage more and more ships gathered at Ulithi. All were training, stocking supplies, repairing. Boats ran constantly from ship to ship, begging, stealing, lying to secure needed items. On the BARR the big item was obtaining additional AA guns. Old 20 MM mounts were welded to the deck between the depth charge racks. Some twelve, ex-airplane 50 caliber guns were pipe mounted in every exposed position. Kamikase, zoomie were the words on everybody's tongue. Liberties each afternoon consisted of beer, swimming, shell gathering and volleyball. Feitabul and Pug a Lug Islands were the areas. The sun was hot, the coconut palms choked off the breeze. Only the hermit crabs seemed to enjoy it.

From late January through the 9th of February the ship maneuvered in company with the USS GILMER, BULL, BATES, BLESSMAN and WATERS, all APD's, culminating in a full scale demolition and reconnaissance operation on reefs east of Ulithi Atoll. On 10 February 1945 the advance on Iwo began with a vast group, including the BARR and the other APD's moving out of the anchorage and heading north. At Tinian on the 12th and 13th a rehearsal of Dog-Day movements was held with the transports involved, and on the fourteenth the advance group moved on to Iwo Jima.

At 0600 on the 16th of February, Dog minus three, the BARR arrived off the southern end of the island. The Minesweeps had arrived the night before and were active, clearing the approaches and the water all about the island. Their daring was startling.

That afternoon the first of the BARR and UDT 13 missions were completed. Higashi Rocks lay 200 yards off the northeast corner of Iwo. They were considered a navigational hazard and our mission was to place a small light upon them. At 1600 we closed the rocks to 1500 yards, sent off the landing group and stood by. On shore the terrain was high, rugged, mottled green and brown. Cave mouths could be seen. The sulphur springs steamed unconcernedly. As the UDT's were completing emplacement of their light, a battery from shore opened fire upon them. They dove between the rocks for cover. Shrapnel tore and rattled about them. More fire followed. On the BARR shrapnel slashed the water and rattled on the decks. Moving in slowly to close the returning boats, our main battery opened fire on the estimated position of the shore guns. A dozen rounds blasted out. The shore battery did not reopen fire, and we retrieved our boats. A rubber life raft, with gear, had been lost in the surging water off the rocks, but there were no casualties to personnel.

Next morning, at 0900, 17 February, following intense shelling by fire support ships and aircraft, the APD's fanned out of column and in parallel lanes approached the eastern beaches of Iwo for a reconn by the UDT's. Team 13 had been assigned what was expected to be the hottest beach, directly under the gun caves of Suribachi. Latest photographs showed that the entire island was two to three times as heavily emplaced with guns as had been believed. At 0830 all boats were lowered and loaded with rubber rafts, buoys, swim fins, face masks, all the stock and trade of the UDT. As the LCI(C)'s (rocket and 40 mm ships) churned in past the line of destroyers to the 1000 yard range, the defenders opened fire with mortars and emplaced guns, presumably mistaking this for the invasion landing. The LCP(R)'s manned by UDT's streaked past the LCI(G)'s and commenced getting swimmers into the water. The LCI's, having rocketed the beach into a dense cloud of smoke, lay to and sprayed 40 mm shells at the shore. They drew all the return fire. One after the other was hit and hit again. All but a few were disabled completely. Several sank. The remaining ones were ordered to withdraw. Some had lost power, some had lost steering control. Almost all had casualties. It was one of the most fearful, pointblank beatings Navy ships had had to take. Slowly they drifted out past us, white blankets of the dead and injured on deck all too visible.

That the UDT's escaped from the rain of cross shelling with few losses was amazingly fortunate. Team #13 had no casualties. The swimmers felt less safe aboard than they did in the water, where they could dive to four or five feet and be safe from all but heavy near hits. The use of phosphorus shells by the support ships was called for as soon as the fierceness of the Jap fire developed. The smoke cover saved greater carnage. By 1130 the reconn was completed. Underwater teams working the beaches in the center had several injuries and a few losses. No underwater mines or boat traps were detected.

The reconn on the western beaches in the afternoon followed the same pattern, with the LCI(G) rocket attack omitted, and the use of plane-laid smoke screens substituted. Destroyers closed to 2000 and 1500 yards and following the direction of UDT spotters, shelled emplacements for several hours. Team 13, again operating directly under Mt. Suribachi, had no casualties. Recovering the boats, the BARR delivered photographic film taken by the UDT's to the USS ESTES, command ship of Adm. Blandy, then retired with a group for the night.

The 18th of February was to many aboard the roughest on the nerves of any day experienced. Operating 8000 yards off shore in the area of Higashi Rocks, the USS PENSACOLA, cruiser, had taken numerous hits from 6 and 8 inch shore batteries, with considerable damage and many casualties. The BARR received orders to put UDT 13 back on Higashi Rocks in the afternoon to re-establish the navigational light, reported out of commission. The operation came off without incident. The light was found to be operative.

The ship fueled and joined a retirement group for the night. During darkness a Jap Betty bomber passed close aboard. The BLESSMAN, joining up at full speed, several miles astern of us, reported taking two bomb hits directly after the Betty had flown past us.

Her damage and casualties were heavy. This marked our first awakening to the give-away visibility of wake at night and to the need for reducing wake by slowing speed whenever enemy aircraft were in the vicinity after dark. Thus ended the day of the jitters.

February 19th, Dog Day, was spent in the transport area 6000 yards off shore. Occasional shrapnel struck the water nearby, but we felt easier in mind than during the closer approach on the reconns earlier in the invasion. Our boats, manned by UDT #13 personnel, assisted in guiding the Marine forces to the landing beaches. At night we took Anti-submarine screening station and continued screening through the 20th and 21st. On the 22nd the UDT's, operating with the beachmaster, broached one LCP(R) in the heavy surf. On the 26th the body of a Marine was found floating in the water. Identification was removed and the long exposed remains weighted and sunk.

On March 1st, an air alert occurred from 0200 to 0400. Several sticks of bombs were dropped in the beach areas. We screened until the 4th, when we received orders to escort, with the USS BATES, the USS MALIPHEN and BARRIEN.

Enroute to Saipan, on the 6th, we investigated with negative results an emergency IFF 30 miles abeam of our group. At 0700 on the 7th, we arrived at Saipan, and then with the BATES left for Guam, arriving in Apra Harbor at 1500.

The eighth, ninth and tenth of March were chiefly occupied with liberty and recreation, ball games, beer, sightseeing, and B29 talk. The BARR defeated UDT #13 at softball in the tightest competition yet offered.

On the 11th we were ordered to Ulithi and departed escorting with the KNUDSEN (APD101) and the USS CELILO.

Arriving at Ulithi on the 12th, we anchored in the Southern Anchorage again and commenced preparations for the Okinawa invasion. UDT #13 swam, paddled and did calisthenics. Stores were replenished from the USS CASCADE and DIXIE. Repairs were made and additional small caliber automatic weapons were secured and mounted.

On the 21st we sortied from Ulithi as part of the Gun Fire and Covering Force under Rear Admiral Deyo (ComBatRon ONE), setting course directly for Okinawa.

Early in the morning of the 25th of March, Love minus 7 days, we arrived off Okinawa. As in Iwo, the minesweeps proceeded, and were busily sweeping the inshore waters of the Rhetto islands. At 1510 the APD group Able (BARR, BATES, GILMER, KNUDSEN and BULL) in company with fire support destroyers, EDWARDS, PORTERFIELD AND PRESTON, and with the USS ESTES (Rear Admiral Blandy) attending, made approach to Kerama Rhetto. The BARR, the EDWARDS and LCI(G)'s 440 and 475 arrived off the southern tip of Tokashiki at 0700. UDT #13 reconned the southwestern beaches there, completing the operation with no casualties at 1500. Two men on one of the LCI(G)'s were killed by the explosion of a 40 MM shell in a gun casualty. That night we retired with TF 54. Apparently the Kerama Rhetto approach had been a surprise to the Japanese. Opposition had been negligible.

Closing the Rhetto at 0600 on the 26th, Jap planes were spotted. Our guns opened fire. One plane dropped a bomb near the KNUDSEN, half a mile to starboard, and the other plane, a Val possibly, suicided over us and at the GILMER on our portside, missing the GILMER narrowly, but killing two men by strafing.

The rest of the day and the following three days were spent in putting UDT #13 ashore on Keise Shima, a group of small, sand and coral islands between the Rhetto and Okinawa. The mission was delayed by minesweeping. On our first approach, the sweeps were exploding mines in the area as we closed. Once swept, the BARR closed to 2000 yards and the swimmers reconned without incident other than strafing by two of our own fighters. The swimmers dove deep and hugged the coral until the planes passed. In the course of the Keise mission three demolitions were carried out in order to clear the reef and make passage for LST's to the beach.

Each night during the early weeks the BARR retired with one unit or another from the beach areas. On 31 March destroyers in the retirement group opened fire on enemy aircraft. Two bombs exploded 1000 yards from us during this raid. Seldom a night passed without bogies in the vicinity and the GQ alarm clang, clang, clanging away.

April 1st. Easter Sunday, Invasion Day, was relatively quiet for the BARR. We stayed in the Kerama Rhetto area, and did not close Okinawa.

On the 6th of April UDT #13 was transferred to the USS WAYNE, APA 54, for return to Maui. The BARR was fueling and replenishing ammunition inside the Rhetto at the same time. The Japs chose this time for one of their heaviest daylight suicide raids. Our CAP knocked down many, but others broke through. One plane was shot down by a DE just northwest of the Rhetto a few miles. Another crashed into an LST ammunition ship and left it ablaze with many casualties. A third was shot down inside the anchorage by AA fire.

By next morning the UDT's were entirely transferred. In spite of the crowded conditions aboard, they had been good companions aboard and the severance of relations was regretted. So the BARR reported to the screen commander for duty.

Steam 7000 yards, turn and steam 7000 yards back and turn. Ping, ping. Keep in phase, turn early to correct position, turn late to open the interval, etc. etc. Flash white, control green, no bogies on the screen. Flash yellow, flash red, all hands man your battle stations. Day in and day out. Scarcely a station in the screen that the BARR did not patrol. Four days on patrol, fuel, patrol, fuel, patrol, then--big break--into Wiseman's Cove to provision and to lie overnight in the anonymity of the smoke, or later on, into Hagushi anchorage, and still later, into Buckner Bay.

AND WE WERE LUCKY. Oh how Lucky! Up in the Able stations when the GOSSELIN had two near bomb misses; the night the SIMS, directly ahead of us, was crash dived by a Betty as they opened fire. It flew down our side to crash them, missing and hitting the water in a blaze. On 13 May, the USS CROSBY (APD 17) relieved us on station at dusk, and half an hour later was crashed by a zoomie. Very lucky we were. Then there was night after night that we stayed at GQ while planes, clearly audible, passed overhead and on to other targets.

Best break, (and we deserved it) were the orders dispatching us to Saipan on 9 April. We arrived on 15 April. Liberty, beer and ball games, and gassing with the B29 boys. The old routine. On the way down a sonar contact and attack by the USS FEIBERLING (DE640) gave notice that Jap subs were not out of the war as yet.

Underway on 22 April, back to Okinawa as a convoy escort. On 27 April the RINGNESS (APD 100) spotted a periscope and torpedo wake and went in and sank a smaller type Jap sub. More sonar contacts in the next 24 hours, evasive courses, false reports. Floating mines were sighted and sunk. But no zoomies. So back at Okinawa on 29 April and screening again on the 30th.

Again on 27 May we made the Saipan run and thence on to Leyte for sonar repairs and availability. More beer, but no ball games, and lousy stockade of a liberty area. The climate sultry, steamy, stifling. The undercut, off Balance Islands, their outlines soft with heavy greenery, the native proas and other odd sailing craft, shell necklaces, --these the features of Leyte.

Underway on 17 June to Manila, the BARR carried a ship-full of Filipino U.S. Naval personnel on leave from Task Force 38 to their homes. They were delivered at Manila on the 19th, the ship anchoring there for four hours. Manila was bombed, burned and torn, noisy with U.S. jeeps and trucks, the harbor a mass of sunken vessels, spars sticking from the askew, hulks aground, burned and rusted.

From Manila it was a short day's run to Lingayen Gulf, San Fernando. A morning here and out at noon convoying a group of LST's to initiate the route from Lingayen to Okinawa. Except for a depth charge attack by the USS VAMMEN (DE644), the run was without event, and Okinawa was sighted on 24 June and we were once again screening with bogies coming in every night, but staying clear of the area during the day for the most part. Submarine contacts seemed to be more numerous, but sinkings were rare. Around Ie Shima the bogies were still crashing into shipping.

On July 7 the BARR met Brass Hats. She was assigned to assist the USS PRICHETT (DD561) in carrying Army Generals and Colonels on a tour of the adjacent Nansei Shoto Islands. All hands spruced up and for a day and a half we steamed at full speed from one island to another, --Tori, Xamami, Theya, Kume, and Ie Shima, Tokashiki, Mae, Keise--familiar names by now.

On the 19th of July a long dormant worry came to the fore. Typhoon warnings began to make their appearance in the day's dispatches. Typhoon sortie plans were studied, and from the 19th through the 21st July we rolled and pitched convoying a group at 4-5 knots on retirement from Okinawa, wondering if the aerographers had guessed correctly this time.

Screening again by 23 July, with peace rumors making their first appearance and the tension and seat-out just beginning, that night a bogie flying low, swept up our port side at half a mile, turned and pinned us down moon, and came in. A splash in the water, --torpedo? Perhaps--then he veered up and away down our starboard side, engines sputtering and coughing.

By now air raids were fewer. The peak definitely was past, but with the screen reduced to a handful of vessels, and single planes effecting sneak approaches by night, the screening ships were sweating it out. Knock wood a plenty these days.

Finally orders were received assigning availability at Buckner Bay, but from Aug. 1 to the 3rd a typhoon sent all ships rocking out the harbor in an evasive maneuver. Back again and at anchor there was opportunity for liberty on an island at the entrance to Buckner Bay, with the swimming good, shell hunting especially fine, and beer, hot dogs and fruit for a picnic lunch. And out again to screen for a few days before being suddenly called into Buckner Bay for unknown duty involving an operation against Tokyo. All the APD's in the area assembled. Stock up with provisions, rumors, questions, suppositions, but no answers. Then while at anchor on the 13 August, at dusk, an APA several berths away was bombed and suicided by planes without warning. The night before the USS PENNSYLVANIA had been blasted while at anchor. Peace terms practically signed. The sweat-out was easing up, almost over, after 140 days. Of the 140, the BARR had spent almost 100 days at Okinawa and most of them on the exposed screening stations.

Highly uncertain as to the actual duty involved the BARR, SIMS, PAVLIC, BASS, REEVES and RUNELS, all APD's, left Buckner Bay under command of Capt. J.M. Kennaday with orders to rendezvous with TF 31 off Tokyo.

For 15 days, with British Landing Parties of Royal Marines and Sailors from the KING GEORGE V and the New Zealand manner HMS GAMBIA, CL. aboard, the BARR steamed through storm after storm with one task group and another, delivering mail, passengers, fueling, closing 19 ships in one day's steaming. Delayed several days by typhoons, the group closed Tokyo and entered Sagami Wan on Aug. 27th, the APD's, as usual out in front. Anchoring two nights, on 30 Aug. the six APD's with various assignments, made their entrance into Tokyo Bay and closed the Yokosuka Naval Base, the BARR coming alongside a pier on Azuma Peninsula, the fuel and ammunition storage of the base, and putting the Royal Marines ashore without difficulty.

Mission completed, the BARR was assigned that night to TU 30.6 for duty evacuating allied POW's from the central Honshu areas. During the next twenty days the BARR received 1,135 repatriates aboard for further transfer. Most were processed aboard the USS BENEVOLENCE, some the BARR Medical Officer processed with the assistance of Lt. Colonel Gunery, USA. The operations took place in Tokyo Harbor, Yokohama, Khizarasu, Hamamatsu, Sendai and Kamaishi, with our anchor down seldom longer than a day at a time, and with the boats and boat crews operating late into each night.

Of special interest were the operations of September 1st. With correspondents aboard, the BARR was ordered to follow the REEVES (APD 52) into inner Tokyo Harbor to take aboard POW's of the allied nations being brought into that area. Preceding this vessel by half an hour the REEVES passed between the small fortress islands with their dummy gun emplacements and moored to a buoy inside. The BARR attempted to come alongside the REEVES but was ordered to tie up to the dock. Thus this ship was the first U.S. major or minor war vessel to tie along-side in Tokyo, the goal of the entire U.S. Navy for four years. We remained there throughout the day. Entertainment of a peculiar sort was provided by an idiot Japanese girl. After dark, in a thick fog, we moved out the channel and closed the BENEVOLENCE to transfer a group of missionaries of all nationalities, including three women and two girls. One woman was 80 years old, the girls about eight and ten. They are believed to be the first women evacuated from the area.

Hoping to remain at anchor for a few days for maintenance work, heavy winds struck the Tokyo area on the 18th Sept. Our anchor dragging we were forced to get underway and shift berths. The black gang did excellent work get-ting both engines operating in short order. By afternoon the Bay was calm.

On 20 Sept. evacuation mission completed with a well done for all ships con-cerned, the BARR was assigned to TU 53.4, the local command at Yokosuka. On the 24th, the BARR left for Iwo Jima on a mail run, returning in the midst of a good blow on 28 Sept. Iwo wasn't the same Iwo of our memory.

With the ship reduced to 80% of compliment by the transfer of discharges, including most of the oldest, highest rated men aboard, with Lt. Cdr. Dickie detached (as of 4 Sept.) and Lt. Gordon as C.O., the BARR was assigned to duty with the United States Strategic Bomb Survey as a--barracks ship, taking orders directly from ComFifthFleet. On 12 October, jeeps and trailers were loaded aboard at the dock in Tokyo and the BARR got underway for Nagasaki, arriving on the 15th of October. Nagasaki---bad odors, ruins, Marine MP's, the recreation area rebuilt by the BARR near the Mitsuibishi submarine ways, the pathetic, dirty shivering Japs, good beer, basketball--and no sign of orders to return to the States.

Chronological History of the USS Barr (DE 576-APD 39)

The USS BARR is named for Private W.W. Barr, U.S.M.C. Private Barr was killed on Tulagi. The BARR was built by Bethlehem Hingham Shipyard Inc., at Hingham, Mass.

5 November 1943…...Keel laid.

28 December 1943….Launched

15 February 1944…...Commissioned USS BARR (DE 576). Lt. Cdr. H.H. Love, U.S.N.R., Commanding.

22 February 1944…...Underway on own power to Charlestown Navy Yard, Boston.

26 Feb. - 4 March…...Trial runs for calibration of instruments, test firing of guns.

5 March 1944……….Underway to New London, Conn. for further calibration, sailing via Cape Cod Canal.

9 March 1944……….Underway for Bermuda on shakedown cruise.

11 March 1944……...Arrived at Bermuda - commenced training with emphasis on A.A.warfare.

6 April 1944………...Departed Bermuda following inspection by Captain D.L. Madiera. In company with USS AHRENS (DE 575) and USS Osmus (DE701).

8 April 1944………...Arrived Boston, Charlestown Navy Yard for post shake-down availability, repairs, alterations and complete paint job.

17 April 1944……….Underway for Casco Bay, Maine for Destroyer - Atlantic Fleet Training.

19 April 1944……….In company with DE 575 and DE 686; underway for Norfolk, Va.

21 April 1944……….Arrived at Norfolk, Va. Reported to Commander Task Group 21.11 for duty with Killer Group.

22 April 1944……….Underway with Task Group 21.11, consisting of USS BLOCK ISLAND (CVE 21), escorted by USS AHRENS (DE 575), USS ELMORE (DE686), USS BUCKLEY (DE51), for area off CapeVerde Islands.

24 April 1944……….Put back (independently) to Bermuda for Sonar repairs. Repairs made and departed to rejoin same day.

25 April 1944……….Rejoined Task Group 21.11.

29 April 1944……….Task Group 21.11 relieved Task Group of one CVE and five Destroyer Escorts at 19-55 N - 38-14 W.

1 May 1944............ With USS ELMORE, dispatched to search sub contact. Results negative although two hedgehog patterns were fired. Rejoined and Task Group continued searches.

6 May 1944............ At 0230, USS BUCKLEY joined air-craft attacking surface sub. BUCKLEY rammed and sank submarine, taking prisoners. BUCKLEY departed for Boston for repairs.

7 May 1944............ Made two attacks with hedgehogs on a sonar contact. No results.

8 May 1944............ Made hedgehog attack on sonar contact. Negative results.

9 May 1944............ With USS AHRENS investigated reported sub contact. No results.

11 May 1944........... Five Sonar contacts. All negative.

13 May 1944........... Relieved by Task Group 22.2 (USS BOGUE and five (DE's); Task Group 21.11 at minimum fuel limit. Set course for Casablanca.

15 May 1944........... USS PAINE (DE 578) joined Task Group 21.11.

18 May 1944........... Arrived at Casablanca. Beer parties, ball games, etc.

22 May 1944........... Underway with USS PAINE to search for sub reported near channel entrance.

23 May 1944........... Returned to Casablanca for fuel and underway with Task Group 21.11 to continue operations.

29 May 1944........... Near 32-09 N - 22-15 W, at 2014 while closing reported sub contact, BLOCK ISLAND torpedoed, taking three hits. At 2030, while chasing down contact, BARR took a torpedo astern totally wrecking ship aft of #2 engine room. BLOCK ISLAND sank at 2155 with six casualties. BARR had eleven injured, twelve missing, and five dead. USS ELMORE sank sub acting on information from USS AHRENS. AHRENS and PAINE took aboard BLOCK ISLAND survivors. Injured and half the crew transferred to ELMORE for transportation to Casablanca.

30 May 1944........... BARR undertow by ELMORE enroute to Casablanca.

1 June 1944............ USS WILHOITE (DE) relieved ELMORE as towing ship.

2 June 1944............ Dutch tug, ANTIC, relieved USS WILHOITE.

5 June 1944............ Arrived Casablanca.

8 June 1944............ All but nucleus crew transferred for transportation to United States. BARR in drydock until 2 July; wreckage burned off and stern plates welded on. Lt. Comdr. P.T. Dickie, USNR, relieved Lt. Comdr. H.H. Love as Commanding Officer.

3 July 1944............. Underway to Boston in tow by USS CHEROKEE, Fleet Tug.

4 July 1944...............Joined convoy G.U.S. #44 west of Gibraltar.

17 July 1944............Arrived Bermuda to avoid storm.

22 July 1944............Underway for Boston in tow of CHEROKEE.

25 July 1944............Fishing Boat collided with CHEROKEE off Cape Cod at night losing one man overboard from fishing vessel.

Aug., Sept.,............ BARR converted at South Boston Dry Docks Oct. to APD;
and Oct., 1944   repairs to stern made. All hands received 30 days leave.

31 October 1944.......Trial runs in Massachusetts Bay.

3 November 1944......Underway for shake-down cruise at Norfolk, Virginia.

5 November 1944......Arrived at Norfolk.

6-11 November 1944. Exercised at night boat landings, shore bombardment, etc.

12 November 1944....Moored at Norfolk, Convoy Escort Pier #21.

15 November 1944....Underway, enroute Panama Canal, escorting USS TETON (AGC14) and transporting 72 enlisted men bound for Pearl Harbor.

21 November 1944... Arrived at Christobal, C.Z.

22 November 1944....Passed through canal and departed with TETON for San Francisco.

1 December 1944...... Arrived at San Francisco.

3 December 1944...... Departed for Pearl Harbor, escorting USS CECIL (APA96).

9 December 1944...... Arrived Pearl Harbor, T.H.

11 December 1944.... Shifted to Maui, T.H. for training with Underwater Demolition Teams. Practiced night and day demolitions, and shore bombardment with Team16 in Maalae Bay.

18 December 1944.... Returned to Pearl Harbor for supplies and maintenance.

28 December 1944.... To Maui. Took aboard U.D.T. #13. Through January 6, 1945, exercised with UDT's in company with USS BATES, USS GILMER, and LCI's. Team #16 suffered minor casualties in demolition operation the night of 2 January, 1945.

7 January 1945......... Moved to Pearl Harbor with BATES, GILMER, and WATERS. Took aboard 50 tons of tetrytol and supplies.

10 January 1945.......Underway in large Task Group under Rear Admiral Blandy, in the USS ESTES. Battlewagons, cruisers, Destroyers, and APD's, enroute to Ulithi.

15 January 1945.......Crossed the 180th Meridian.

23 January 1945.......Entered Ulithi anchorage, Anchored in Southern Area. Until 9 February 1945, trained, prepared and loaded supplies for the invasion of Iwo Jima. Le Blanc, SF1c of UDT #13, electrocuted while welding over the side.

10 February 1945...... Underway as part of advance movement group for Iwo with USS GILMER, WATERS, BATES, BULL, and BLESS MAN forming the APD group.

12 February 1945...... Arrived Tinian and rehearsed D-Day operations with transport groups.

14 February 1945...... Joined movement group enroute to Iwo.

16 February 1945...... D-3 - Arrived off Southern end of Iwo Jima at 0600. Took screening station. At 1600, closed Higashi rocks to 1500 yards; two thousand yards off NW end of Iwo, while U.D.T.'s emplaced Navigation Light on the rocks. U.D.T. men on rocks taken under fire by shore battery. No casualties. BARR closed rocks to 1000 yards to pick up U.D.T. men and fired 10 rounds from 5" main battery at the shore. Shore fire ceased.

17 February 1945...... U.D.T. reconned eastern beaches. Team # 13 doing beach adjacent to Suribachi. BARR launched boats at 4000 yards. Heavy shore fire sunk or completely disabled 8 of 10 LCI (G)'s with many casualties. U.D.T. #13 had no casualties. Western beaches reconned at 1400. No casualties to Team #13. Destroyers and aircraft made increased use of smoke and phosphorous shells. U.D.T.'s did excellent close-in spotting for Destroyers' fire.

18 February 1945...... BARR ordered to close Higashi Rocks for U.D.T. #13 to replace light. USS PENSACOLA heavily damaged by 6" and 8" shore fire that morning in same area at greater range. BARR closed rocks to 1500 yards and U.D.T.'s investigated and relighted navigation aid. During night retirement, USS BLESSMAN astern of BARR, while speeding to join retirement group was bombed by Jap Betty which passed low alongside BARR at 2120, just prior to the bombing. Many casualties aboard the BLESSMAN.

19 February 1945...... DOG DAY - BARR in transport areas, about 6000 yards off Eastern beaches. U.D.T. #13 furnished boat and men to guide 4th and 5th Marines ashore at 0900. Took screening station at night. From this time through 3 March 1945 BARR screened or anchored while U.D.T.'s worked with the beachmasters and removed underwater obstacles.

4 March 1945.......... After 20 days at Iwo Jima, BARR departed for Saipan with USS BATES, escorting USS MULIPHEN and BARRIEN.

6 March 1945.......... 0900 Left convoy to investigate emergency IFF contact. Negative result. Rejoined at 1700.

7 March 1945………. Arrived Saipan and then with BATES steamed to Guam, making Apra Harbor at 1500.

8 - 10 March 1945…..Beer, ball games and liberty at Guam.

11 March 1945…….. Departed Guam with USS KNUDSEN (APD 101) escorting tanker USS CELILO.

12 March 1945…….. Anchored in Southern Anchorage, Ulithi.

13 - 20 March 1945…Preparation for the invasion of Okinawa.

21 March 1945…….. Sortied from Ulithi as part of Gun Fire and Covering Force under Rear Admiral Deyo (ComBatRonOne) setting course for Okinawa. GILMER, WATERS, BATES, KNUDSEN, BULL and BARR comprised the APD group. Task Group 52.11.

25 March 1945…….. Love minus seven. Arrived off Okinawa at 0510 - APD group ABLE, fire support destroyers, EDWARDS, PORTERFIELD, PRESTON, and USS ESTES (Rear Admiral Blandy) approached Kerama Rhetto. BARR, with EDWARDS and LCI (G)'s 440 and 475 closed southwestern tip of Tokashiki. U.D.T. #13 reconned these beaches. Task completed at 1530 with no opposition from shore. One LCI (G) had two men killed when 40 MM gun functioned improperly. Retired with Task Force 54 at night.

26 March 1945…….. Approaching Kerama Rhetto at 0600, the KNUDSEN, 1000 yards to starboard, received near bomb miss and Jap Val made suicide dive passing over BARR and just missing USS GILMER, 1000 yards on our port side. USS GILMER lost two men by strafing. BARR opened fire early and may have deflected pilot from this vessel. At 0730, transferred Army Officers to SC 1330 to enable them to accompany leading waves of troops to Rhetto Beaches. Retired at night with tractor group.

27 March 1945…….. Proceeded to area South of Keise Shima, but operations were delayed because waters had not been swept. Enemy aircraft in vicinity during the night retirement.

28 March 1945…….. At 1230, we followed mine sweeps into area south of Keise Shima. Mines were exploded in that area while we waited for the sweeps to finish. U.D.T. swimmers investigated small sand island of Waganna. Demolition charges on reefs set off at 1610. No casualties. At 1820 joined tractor group and retired. Enemy planes in area all night.

29 March 1945…….. Further blasting of Keise Shima reefs by U.D.T. #13 to make channel for an LST to land. Blasts set off at 1130 and again at1600. Retired for the night.

30 March 1945.........Further blasting of Keise Shima reefs by U.D.T. #13. Retired for the night.

31 March 1945.........Enemy aircraft drew fire of screening Destroyers. Two bombs dropped 1000 yards from the BARR. Spent day off Keise Shima during emplacement of equipment and troops on the island by the Army. Took night screening station north of the Rhetto.

1 April 1945............Reported to Commander Task Force 53, then to Commander Task Group 51.5, transport screen. Joined transports retiring for the night as part of A.S. screen.

2 April 1945............Enemy aircraft in area all night. 1000 - Took screening station 10 miles off Okinawa.

3 April 1945............Patrolled station north of Mae Shima. Sonar gear out of order.

5 April 1945............Sonar gear temporarily repaired.

6 April 1945............At G.Q. from 0300 to 0700. Flash Red on and off all day. At 1540, fueled and while alongside tanker, taking aboard fuel and ammunition and transferring U.D.T. #13, and equipment, to USS WAYNE (APA54) enemy planes closed Kerama Rhetto. Several shot down. One suicide hit an LST just off the anchorage. At 1840, AA fire downed one plane in the anchorage. 1930 - Secured from General Quarters.

7 April 1945............At G.Q. from 0400 to 0615. Completed transferring of U.D.T. #13. Screening station for the night.

8 April 1945............G.Q. on and off all day. On screening station.

9 April 1945............G.Q. in early morning. Departed for Saipan at 1200 with convoy of Task Unit 51.29.11 and five escorts.

10 April 1945..........1620 - USS FEIBERLING (DE640) and BARR investigated sonar contact by FEIBERLING. Made several hedgehog and depth charge attacks. BARR dropped pattern of D.C.'s on possible contact. No results.

13 April 1945..........Arrived Saipan. Reported to SERVRON TEN for repairs.

14 - 22 April 1945.....At Saipan for upkeep and repairs to sonar gear.

23 April 1945..........Underway for Okinawa, screening 13 LST's and 6 LSM's; part of Task Unit 94.19.14.

27 April 1945..........0825 - USS RINGNESS (APD100) reported torpedo wake and a periscope. She made an urgent attack and destroyed a midget submarine. Four other contacts reported during the day with negative results.

28 April 1945..........BARR sunk horned mine by gunfire at 1830. 2215 - Air alert; AA screen formed.

29 April 1945.......... Arrived Okinawa. 2110 - An air alert while in smoke screen off Hagushi anchorage.

30 April 1945.......... On screening station at 0700. 2200 - Air alert.

1 May 1945............ A.S. screening. 1900 - An air alert.

2 May 1945............ Screening.

3 May 1945............ Screening. Three flash red alerts.

4 May 1945............ Screening. 0251 - USS GOSSELIN (APD) in adjoining station missed by bomb; 0352 - Enemy planes dropped flares nearby. Many planes in vicinity. 0800 - Flash red alert. Felt underwater explosion at a distance. 1030 - Flash red. 1900 - Flash red.

5 May 1945............ Screening. 0215 Flash red. 0250 Jap plane showing red light passed 2 miles ahead. 2240 Flash red.

6 May 1945............ Screening. 0200 Flash red. 0850 Flash red. 1900 Flash red.

7 May 1945............ Screening. 0200 Flash red. 1100 Flash red.

8 May 1945............ Screening.

9 May 1945............ Screening. Relieved by USS SWEARER (DE 186). 1900 Flash red.

10 May 1945.......... Screening. 0000 - Flash red. 0310 - Low flying plane passed less than 2 miles abeam. 1430 Relieved by USS LAWRENCE (APD 37). Anchored off Hagushi beaches in smoke.

11 May 1945.......... 0830 Flash red. Joined AA screen at 0930. Heavy raid ended at 1015. All Jap planes intercepted by C.A.P.

12 May 1945.......... Screening. 1900 Flash red. At 1915 low flying plane passed at four miles.

13 May 1945.......... Screening. 0300 Flash red. 1500 Sonar gear shorted out. Relieved at 1900 during flash red alert. At 1930 USS CROSBY (APD 17) relieving ship was hit by suicide plane. 2030 Flash red. 2100 BARR relieved USS CROSELY (APD 87) on screening station.

14 May 1945.......... Screening. 0300 Flash red. 1800 Underway to join and escort USS SAMARITAN to Okinawa. 1950 Enemy plane approached within 3 miles, but circled away.

15 May 1945.......... Joined USS SAMARITAN at 1400.

16 May 1945.......... Arrived Okinawa. 1600 Screening. 2000 Flash red with several planes flying low close by RINGNESS (APD 100) missed by suicider at 5 miles from BARR.

17 May 1945.......... Screening. 1400 Relieved to provision. 1930 Flash red.

18 May 1945.......... In anchorage. 1900 Flash red.

19 May 1945........... At anchor.

20 May 1945........... Underway at 0400 with USS LOY (APD 56) to rendezvous with convoy approaching Okinawa. 1600 Joined convoy Task Unit 94.18.10.

21 May 1945........... 0800 USS LOY (APD 56) destroyed floating mine off southern tip of Okinawa. 1600 Screening. 1900 Flash red.

22 May 1945........... Screening. 1940 Flash red.

23 May 1945........... Screening. 2350 Flash red.

24 May 1945........... Screening. 1920 Flash red.

25 May 1945........... Screening. 0030 Plane crashed close aboard USS SIMS (APD50) in adjoining station, 2 miles from us. USS BARRY (APD29), 5 miles NE, hit by suicide plane. Air alerts all day.

26 May 1945........... Screening - Relieved by USS FLEMMING at 1700. At anchor 1830.

27 May 1945........... 0750 Flash red. Underway to Saipan escorting convoy Task Unit 51.29.18.

2 June 1945............ Arrived Saipan.

4 June 1945............ Departed Saipan with USS SIMS (APD 50) enroute to Leyte.

8 June 1945............ Arrived San Pedro Bay Leyte for repairs and maintenance.

17 June 1945........... Departed San Pedro Bay for Manila with 55 Filipino enlisted passengers from Task Force 38. Proceeding via San Bernadino Straits.

19 June 1945........... Arrived Manila. Transferred passengers. Departed Manila 1250.

20 June 1945........... 0850 Arrived San Fernando, Lingayen Gulf. Underway at 1200 with Lingayen - Okinawa convoy #1 of 11 LST's and 4 escorts.

23 June 1945........... USS VAMMEN (DE 644) made D.C. attack on doubtful sonar contact.

24 June 1945........... Arrived Okinawa. Screening. Several enemy aircraft in vicinity at night.

25 June 1945........... Screening. Enemy aircraft in vicinity at night.

26 June 1945........... Screening.

27 June 1945........... Screening.

28 June 1945........... Screening. Relieved at 1700.

29 June 1945........... 0500 Screening. Sub reported sighted nearby.

30 June 1945........... Screening.

1 July 1945............. Screening. 0330 Flash red.

2 July 1945............. Screening. Several Flash red alerts at night. USS PAVLIC in next station reported object splashed near them at 0200.

3 July 1945..............Screening. Several red alerts. Aircraft shot down and sub reported in vicinity.

4 July 1945..............Screening. Relieved at 1700.

5 July 1945..............Screening.

6 July 1945..............0320 Screening ship in adjoining station dropped D.C. pattern on sonar contact. Negative results.

7 July 1945..............0630 Underway in company with USS PRICHETT (APD 561). U.S. Army Generals and colonels embarked for tour of islands in the area.

8 July 1945..............1800 Completed tour. Resumed screening duties.

9-10-11 July 1945….. Screening.

12 July 1945............Screening. 0315 Red air alert for two hours.

13 July 1945............Screening.

14 July 1945............0400 Flash red alert. Screening.

15-16 July 1945....... Screening.

17 July 1945............2200 Flash red alert. Screening.

18 July 1945............2100 Flash red alert. Screening.

19 July 1945............Screening. 0600 Retired east and then south of Okinawa.

20 July 1945............Screening task group during evasive maneuvers in the execution of typhoon plan X Ray.

21 July 1945........... 0900 Returned to Okinawa. 1130 Took screening station.

22 July 1945............Screening. 0200 Flash red alert.

23 July 1945............Screening. 0110 Low flying unidentified plane sighted visually to port at two miles. Plane crossed bow and came in on starboard bow, altitude 50 feet or less. At 400 yards plane appeared to drop something in the water. Plane veered off. Ship was up moon from plane. Plane showed no IFF.

24 July 1945............Screening.

25 July 1945............Screening. Escorted LST's to Buckner Bay and anchored for the night.

26 July 1945........... Screening.

27 July 1945   Screening. 2245 Flash red alert.

28 July 1945............Screening. 2030 Anchored at Hagushi.

29 July 1945............Escorted small convoy to Buckner Bay. 1715 At anchor at Buckner Bay.

30-31 July 1945....... Anchored Buckner Bay for supplies and maintenance.

1 August 1945.........1700 Underway from Buckner Bay as escort for group taking evasive maneuvers to avoid approaching typhoon.

3-7 August 1945.......0830 Returned to Buckner Bay and anchored for completion of assigned availability.

8 August 1945......... Took screening station.

9 August 1945......... Drone target practice while screening.

10 August 1945........ Screening. Personnel and material inspection held by Division Commander, Capt. J.M. Kennaday, while patrolling station.

11 August 1945........ Screening.

12 August 1945........ Screening - Investigated reported crash of plane. Anchored at Hagushi overnight.

13 August 1945........ Screened then proceeded to Buckner Bay. 1942 APA 124 struck by bomb and suicide plane. Flash red until 2130.

14 August 1945........ Underway with APD's 50, 70, 85, 124, 125, OTC, Capt. J.M. Kennaday in USS SIMS (APD 50), as Commander Task Unit 95.5.39 enroute to rendezvous with Task Force 31 in area East of Tokyo.

15 August 1945........ Task Unit changed to 30.6.

16,17 August 1945.... Joined with Task Force 31, assigned to screen Task Unit 30.8.1.

18 August 1945........ Joined Task Unit 30.8 as part of screen.

19 August 1945........ Attached to Task Unit 12.1.2.

20 August 1945........ 0730 Closed Task Group 38.5. Took aboard from HMS KING GEORGE V and HMS GAMBIA a landing force of 177 men and 6 officers. Rejoined previous unit now designated as Task Group 31.4.

20-25 August 1945.... Operating as part of screen. Assisting in transfer of officers from ships of the Task Group. All units maneuvered to avoid approaching typhoons.

26 August 1945........ Tokyo approach delayed to avoid typhoons.

27 August 1945........ Entered Sagami Wan.

30 August 1945........ 0900 Entered Tokyo Bay as part of Task Group 31.4. Disembarked Royal Marines at pier on Aguma Peninsula, Yokosuka Naval Base. 1500 Underway to North end of Tokyo Bay. Reported to Commander Task Group 30.6 on USS SAN JUAN for duty evacuating Allied P.O.W.'s.

30 August 1945........ Evacuation of Allied P.O.W.'s Yokohama, Tokyo districts.
   to   Received aboard and transported 565 such personnel.

6 September 1945..... Operating with USS BENEVOLENCE, SAN JUAN, REEVES (APD 52), RUNELS (APD 85), LSV 2 and 5.

1 September 1945..... At noon we followed USS REEVES (APD 52) into Tokyo Harbor. The REEVES was the first U.S. vessel of any sort to enter the harbor. BARR tied to the dock and was the first U.S. vessel of any sort to tie up in Tokyo Harbor.

6 September 1945.....1930 Underway for Hamamatsu evacuation area.

7 September 1945......0700 Arrived Hamamatsu.

9 September 1945......0700 Departed Hamamatsu with 110 Allied P.O.W.'s aboard. Being processed by ship's facilities. 2000 Arrived Yokohama.

10 September 1945....1700 Underway to Sendai area.

11 September 1945....1300 Arrived Sendai.

13 September 1945....1500 Transported landing party out the harbor of Shiogama Ko for an exploratory of adjacent coast line.

14 September 1945....1730 Underway for Kamaishi, Honshu.

15 September 1945....0600 At anchor Kamaishi Wan.

16 September 1945....Underway for Tokyo with 150 Repatriates aboard.

17 September 1945....Arrived Tokyo Bay, disembarked Allied P.O.W.'s

18 September 1945....Typhoon felt in Tokyo Bay. Shifted berth for better anchorage.

19 September 1945....Evacuation of Allied P.O.W.'s operation completed - BARR participating in all but one day of the complete operations for the area. 1135 Allied P.O.W.'s received aboard and transferred.

20 September 1945....Assigned to Tokyo Mail run. Four days at moorings spent in maintenance, logistics and liberty.

24 September 1945....Underway for Iwo - no freight, mail or passengers aboard.

26 September 1945....0700 Arrived Iwo Jima. 1800 Departed Iwo for Tokyo with nine passengers aboard.

28 September 1945....Two approaching typhoons; restricted liberty and logistics
   to   progress. On 11 October moved to dockside in Tokyo
11 October 1945   Harbor and under orders from Commander Fifth Fleet, loaded equipment and personnel aboard.

12 October 1945.......Departed at 2200 (Item) for Nagasaki to act as base of operations for United States Strategic Bomb Survey in that area.

15 October 1945.......Arrived Nagasaki, unloaded equipment and commenced operations as Barracks Ship for U.S.S.B.S. in Nagasaki. Estimated duration of operation November 15th - 30th, 1945.

END

Present Date 15 October 1945

APPENDIX B

OFFICERS AND CREW OF THE USS *BARR*

Information for this appendix was derived from Muster Roll documents on U.S. National Archives microfilm, which was provided by Ned Marrow. Some of the documents were illegible and a few monthly Muster Rolls were missing, so the list may be incomplete.

Many of the officers and crew changed when the *Barr* was converted to an APD; thus the list is separated into three parts. The highest ranks or ratings for the men and their places of entry into active service found on these documents are also given (see Appendix E for information on ratings). Those who were killed in action (KIA) or missing in action (MIA) when the *Barr* was torpedoed in the Atlantic are designated.

Men who served on the *Barr* as a DE only:

James Edward Adams S1c Pittsburgh, PA, MIA
James Vernon Allen S2c Raleigh, NC
Raymond VanDyck Barnes RM3c Balto, MD
Carl I. Bennett GM1c Pearl Harbor, MIA
Meredith Kilsworth Brady GM2c Greensburg, PA, KIA
John Edward Bray S1c Louisville, KY
Carl Nelson Burdett GM3c Toledo, OH, MIA
Junior Vaughn Byrd F1c Spartanburg, SC
Carl Caldwell MM1c St.Louis, MO
Bennie Cannata S2c Chicago, IL
Fred Alfred Carver EM2c New Orleans, LA
Francis Paul Christopher GM3c Detroit, MI
James Wesley Christy GM3c Greensburg, PA
Joseph Paul Ciffizari SC3c Springfield, MA
Harold Robert Clyde RM3c New York, NY

Harold Harry Cohen S2c Pittsburgh PA
Lewis Luke Collins RM3c Boston, MA
Robert W. Cook PhM2c New York, NY, MIA
Benjamin Andrew Copass III Ensign
James LeRoy Coplan S1c Minneapolis, MN
Carl Ray Dailey S2c Columbus, OH
Joseph Gabriel (Joe) Dalesandry RM3c Pittsburgh, PA
Robert Charles Daugherty RM3c Oklahoma City, OK
Eldin Obert Davenport CNT(PA) San Pedro, CA
Edward Leonard Demski S1c Detroit, MI
Wade Denny S2c Louisville, KY
Daniel Leonard DiBono EM3c Philadelphia, PA
Addison W. Dixon Ensign
Henry Lawrence Earle EM3c Washington, DC
John Archibald Earle FC3c Dallas, TX
Ernest Robert Edwards S1c Raleigh, NC
Robert Carrington Ellenwood RT1c Cincinnati, OH
Robert Ameden Ellis S2c (TM) Boston, MA
Thomas George Ellis S1c(TM) Richmond, VA, MIA
Donald Eugene Elswick S1c Abingden, VA
Michael Joseph Flynn TM3c Philadelphia, PA
Alexander Gershman MM3c New Haven, CT
Michael Harry Gorchyca F1c(EM) Phila., PA, MIA
Haynes B. Gordon CSKA, MIA
Walter Lee Goss S1c Atlanta, GA
George Franklin Haigler, Jr. S2c Hattiesburg, MS
Gerald Emerson Haile S1c Los Angeles, CA
Theodore Handel EM3c New York, NY
Gordon Boyd Haynes Sk1c Chicago, IL, KIA
Henry Heintz, Jr. EM3c Albany, NY
Kenneth Emil Hendricks S1c Baltimore MD
Adolph Campbell Herlitze RdM3c Pittsburgh, PA
John W. Hird, Jr. Ensign
Irving Hochstein S1c Wilmington, DE
Elmer Truman Hulbert S2c Utica, NY
David Meredith Jenkins F1c Columbus, OH, MIA
William Jesse Jennings Cox Macon, GA
Clyde Henderson Johnson S2c Atlanta, GA, KIA
Henry Bernard Johnson RdM3c Milwaukee, WI
Marvin Autry Johnston EM1c Dallas, TX
Awtry Marion Jones S2c Atlanta, GA

Kenneth Kline Kauffman SM1c Pittsburgh, PA
Alfred Daniel Kawalec S1c Buffalo, NY
Richard Floyd Kidwell CEM(PA) New Orleans, LA
Victor Daniel Knutsen WT3c NY,NY
Solon Gust Koclanes GM3c Chicago, IL
Walter Irvin Kresge EM3c Wilkes-Barre, PA
Alfred William Kunkel EM2c Cincinnati, OH
Corbitt Horace Lamb S2c Raleigh, NC
Nathan Paul Lawhead S2c Altoona, PA
Edmond Ernest Lefebvre MM3c Manchester, NH
Frank Adam Lehner EM3c Pittsburgh, PA
Frederick John Linroth QM3c Chicago, IL
James Zimmerman Logan Lt.(jg)
Henry Hamilton Love Lt Cmdr.USNR, C.O.
Bernard Anthony Lyman TM2c New York, NY
Harold Edward MacNeill TM2c Utica, NY
Harold Clinton Main F1c Columbus, OH
Winston Vancy Mantooth S1c Chattanooga, TN
Louis Frederick Marano S2c New Haven, CT
Phillip Edward Marion F1c Newark, NJ, MIA
Neddy John (Ned) Marrow S1c Erie, PA
Edwin Mathias Marsh FCR3c Albany, NY
Joseph Marzitelli F2c Providence, RI
Leland Alva McCabe EM3c Albany, NY, MIA
Willie Rudolph McGraw S2c Raleigh, NC
Warren Soper McHenry Y3c Chicago, IL
Emmett McLeod StM2c
John Patrick McNeill S2c New York, NY
Joseph Richard Millette S2c Boston, MA
Thomas Morrison F1c
George Edward Murray PhM3c Chicago, IL
Frederick George Musitano S2c New York, NY
Franklin R. Navaro Ensign Lt(jg)
Richard C. Newcomb Lt Comdr.
Donald O'Keefe S1c Boston, MA
Steven Onda S2c Newark, NJ
Harry Alfred Osberg S1c(Y) Kalamazoo, MI
Charles Joseph Pabst MM3c Newark, NJ
Robert Franklin Pabst F1c(MM) Newark, NJ
Austin Jerry Page S1c Boston, MA
John Patrick F2c Greensburg, PA

Robert Franklin Payne, Sr. CBM(AA) Jacksonville, FL
John Murphy Pearson M1c Washington, DC
Anthony John Petti S2c Baltimore, MD
William Percy Pettry S2c Huntington, WV
Ernest Joseph Pheiffer WT3c Newark, NJ
John Henry Phillips, Jr. CM2c Raleigh, NC
Joseph Polkowski S2c Newark, NJ
George James Porter S2c Lowell, MA
Victor J. Pra-Sisto Lt(jg)
Warren C. Quinn S1c Raleigh, NC
Edmund Julian Rabitski MM3c Boston, MA
William Hector Rankin CMM(AA) Tampa, FL
Leon Rezet WT3c Philadelphia, PA
James Whitcomb Riley CTM(AA) New York, NY
William Andrew Roddy S2c Boston, MA, MIA
James Alexander Rouse SM2c, KIA
Alfred Daniel Roy F1c(MM) Boston, MA
Wayne Carlyle Salls S1c Jacksonville, FL
Wayne Sanders SC2c Birmingham, AL
Charles E. Sapp S2c S1c
George Page Sark S2c Columbus, OH
William James Scott S2c Boston, MA
David Lewis Sellmann WT3c Newark, NJ
Thomas Silas, Jr. MM1c East Boston, MA
Charles Silverstein S2c(RdM) Philadelphia, PA
James Simmons, Jr StM1c Okla. City, OK, MIA
Robert Perion Sitzlar S2c Chattanooga, TN
Amos Wilbur Smith S2c Columbus, OH
Charles Thomas Smith MM2c New Haven, CT
Jack Chauncey Smith RdM3c Pittsburgh, PA
Raymond Lee Sokolovske S1c Cox DesMoines, IO
John Spears, Jr. StM2c Columbia, SC
Anderson C. Spencer, Jr StM2c Little Rock, Ark.
David Spivack S2c(RdM) New York, NY
Ernest Wade Stapleton S2c Huntington, WV
Robert Andrew Streets S2c Clarksburg, WV
Jessie Calvin Strong StM2c Chicago, IL, MIA
Ralph Vern Taylor S2c Columbus, OH
Junior Beecher Trail F1c Charleston, WV
Raymond Philip Wallace SoM3c Hartford, CT
James Edward Ware S1c Spartanburg, SC

Park Albert Warner F1c(MM) Pittsburgh, PA
Tony John Virag S2c New York, NY
Robert Glenn Watkins BM1c Richmond, VA
S. Will Welch SoM3c Toledo, OH
William Thomas Wenke S1c Buffalo, NY
Joseph Howard West F1c(MM) Richmond, VA
Robert Wetzel F1c
Thomas Weisner Williams Cox Balto, MD, KIA
Robert Loring Wilson SoM3c Chicago, IL
Donald Leroy Winterrowd SC3c Indianapolis, IN
Eugene R. Yeager Ensign
Virgil Francis Young Ck3c Macon GA

Men who served on the *Barr* as an APD only:

Cyrus B. Aldinger Lt.
Reuben Leslie Allendorf EM1c Indianapolis, IN
Loyd Ashley S2c
Edward L. Bartlett Ensign
Jesse Clifford Blackmon WT2c(T) Nashville, TN
Henry Julian Bonnabel CBM(PA)
Kenneth Wesley Boyd S1c
Sidney Johnston Braxton MoMM3c
Ralph Edward Brown RM2c Boston, MA
Carl Bryson, Jr. S1c
Joseph Stanley Buller Ensign
Jerry Calemmo F1c(EM) New York, NY
Joe Bailey Callahan S1c
Joseph Canterini MM3c (T) Wilkes-Barre, PA
Rodger Melvin Coffman M3c M2c(T)
Ezekiel Gidon Copenhaver EM3c(T)
Samuel Costanzo, Jr. EM3c New York, NY
James Edward Cunningham S1c Little Rock, AR
Donald Howard Dahman GM3c(T)
John William Davidson, S1c
Robert Melvin Davidson EM2c
Curtis Eugene Davis F1c Richmond, VA
Jesse Odell Davis S1c Birmingham, AL
Vernard Franklin Davis S2c Indianapolis, IN
George Newton Decker S2c Wilkes-Barre, PA
John William DeMoss Bkr3c(T) Sheridan, AR

James Anthony DeSanto EM2c
Marion Douglas Dumas SF1c
Donald Vernon Erickson MMS3c Minneapolis, MN
Julius Estes S1c
Guy Eldridge Farley RM3c
Irving Feuer F1c New York, NY
Charles P. Filpazzo BM2c
John Michael Flannery Y1c Albany, NY
Floyd Titus Fogle S1c
Joseph James Fontano MM3c New York, NY
John Frampton Freeman CCM(AA) Birmingham, AL
Willie Gadlin StM1c(T)
John Angelese Gage EM3c(T) Boston, MA
Wilfer Walter Gengler S2c
Lowell Charles Gerard F1c
George Elken Gerlach F1c
Matthew Gerlach, Jr. F1c
Romie Gene Gillis F1c MM3c
William Russell Gladhill QM3c(T)
Thurl Edward Graham F1c
James Benjamin Grenga Y1c Macon, GA
Lester Eugene Griffin, Jr. RdM1c Chattanooga, TN
Orville Laverne Haiss S1c
Talmadge Franklin Grubbs S1c
Burton Wilbur Haglan FC(O)2c
Francis Patrick Hallisey CMM Philadelphia, PA
Glenn Peter Hansford MM3c Chicago, IL
Emmett O. Hanson S2c
Wilfred Pearsall Hasbrouk F1c New York, NY
Sonny Arnitt Hatfield FC1c Richmond, VA
Louis Claran Haynie, Jr. EM3c
Morris Eugene Heaton RM3c(T)
Harold Sheldon Hemmingson EM3c
Clarence Robert Herechski S2c
Darrell Gordon Hohlt CRM
Edward Floyd Holley S1c
Thomas Francis Houghton EM2c
John W. Hubenthal Ensign Lt.(jg)
Gordon F. Huber Ensign
William Earle Humphrey F1c Detroit, MI
Donald Clayton Humphreys F1c

James Rees Jarvis S1c
James William Johnson, Sr. F2c F1c
John Francis Johnson GM3c Philadelphia, PA
Philip Paul Jones Lt.
George M. Joseph F1c Philadelphia, PA
Walter Neavin Jowers WT3c Jacksonville, FL
Thomas F. Kaiser Lt(jg)
Jack Karp SSM(L)3c New York, NY
Leo Herbert Kerchner RM3c
Charles Richard Keys Ensign Lt.(jg), E.O., C.O.
Edward Lee Kiger S2c
Ira Harless Killgore S1c Anniston, AL
Milford F. Kostman Ensign
George Ellis Lawrence Ck3c
Norman LeMere MM3c Providence, RI
Emile Arthur Levesque F1c Boston, MA
Walter Thomas Linley MM2c Detroit, MI
Garrison Daniel Loudermilk F1c Atlanta, GA
Casmer Edward Majka S1c
James Vincent Malandra F1c Philadelphia, PA
Walter Arthur Marsch CRTChicago, IL
LeRoy Martin SoM2c
Donald Pray Mavro S1c Boston, MA
Robert Eugene Mawyer CBM
Bellfield McCormich S1c
Donald C. McKinlay Lt
Wallace Frederick Mellum EM1c Minneapolis, MN
Lee Orvin Moyer S1c
Edward Paul Muha F1c New Haven, CT
Richard Leroyd Nichols EM3c(T) New Haven, CT
Timothy Patrick Joseph Nolan EM3c New York, NY
William Kulp O'Brien CM3c Philadelphia, PA
James Lee Odell F1c Chattanooga, TN
William Joseph O'Donnell QM3c San Francisco, CA
Charles Francis O'Neill EM2c Boston, MA
Joseph Palozzi, Jr. S1c Akron, OH
Leonard Edward Parise CSK
Preston A. Peak Ensign
John Pennington, Jr. FC3c Baltimore, MD
Donald Irving Peoples SK3c
David Neely Peterman S1c

William Darrell Phelps RM2c Erie, PA
Charles Hiram Phillips WT2c Cleveland, OH
Warren Thomas Pierce SoM3c
Melvin Lee Ray S1c
William Redmond SM3c New York, NY
Gilbert Timothy Regan RdM3c New Haven, CT
John J. Reilly, Ensign
John Allen Reph, Jr. EM2c Philadelphia, PA
Hollis William Rhodus MM3c San Francisco, CA
Victor Philip Rislow S2c Abingdon, VA
Gottlieb Reinhold Roessler S1c
George M Rowan Lt, E.O., C.O.
William Cornelius Sargent S1c Spartanburg, SC
Ivan Wayne Satterthwaite F1c (MoMM)
John George Scerbak S1c
Edward Lee Schappert S1c Wilkes-Barre, PA
George Schley, Jr. S1c Harrisburg, PA
Edward Joseph Schueller MMS3c Des Moines, IO
Virgil Huber Schulte F1c
Robert Earl Schultz EM3c
Claude David Seeley, Jr. GM3c Wilkes-Barre, PA
Ralph Elmer Shireman SC1c
Alexander John Shvedoff F1c New York, NY
Roy Melvin Skipton, MoMM3c
Clifton Jerome Skjonsby MM3c
Bernard Skolnick QM2c
Richard John Skovira RM3c
Lee William Sledd RdM3c Richmond, VA
Bernard Slotkin F1c New York, NY
Daniel Gerald Smale S1c Philadelphia, PA
Charles Smith, Jr. S1c Philadelphia, PA
Joseph Linden Smith RdM3c Columbia, SC
Keith Hamilton Smith S2c Roanoke, VA
Robert Thomas Smith S1c Wilkes-Barre, PA
Roy Clifton Smith S2c
Harry Garner Sonntag WT3c(T) Philadelphia, PA
Raymond Thomas Stefancin S1c
William Carl Stein Y2c
Chester Stanley Stepkovitch S1c Wilkes-Barre, PA
James Francis Stillwell GM2c
Frank Elmer Strmiska MoMM3c New Haven, CT

Eugene E. Swearingen Ensign
Robert John Sweatt PhM2c
Royce Talbert CGM
Charles Desota Tucker Sc3c Jacksonville, FL
Raymond James Updegraff MM3cLos Angeles, CA
Guy Walker ST3c
Frank Whaley Ensign, C.O. for Decommissioning, 7/12/46
Ned Lewis White Y2c
Maurice William Wilkins S1c Baltimore, MD
Jesse Aubry Williams S1c Richmond, VA
Louie Burns Wilson MM3c(T) New York, NY
Zenon Casimir Wolan EM2c New York, NY

Men who served on the *Barr* as a DE and an APD:

William Rufus Armstrong QM1c Hartford, CT
Jack Baker Cox Raleigh, NC
Pedro Baccay Balawag CCk Norfolk,VA
James Hughel Barnett CWT Birmingham, AL
Jack William Borgeld SoM3c St. Louis, MO
Berthol Adrian Bowman RM2c Springfield, IL
Alton Ilmer Brown S1c Raleigh, NC
George Budak SM2c Cleveland, OH
Charles Thomas Burgess RM2c St.Louis, MO
Charles Henry Burnett GM1c Kalamazoo, MI
William Edward Card MM1c New Haven, CT
Frank Celestin StM2c
Porter Tirrill Dickie Lt. Comdr., C.O. (7/1/44 to 9/4/45)
James Robert Dougherty B1c Philadelphia, PA
John Joseph Ferraro SC3c Buffalo, NY
Robert Eugene Gallant BM1c Boston, MA
Max Glaser Y2c Boston, MA
Milton Goldman EM1c NY, NY
William Harold Gordon Lt. Cdr., C.O.(9/4/45 to 11/22/45)
Preston Hiatt (Pete) Groppenbacher Cox
George John Harobin EM2c Allentown, PA
Garvey Alex Haynes CSK Spartanburg, SC
John Wesley Howk BM2c Kansas City, MO
Golding Theodore Huber CPhM Fargo, ND
Paul Loren Kennedy RdM2c Cleveland, OH
Charles Kowers CEM

Henry Peter Krawiec SM2c Hartford, CT
Charles Casimir Kwiatkowski CEM Chicago, IL
Christian Henry Lippert SoM1c Newark, NJ
Robert Little Cox Cincinnati, OH
James Robert Mack WT3c Wilkes-Barre, PA
Richard Peter Madanjian EM1c Boston, MA
Armand Joseph Marion MM1c Albany, NY
John J. McEwen, Jr. Ensign Lt.
James Anthony McMahon MaM3c New York, NY
Raymond Leonard Meadors SC2c Cincinnatti, OH
James Robert Meehan S1c Boston, MA
Elwood Walter Michaelis RM2c Chicago, IL
William Elwood Overstreet SC3c Jackson, AL
Cornelius Joseph Owens MM1c Camden, NJ
Noman Ollie Pearce MM2c Atlanta, GA
Grant Cole Perry (A) CWT Chicago, IL
Clarence Irving Priest, Jr. S1c Boston, MA
Edwin Walter Prus Sk2c Indianapolis, IN
Joseph Edward Purgatorio GM1c Phila., PA
Glenn Sam Richardson BM2cRaleigh, NC
Chester Roberts SF1c Louisville, KY
Edward Perry Romer, Jr. MMS1c
Erik Leonard Rosengren SM1c NY,NY
Paul Calvin Royar WT2c New York, NY
Stephen Rushalk Bkr1c NY, NY
Thomas Francis Ryan CQM NY, NY
Donald Joseph Shannon FC2c Los Angeles, CA
Russell McKenney Shea Cox
John Andrew Simon RdM2c Cleveland, OH
Dan Chandler Simpson CMM Los Angeles, CA
Francis John Skotko GM2c NY, NY
Edward John Sliwinski CRM Miami, FL
Glen Dale Smeltzer CCS Long Beach, CA
Andrew Charles Soucy WT2c Lowell, MA
Douglas George Stephen RdM2c Chattanooga, TN
William Edward Storms GM3c Albany, NY
Robert Samuel Stout SF3c Chattanooga, TN
Harold Arthur Thomas CCS St. Louis, MO
John Leroy Thompson WT2c Erie, PA
John Wesley Thornburg S1c Atlanta, GA
Harold French Toler S1c Huntington, WV

Lawrence Jacob Unzicker Lt.
Manuel Verissimo, Jr. WT1c Boston, MA
James Anthony Vertes MM2c Newark, NJ
Elton Frank Watkins BM2c Raleigh, NC
Frank Lewis Whitman, Jr. CY New Haven, CT
Odis T. Williams StM1c
Edward Chester Wilson S1c New York, NY
John Wolthers SoM3c New York, NY
Michael Yarenbinsky SoM3c New York, NY
Julian Gregory Zeloski CMM Boston, MA

APPENDIX C

HISTORY OF UNDERWATER DEMOLITION TEAM #13

(The following history of UDT #13 was written by Marvin Cooper and is included here with his permission.)

UNDERWATER DEMOLITION TEAM THIRTEEN
THE "BLACK CAT TEAM"

In late June of 1944, Naval Combat Demolition's Class Seven began its training at the Naval Amphibious Training Base at Fort Pierce, Florida. Class Seven was the "mother of all classes", and from its ranks the great Underwater Demolition Teams 11, 12, 13 and 15 were later formed. Class Seven began its training with personnel from many sources which included some residual base personnel and men left over from other classes (mostly Seabees), men from other amphibious bases, men from the fleet, men out of service schools, and men right out of boot camp. The officers were all from similar backgrounds. There was about one officer for every five enlisted men. This provided the 1 to 5 ratio needed for 6 man rubber boat crews of Naval Combat Demolition Units (NCDU). The class consisted of 360 men, more or less, equivalent to about 60 rubber boat crews.

The training period for Class Seven was about six weeks of night and day "commando" type training for which Fort Pierce was noted. The class started with "Hellweek" and ended with "Payoff Week", and during this training period, its personnel had learned the "asics" of demolition methods and all the "boys" were now men called "Demolitionairs" or "Demos".

In early August, the entire class was granted a 10 day leave plus travel time. Returning from leave during the last week in August, the Demolition Units had little to do except to continue physical training informally arranged by their officers and the training staff. In early September, seventeen crews left the Class and moved to the west coast by troop train. Those seventeen NCDU crews later became Underwater Demolition Team Fifteen.

During the hot muggy month of September, the remaining crews fought the sandflies, mosquitoes, and the threat of one hurricane. The Demolition Area was separated from the beach by the Navy Scouts and Raiders Area, and with more free time came more liberties, and fights between the Demolition people and the Scouts and Raiders were common events in the bars of downtown Fort Pierce. Some of the guys took weekend excursions to West Palm Beach or Miami.

September was not all liberty and play for the "Demos". They went down to Camp Murphy for rifle range practice and had a session of gunnery practice off the beach of South Island. A Navy plane went into the ocean off North Island, and the crews swam from rubber boats trying to locate the wreckage, but their efforts failed and the plane was never found. One day was spent deepening the inlet to Stuart, Florida near Jensen Beach. The channel was deepened by well placed explosive charges. Another day was spent practicing diving with deep sea suits in the Atlantic Ocean.

September passed but Class 7 was not destined to spend the war years in Florida. On October 3, following the long awaited orders, the remaining crews of Class 7 boarded a troop train at Fort Pierce and began the long 3000 mile journey to the San Francisco Bay area in California. About 250 men and officers started a journey across the country that must have set a new record for slowness since the days of the 19th Century wagon trains.

Seven long days and nights the troop train inched northward and then westward in a stop and go fashion. It pulled on to sidings letting express trains, passenger trains, freight trains, and cattle trains have the right of way. Jacksonville and Birmingham were passed the first couple of days. On the third afternoon the train lumbered through the rail yards of St. Louis. The St. Louis Browns were playing the St. Louis Cardinals in the 1944 World Series, and many of the Demos believed they should have had a layover for a chance to see a World Series game. Of course, that did not happen, and the train edged along the Missouri River towards Kansas City.

Dodge City, Kansas furnished a place for a short stop. There were no Matt Dillon gunfights, but the crews had breakfast off the train at one of Fred Harvey's famous diners. Next the train moved through a prairie dog "town" in eastern Colorado, and the Demos viewed the prairie dogs standing at attention beside their burrows. The dining car had been pulled from the train someplace in Missouri, and that night, dinner was in Denver at another Harvey's restaurant.

From Denver to Cheyenne, the train crept through the night until it met the Union Pacific railroad line heading west towards Utah. A diner was again added to the train. At Ogden, there was a long stop, and the crews were all ordered to disembark for some long needed calisthenics. That is, all except one Demo. He had somehow acquired a bottle early in the journey, became slightly inebriated, was put on report, and confined to the train. That young man would later be one of the stalwart men of UDT 13.

Westward, skirting the fringes of the Great Salt Lake, into Nevada, and over the steep slopes of Donner Pass in California, the train approached its destination. On the morning of the seventh day of travel, October 10, seabags and Demos poured off the train at Camp Shoemaker, California. The men were very hungry, but the messhalls were closed, and they were told they would have to wait for the noon meal. The officers went to bat for the men, and after conferring, pulling rank and arm-twisting with the base officers, food was prepared for everyone.

The stay in the "Bay Area" was short. A short liberty in Oakland and San Francisco was granted from Shoemaker. Then the men were moved to Treasure Island in the Bay where they were given a multitude of shots for the hazards facing them in the south Pacific. No inoculations were given to protect them from the greatest danger they would face, the Japanese gunners and mortar launchers.

On October 14, 1944 the crews boarded the USS General Patrick (APA) and sailed out of the San Francisco Bay under the Golden Gate Bridge into the broad Pacific. Men wondered when they would return, and speculations like "a Frisco dive in forty-five" and "the Golden Gate in forty-eight" were some opinions expressed.

The General Patrick was a nearly new Kaiser built "liberty ship" that seemed to have a characteristic to leak water in heavy seas. By the following morning, the ship was moving through heavy swells west of San Francisco, and many Demos developed their "sea legs" during the next few days. Many suffered from sea-sickness before the ship moved into more placid waters as it approached the Hawaiian Islands.

On the 19th of October, the General Patrick entered Pearl Harbor in Oahu, Territory of Hawaii. The men could see the super-structure of the Arizona protruding from the water, and this was about the only evidence of the infamous bombing raid of December 7, 1941 that could be seen in the harbor area. The crews were moved aboard an LCI which was to move them to the Naval Underwater Demolition Training and Experimental Base on the island of Maui a hundred or so miles to the south and east.

Leaving Pearl Harbor, the LCI moved south and east skirting the southern shores of Molokai, and soon the mountains of west Maui appeared on the eastern horizon. Turning more towards the south it passed the town of Lahaina, and then almost due east 10,000 foot Haleakala loomed skyward. The Underwater Demolition Base was located at the foot of Mt. Haleakala about 10 miles or more south of Kahulai, Maui's main seaport.

The crews left the LCI, mustered, and were assigned tent quarters in what was called the Maui "dust bowl". To the north of the tent area some "smelly" toilets were located, and south of the tent area some luxurious open cold showers were convenient to the area. To the west towards the beach, an outdoor theatre, laundry facilities, administration offices, officers' quarters, messhall, and other facilities were located. There was no electricity provided in the "dust bowl", but later it was provided after the Demos dug some of the holes for the poles.

This was where Teams 11, 12 and 13 were organized from the Fort Pierce boat crews. Generally, the enlisted men were assigned to the same team that their crew officer was assigned, but in some cases crew members were moved into different teams, and this might have been a matter of creating equal numbers for the three teams. Eventually the three teams received men from Team Able, an earlier team that had been in combat in the Solomons, and had their ship sunk just before the invasion of Pelelui.

Lieutenant Commander Vincent Moranz became Team 13's commanding officer and Ensign Moore was the Executive Officer. Moore was later replaced by Lieutenant Donald Walker as Executive Officer. Lieutenant Walker was an officer from the Team Able group. Team 13 had several Team Able men in their ranks.

The six man crew system was dropped and replaced by a five platoon system, four operational platoons and one headquarters platoon. The four operational platoons were labeled Able, Baker, Charley and Dog (A, B, C and D) and each platoon was an LCPR boat crew consisting of 2 platoon officers, a coxswain, 2 gunners, a radioman, a machinist, and about 10 or 12 swimmers. All members of the crew were trained as UDT swimmers and demolition specialists, and there were overlapping and changing assignments. The headquarters platoon consisted of specialists including the Team pharmacist mate, yeoman, photographer, operations officer, and supply officer. This was the general organizational structure of the Underwater Demolition Teams of the Pacific Fleet.

The change in organizational structure from the NCDU's of Fort Pierce was a no more radical change than the change in the training program at Maui. Swimming became paramount in the training program along with the dropping and retrieving of swimmers at high speeds from rubber boats attached to the fast LCPR's. Swim fins and face masks were added equipment. Team 13 trained through most of the months of November and December, and everyone had experiences to remember like the day and night reconnaissance missions, day and night demolition missions, and the high jumps from the base pier with no parachute. The extensive physical training only increased the camaraderie and organizational pride among the men. The competition with the other teams - Teams 11 and 12 - was also a factor in developing "team spirit".

During December, Team 11 had what every Demolition man fears. They had an accident with explosives on a night demolition training mission. A boat crew failed to leave the target beach at the scheduled time, and they were there when the beach exploded. Fortunately, it was only a dry run using primacord, but still an officer lost a leg and several men were wounded. The team was demoralized and when it was time to move to the western Pacific, Team 11 was left in Maui to recuperate. The accident was also dispiriting to the men of Teams 12 and 13 because many men in Team 11 were friends from the Florida training period.

On January 3, 1945, Team 13 boarded the USS Barr (APD39) at Maui. Their training had been completed in late December, and they were heading west. The Assault Personnel Destroyer Barr, converted from a destroyer escort, was UDT 13's transport into combat. Loaded with many tons of tetrytol, hundreds of rolls of primacord, fuses, fuse igniters, 45 caliber handguns, Thompson submachine guns, Navy knives, dive masks, swimfins, rubber boats, and the many other items needed for demolition operations, the team headed for the Caroline Islands. The Barr was part of the screen force for a convoy of APA's. With the Barr on the right flank, the USS Bates on the left, and the battleship USS Nevada as flag, the convoy proceeded across the central Pacific. On the Bates (APD47) was Team 13's sister team, UDT 12.

The convoy moved close by the Japanese held island of Truk, and all hands were warned to be prepared for possible Japanese air patrols. In late January, they reached Ulithi, the large atoll anchorage which UDT 10 and Marine assault troops had taken from Japanese forces a few months earlier. This was the staging area for the assault on Iwo Jima in the Volcano Islands about 750 miles from Tokyo, Japan.

Teams 12 and 13 were just comfortably anchored down in the calm waters of Ulithi's inner lagoon, and who should appear but their old buddies in UDT 15. Team 15 had left Fort Pierce a month earlier, trained quickly at Maui and had helped open the beaches at Lingayen Gulf on the Philippine island of Luzon. With Team 15 was Team 14, one of the fleet teams that had not trained at Fort Pierce.

From Team 15, Team 14 and other sources came the word about the "Divine Wind" or kamikaze planes, and to the Navy this meant suicide planes. The Japanese were training young men to fly fighter type planes one way - to take off but never to land. Loaded with a bomb and plenty of gasoline they crashed into many ships in the American forces during the invasion of Luzon. The war had taken an unexpected turn. It was decided that to help face the problem of the suicide planes fire power on the Barr would be increased by adding several fifty caliber machine guns on the fantail of the ship.

Raymond Le Blanc, a Team 13 member and one of those who had come from Team Able, was one of the team members who volunteered to help build the gun mounts. Ray was a welder, and while welding over the side on a repair patch, a wave from a passing vessel splashed upon him and his welding equipment. Ray fell into the water, and apparently stunned or already dead, drifted under the ship. Teammates immediately jumped into the water to try to save him, but when he was finally pulled from the water, it was from the opposite side of the ship. Ray either died from electrocution or drowning. Ceremonies were held on the Barr and Ray was temporarily buried in a small military cemetery on the island of Asor, one of the many islands of the Ulithi atoll.

The accidental death of Ray Le Blanc, who was well liked by his new teammates as well as those from Team Able who had known him much longer, brought the realities of the war to the entire Team as they pondered the shores of Iwo Jima. In a way, the waters of Ulithi were a playground for the swimmers of UDT 13. They dived from the fantail of the Barr into 85 degree water; they took rubber boats to the edge of the eastern ring of islands in a search for shells and a possible pearl; and most important with these activities they were staying in physical shape for what they would face in a few weeks.

Team 13 was briefed on their assignment at Iwo Jima, and they made a practice swimming reconnaissance from the open ocean into the beaches of the eastern islands of Ulithi.

On February 10, Teams 12, 13, 14 and 15, on their respective APD's, left Ulithi with the bombardment force for the invasion of Iwo Jima. Team 11 would have been with them except for the training accident in Maui a couple of months before. Six days later on February 16, they arrived off the island of Iwo Jima. The weather was cool, partly cloudy, and gloomy. The island looked ominous. To the south rose Mt. Suribachi a thousand or so feet, to the north was a long ridge with a lower elevation. Six miles long and one to three miles wide, Iwo even before the start of the battle looked devastated. It had been bombed daily for sixty consecutive days by U.S. Army Air Corps bombers stationed at Saipan, and yet on that very day 20,000 Japanese troops were living in the caves and pillboxes which ringed the island.

Underwater Demolition Team Thirteen drew the first assignment. On the north end of Iwo, a cluster of rocks protruded from the water a few hundred yards from the mainland. Strangely enough, they even had a name and were called Higashi Iwo. UDT 13's assignment was to put a navigational light emplacement in the rocks to warn the ships of the invasion fleet of their presence in the darkness of night. On the afternoon of February 16, the team sent an LCPR from the Barr carrying a rubber boat with a crew to mount the light in place. The Japanese didn't quite approve and mortar fire started falling in the area of the LCPR and the rubber boat. The Japanese also opened up with shell fire of 5 inch or above on the Barr. The Barr moved rapidly towards the island and closer to the LCPR with its 5 inch gun blazing at the spotted location of enemy fire. Behind the Barr the USS Pensacola plastered the north end of the island with its full battery of 8 inch guns. The rubber boat crew bravely moved into the surf beaten rocks and calmly placed the navigational light in its designated location. Team 13 had gone to war.

The Barr had a nightly assignment of cruising the "picket lines", which was a screen of ships cruising to form a radar and sonar line to keep enemy submarines and aircraft from entering the U.S. fleet area. This would be especially important when the transports and supply ships arrived on the day of the invasion. The Barr started this assignment on the night of the 16th, and the night was uneventful.

February 17th, 1945, D-2, was designated the day for the Underwater Demolition Teams to "open" the beaches of Iwo Jima. Although the east beaches were the expected invasion beaches, the west beaches were also to be reconnoitered, and if better suited for the landing they would be used. The four teams would send swimmers into both the east and west beaches. The morning operation would be the east beaches followed by the afternoon reconnaissance on the west beaches.

On the morning of the 17th, Team 13 was assigned Green Beach #1 which was the southern section of the east beaches. Team 13 was to swim in under the near shadow of Mt. Suribachi which towered to the swimmers' immediate left. It appeared to be the most dangerous beach of the entire east side. The only consolation was that Team 13 was to send in 10 swimmers and the other teams were to use 20 swimmers, but to those 10 swimmers the giant "beehive" of a mountain swarming with machine gunners and mortar launchers was little consolation.

The fire support for the Underwater Demolition Teams was awesome. Battleships, cruisers, and destroyers were positioned to rain a withering fire upon the eastern slope of the small island. In close were twelve LCIG gunboats which would pour a continuous flow of rocket fire on the enemy gun positions. Through experience in previous operations the Navy had learned that to have successful daylight reconnaissance missions into heavily fortified beaches this fire support was necessary.

Team 13 sent two LCPR's from the Barr. One with the swimmers aboard and the other as a standby crew to be used only if needed. The LCPR's moved inside the line of LCIG gunboats and started to receive fire from shore. With throttles wide open they turned and moved parallel to the beach dropping the swimmers one by one. Mortar fire and machine gun fire rained down over and around all the reconnaissance boats until they moved out of range beyond the line of LCIG's. So far no boats were hit and there were no casualties.

Things were different on the LCIG line. The Japanese poured everything they had from 8 inchers on down at the 12 LCIG gunboats. Eleven of the 12 were hit and disabled by gunfire, one was sunk, and many crewmen were killed and wounded. Some of the casualties were UDT people who were acting as spotters on the ships. In less than a half hour, the flotilla of gunboats were completely out of the fray. They were too badly mauled to continue their support. This was the worst disaster for their group during the Pacific war.

While the gunboats were being annihilated, Team 13 swimmers swam into their assigned beach braving mortar, machine gun and rifle fire, and very frigid water. Their last swim had been at Ulithi in 85 degree water, but at Iwo it was reported as low as 60 degrees. Their combat uniform was bathing trunks, face mask, swim shoes and fins, webbed belt, knife, mine detonators and a plastic plate to record information. The only protection from cold was a layer of grease over their near naked bodies applied before they left the Barr. The swimmers made their reconnaissance in less than an hour, returned to the swimmer pick up line, and were retrieved by the LCPR in a high speed run. UDT 13's Green Beach #1 was clear of mines and obstacles, and was judged very suitable for landing craft entry.

In the afternoon of the same day, the fire power support group moved to the west side of the island, but they were minus the LCIG gunboats, which the UDT men had expected to give them the badly needed close-in fire support. Air support was added to the plan for the west beaches, and it was hoped that the planes could replace the fire power lost when the gunboats were forced out of the plan. The planes were to lay down heavy smoke screens over the terrain inside the surf line.

Team 13's beach was once again the southern most beach right under the north slope of Mt. Suribachi, and it was coded Purple Beach #1. Without the LCIG's, the men feared the worst. Team 13 once again sent in 10 swimmers. The air temperature was still cold, and the water was no warmer. The LCIG's were under fire while dropping the swimmers, and the swimmers received heavy machine gun and some mortar fire. The Navy planes covered the beach from surf to dune line with a steady machine gun and rocket fire, moving up the dunes as the swimmers approached the shore. The swimmers swam just outside the surf and moved parallel to the beach for about fifty yards per swimmer. The beach was clear of obstacles, steep sloped, and appeared suitable for all types of landing craft. Occasional rifle or machine gun bullets sprayed around them, and they swam under the water as much as possible. They gathered and logged the information on their slates and swam seaward. The LCPR's came in to the swimmer pickup area to make their retrieval pass. This part of the mission did not work as planned. Some swimmers had cramps from the cold water, the seas were high, some swimmers were not in line, and there seemed some confusion in location of the pickup area. At least one Team 13 swimmer was picked up by a Team 12 LCPR, and a Team 15 LCPR had to go close to the beach to retrieve two swimmers. Team 12 had one missing swimmer that was never found.

After the two reconnaissance operations, the swimmers had a small shot of brandy and reported their findings. The Barr moved out to sea and resumed their assigned picket line position.

Team 13 was called back into action the next day, February 18. Their light on Higashi Iwo had been shot out by the "friendly" Japanese. Naturally Team 13 was called to reinstall the light, and once again under fire, a boat crew paddled to the rock and replaced the light.

On the night of February 18, Team 13 on the Barr was cruising the picket line. Team 15 was on the USS Blessman (APD48) several miles away and was experiencing the same duty. The ships were cruising condition green meaning that their radar and sonar were receiving no information. On the Blessman, UDT men and ship's crew personnel were playing cards and writing letters. All had the feeling that their tough assignment was behind them. A two engined Japanese bomber flying low under the radar beams dropped a bomb which landed directly on the mess hall. Team 15 had eighteen men killed and twenty-three wounded. Nearly half of the team were casualties. Many of those killed and wounded were friends of men of UDT 13.

February 19, 1945 was D-Day, and Team 13 men directed the first wave of landing craft into Green Beach #1. The other teams did likewise, and the Marines' struggle for Iwo Jima began.

The post assault operations of UDT 13 were numerous. The Barr had about 40 tons of tetrytol aboard, and Team members transported many of those tons to the beach for the Marines to use. The Team worked on clearing the beach and water approaches of disabled boats and landing craft. A special reconnaissance of Mt. Suribachi's south face was made a few days after the initial invasion.

On February 28, after 12 days of pre-assault and post-assault missions, UDT 13 on the good ship Barr left Iwo Jima and headed for Guam. On March 7, the Barr anchored off Guam.

Four days were spent resting and recuperating at Guam. In a suitable channel, Team members played an amateur water polo type game. The water was warm and the cold thoughts and water of Iwo Jima were behind them. A beach party was arranged, and loads of warm beer were served. Celebration was in order and Team 13 Demos lived it up. The supply officer, always searching for bargains, made a foray on the beach for needed supplies.

Next stop was back to Ulithi, that big pond in the Carolines. Team 13 was given a few days "rest and recreation" on the small island of Asor. The R & R was mostly letter writing, swimming, playing cards, and watching an occasional movie in the open air theater.

[Ed. Note: Here Cooper had mentioned that the Barr *was painted "fleet gray" when they returned to the ship, but then struck it out, saying that others had since convinced him this was not correct; however, two other diaries, those of Verissimo and Wolan, both of which were written contemporaneously, say that the* Barr *was painted gray during this period. The importance of this is that the* Barr *had been painted splashes of yellow and green, more for tropical warfare, and may have been painted gray for less visibility by enemy planes on the seas.]*

Like it or not the time had come for Team 13 to move west, and other beaches were awaiting them. On the 20th of March, Team 13 left Ulithi with a bombardment task force bound for the Ryukyu Islands and specifically Okinawa. This task force was the advance group and with Team 13 were Teams 12, 14 and 19. Team 19 had recently arrived from Maui, and this would be their first combat experience. While this advance bombardment group was moving towards the Okinawa area, the larger main group was organizing in the Philippines. Teams 4, 7, 11, 16, 17 and 21 were scheduled to arrive in the Okinawa area later with that task force.

During the night of the 23rd or the morning of the 24th, the advance group moved into the Okinawa area. With all hands at battle stations, Team 13 men on the Barr could see the lights of towns and cities on Okinawa. A battleship and a couple of cruisers sent a few rounds of big ones into the island, and the lights rapidly disappeared. The battle for Okinawa had begun.

Team 13's assignment with the advance force was to open beaches in two groups of islands - Kerama Rhetto and Keisa Shima. Kerama Rhetto Islands were a group of many islands almost enclosing a body of water several miles long and a mile or two wide. The Navy wanted Kerama Rhetto for a safe anchorage for supply ships and transports. The ships would be safe from enemy submarines, suicide boats, and would have better protection from the "Divine Wind' attacks coming from the north.

The largest island in the group was Tokashika Shima, and Team 13 was picked to reconnoiter its beaches. On the morning of March 25, the Team's platoons moved their LCPR's into position to drop their swimmers. The designated beaches were located in a broad inlet with tree covered hills on both sides. The operation went like clockwork. Enemy fire was light, and some swimmers reported none. The swimmers swam to the surf, found no mines or obstacles, but reported many coral heads. Some were less than three feet from the surface. During briefings, there was some disagreement whether the coral would affect landing craft. By using the tides and amtracs, a demolition operation was avoided. The following morning Team 13 men led the assault troops into the shores of Tokashika Shima.

Some swimmers of Team 13 may have been true pioneers in the use of "wet uits". The water was so cold that they wore old-fashioned long underwear while making their mile long swim, and they claimed to be much warmer than those who relied on the coating of axle grease.

The Kerama Rhetto Islands were fifteen to twenty miles off the southwest coast of Okinawa, and by the 27th or the 28th of March they were controlled by U.S. forces. Keisa Shima was much closer to the big island, and at one point Keisa Shima was separated from Okinawa by a narrow straight only one and one-half miles wide. Keisa Shima had a lower profile with less tree covering than Tokashika Shima, and in some places it looked like an overgrown sandbar. UDT 13's assignment was to blast underwater coral to form a channel for the U.S. Army. The Army's plan was to set up batteries of 155 mm guns on the island. Their range not only included some of the planned invasion beaches but also included the city of Naha.

For three days, Team 13 worked in the cold water off Keisa Shima practically under the nose of the Japanese, and well within range of some of their artillery. Beginning the operation on the 27th of March, the Team hand-placed tetrytol satchel charges around giant coral heads, and with their primacord leads and trunk lines they cut the channel shoreward. The Japanese appeared not to care, and no enemy resistance was encountered. It seems some Navy or Marine flyers did care, because while the Demos were working in the water a couple of planes swept over the hill from shoreward, dropped some bombs, strafed the swimmers with machine gun fire, and then flew seaward. Radios hummed, rubber boats and ponchos were cleared from motor boxes to expose U.S. identification. There were no casualties, and it was supposed that the fliers had mistaken the UDT swimmers for Japanese suicide swimmers.

On the afternoon of March 29, Team 13 had completed the channel and had it properly marked with buoys. In those three days, the swimmers had placed over 27 tons of tetrytol in their underwater charges.

Three days later was Love Day, April Fool's Day, Easter Sunday and the day the U.S. Army and Marine Corps invaded Okinawa. Love Day was the code name for the invasion date. Team 13 had no assignment on Love Day, and the Barr cruised the picket lines taking part in the battle against the Japanese suicide planes.

On April 3, 1945, Team 13 received orders that they were to return to Maui, and the men said goodby to their comrades on the Barr. The Team moved from the Barr to a transport anchored in the anchorage at Kerama Rhetto. By this time the anchorage was nearly filled with supply ships, tankers, and crippled ships. They were there a day or two and then left Okinawa and the "Divine Wind" behind as they sailed eastward on the USS Wayne, an APA. The Wayne was being used as a survivor/hospital ship. There were hundreds of badly burned and injured men aboard, and every day the dead would be buried at sea. The men from Team 13 played the role of survivors, and some of them thought by the time they reached Pearl Harbor, that they were lucky to survive. On the Wayne, they were served two meals a day, which consisted of wormy bread and near rotten meat. This was not good food for a demolition man.

In late April or early May, Team 13 finally made it back to their old base under the morning shadow of Haleakala. After being ferried from Pearl to Maui on an LCI, they left the LCI carrying their seabags, and walked back to the "dust bowl" where empty tents were waiting.

Those enlisted men in the "dust bowl" tents had no idea what their next assignment would be, but there was the usual "scuttlebutt" of things to come. The first assignment turned out to be a 10 day inter-island leave. The Demos of Team 13 seemed to scatter in all directions. Some flew over to Honolulu on the mail plane, and some flew down to Hilo on the big island. Others stayed on Maui visiting Hana on the east coast, or Lahaina on the west coast. And then there were those who stayed on base and took day trips to Wailuku or up to see the big crater on Mt. Haleakala.

It was about the middle of May before the Team members found out the reason for their unexpected return to Maui. They were to be assigned as instructors in the base training program at the Underwater Demolition Training and Experimental Base at Maui, Territory of Hawaii. Team 13 replaced Team 9 as an auxiliary group in the training staff. Earlier in the year, Team 9 had received heavy casualties at Luzon and with their complement down about 30 percent had been transferred to the Maui training staff. The Team 9 men received stateside leave and reported to Fort Pierce where they received replacement personnel and were reorganized.

With their assignment in the Maui training staff, the Team moved from the "dust bowl" to "top-side" quarters which were nearer to the beach, mess hall and other important facilities. The men were assigned to various divisions in the training staff. For example, there were small boat operations, swimming, gunnery, demolition blasting, day and night reconnaissance, radio communication, and probably a few more definite areas. Team 13 men were assigned to the training staff from late May until about the first of August. During those two long months, it seemed that the Team was dissolved. Men were assigned to different crews unrelated to the ones their teammates were working with.

August, 1945 was a landmark month for Team 13. Their training classes graduated. Team 27, 28 and 29 completed their training. In July, Teams 11 and 18 had opened the beaches at Balikpapan in Borneo in what turned out as the last major invasion of World War II. Every UDT team in commission on August 1, 1945 was receiving orders to proceed to Oceanside, California to take a course in "cold water training" preparing them for "Operation Olympic" which was the code name for the initial invasion of the Japanese homeland. Team 13 was reorganized and ordered to report to Oceanside.

During the first week of August, an undersized Team 13 was assigned to the USS Burdo (APD133) and left Maui bound for Oceanside. During the cruise to Oceanside, history intervened, an atomic bomb was dropped on Hiroshima and another on Nagasaki, and Japan was in deep trouble. When the Burdo dropped anchor off Oceanside, Team 13 stayed aboard. From the time Team 13 had returned from Okinawa, they had lost about a third of their personnel. Many of the Team Able men, who had been in the Pacific since the end of 1943, had left the Team for stateside leave and other assignments, and others had dropped out of the Team for different reasons. Before they left Maui or at Oceanside, the Team received 27 replacement personnel.

Most of the replacements involved enlisted men, but in the ranks of the commissioned officers there were also big changes. Lieutenant Commander Moranz, who had earned the highest of respect from his men, was forced out of the Team because of the extremely high blood pressure. Moranz had become a "father figure" to his men. He probably was in his forties when he joined the Team. Much older than the designated limit of 30 years. Moranz never swam into enemy beaches with his men like Draper Kaufmann and a few other commanding officers, but he was in the boats under fire directing operations, and his sense of fairness towards the enlisted personnel earned him great respect. Those in the enlisted ranks had affectionately called him "Pinkie" because of his fair complexion, and this was, of course, revealed only in discussions between the men who gave him the most respect.

The Team also lost Lieutenant Walker, their executive officer, who had spent nearly two years in the Pacific with the crews that later became Team Able, then with Team Able and the sinking of the Noa, and then his tenure as Team 13's executive officer.

Lieutenant Commander Moranz and Lieutenant Walker left the Team at Oceanside. Lieutenant Commander Douglas Fane replaced Moranz, and Lieutenant (jg) Robert Gleason, a Team 13 platoon officer, replaced Lieutenant Walker as executive officer. Fane was new in demolition and had recently finished the Fort Pierce training. He was an experienced line officer, regular Navy, and had combat experience in his earlier duties. The enlisted men lost "Pinkie" and gained "Red'. All commanding officers have to have a nickname, and Douglas Fane's had to be "Red" because of the color of his hair.

After one night anchored off Oceanside, the Team and the Burdo moved about 60 miles north and dropped anchor in Long Beach Harbor. The Team 13 Demos received their first stateside liberty in nearly a year, and as the happy men walked away from the fleet landing, they were overwhelmed by noise from horns, sirens, firecrackers and other loud percussions. The war was over, the Japanese had surrendered, and this was V-J Day.

Two nights' liberty in Long Beach, and everyone was sure that a leave awaited them. This was true but not in August. On August 16, two days after V-J Day, the Burdo sailed for Pearl Harbor with Team 13 aboard. Team 13 had unfinished business in Japan.

The stay in Pearl Harbor was for several days, and supplies were gathered and stowed in the holds of the Burdo. Liberty in Honolulu and Pearl City were liberally granted, and those who had not spent all their money in Long Beach took advantage of the opportunity. Some of the Demos came back from a day of liberty looking like they were coming out of combat wearing dress whites. Some of those civilians around Pearl Harbor were pretty tough, but the Demos said, "you ought to see those other guys." Also while at Pearl Harbor there was a day of honor for some of the Team 13 men. On the lush lawn of the Pacific Fleet Command Headquarters, many Team members were presented the Bronze Star Medal or the Silver Star Medal for certain actions performed during the Iwo Jima operation.

On September 1, 1945, Team 13 left Pearl Harbor with a convoy bound for Saipan. The long five or six thousand mile cruise was uneventful. One of the Demos had to be transferred to an APA for a tooth extraction, but he returned to the Team at Saipan.

There was no delay at Saipan for the Burdo and Team 13. They broke convoy and headed northwest towards the Ryukyu Islands. Traveling fast now that they were free of the convoy, they skirted Okinawa, moved into the East China Sea, and turned due north with the bow of the Burdo pointed at Sasebo, Japan. Somewhere in the East China Sea a swamped Japanese fishing boat was sighted. The Japanese fishermen were taken aboard, and Team 13's Japanese interpreter who was with the Team on that cruise, interrogated them. They were in bad shape from lack of food and water. The ship's doctor took over and by the time the Burdo reached Japan, the fishermen were in good condition. The swamped wooden fishing boat had to be destroyed. The Burdo's crew tried to destroy it with 40 mm and 5 inch gunfire, and they even dropped a depth charge set at shallow detonation, but the little wooden boat just dropped a few boards and bounced around in the water. Finally, UDT 13, in their last demolition operation, embarked a rubber boat crew and using tetrytol they blasted the fishing boat into thousands of pieces.

Team 13's assignment at Sasebo was to survey the port and prepare it for the coming occupation forces. This involved sounding water depths, checking piers, wharves, small boats, inland waterways, and small villages along the bay. Most of these operations were handled by the platoons being assigned separate missions. The reconnoitering duties were routine for the Demos, and no problems were reported.

It was the veterans of "Class Seven" who opened Sasebo. Team 11 on the Kline was tied up beside the Burdo, and the two teams worked side by side at Sasebo. This is not an accurate account, because about a third or more of both teams were not from Class Seven but were replacements as the others dropped by the wayside.

When the Burdo left Sasebo, everyone knew that San Diego was their destination. However, their trials were not over for they faced a fearsome typhoon as they left the Japan area. The Burdo tried to outrun the storm, and probably avoided the worst. But the waves were high, and the little ship bravely moved along the troughs, crests and sides of the gigantic waves. Lists of 40 to 50 degrees or more were common. Everyone aboard wore life jackets, because sometimes it seemed likely that the Burdo would bottom up. But she didn't, and by the middle of October, Team 13 was leaving the Burdo in San Diego Bay and moving to the Naval Amphibious Base on Coronado Island.

Team 13 was decommissioned on October 29, 1945 at Coronado. All Team members had an opportunity to "ship over" into the new post-war teams, and some did. One of those was Lieutenant Commander Douglas Fane, Team 13's commanding officer. Fane would be a leader in UDT for many years, and would later write the Naked Warriors, a book about the Underwater Demolition Teams. The majority of Team 13's complement was given leave, reassigned to other bases, and eventually discharged to seek vocations and careers in civilian life. Underwater

Demolition Teams 11, 12 13 and 15, who all started from the core of men in Class Seven at Fort Pierce, were great teams. Teams 11 and 12 both received the Presidential Unit Citation for their work in the Pacific. They were the only Underwater Demolition Teams to receive that honor during World War II.

[Ed. Note: The following excerpts from an article entitled Underwater Demolition Men Decorated at Pearl Harbor (provided by Marvin Cooper) appeared in a Honolulu newspaper in August, 1945:

"Six officers and 26 enlisted men of Underwater Demolition Team No. 13 were decorated here today for the heroic part they played last February during the assault on and capture of Iwo Jima Island.

The officers were presented Silver Star Medals, and the enlisted men, Bronze Star Medals, by Rear Admiral William H. P. Blandy, USN, Commander, Cruisers, Destroyers, Pacific Fleet.

'I believe that no duty in this war required more personal courage than that of the underwater reconnaissance and demolition teams, which performed in advance of our amphibious attack, and that no group contributed more in proportion to its numbers, to the successful conclusion of the war,' Admiral Blandy said.

'I am thoroughly familiar with your work at Iwo Jima because I was there. It was tough and dangerous, but through your efforts our landing craft were enabled to proceed safely through cleared waters to the enemy-held beachhead.'"

The men listed in the article as receiving the medals were as follows:

Silver Star: Ensign Ralph R. Harlan, Ensign Charles F. Hamman, Ensign Lewis A. Robinson, Ensign Harry E. Gardner, Ensign Joseph E. Long, Jr., and Lieutenant Robert E. Gleason.

Bronze Star: Roger E. Miller, John E. Stone, William H. Baker, Edward R. Bryson, Robert E. King, Russell J. Morrow, Thomas L. McElwee, Marvin Cooper, Francis N. Musick, Donald P. Taylor, Thomas E. Owens, James C. Moore, Kenneth J. Dollinger, Charles Rudy, Jr., Donald J. Presson, George N. Rush, Carl N. Lazar, Gary J. Price, Victor G. Taraborrelli, Gilbert A. Reimer, Lawrence A. Johnson, Walter R. Miller, William O. Butler, John A. Barrett, Sherman G. Prince, and Stanley J. Gunshetski.

The paper added that "Silver Star Medals also were awarded by Admiral Blandy to Lieutenant Commander V. J. Moranz, USNR, of Philadelphia who led the team in the Iwo operation, and to Lieutenant (jg) D. M. Walker, USNR, of Woodstown, N.J., the team's executive. Both officers have returned to the United States."]

APPENDIX D

OFFICERS AND ENLISTED MEN OF UDT 13

Information for this section was provided by Marvin Cooper. The following UDT 13 men served on the U.S.S. Barr. (see Appendix E for information on ratings, e.g., MM2c, Cox).

Officers:

A.C. Allen, Jr., Ensign
Edwin I. Cleveland, Ensign
Harry E. Gardner, Ensign
Robert E. Gleason, Ensign
Charles F. Hamman
Ralph R. Harlan, Ensign
Robert V. Hehli, Lt.(jg)

Leo N. Huddleston
J.E. Long, Jr., Ensign
Vincent J. Moranz, Comm. Off.
Donald H. Murray, Lt.(jg)
Lewis A. Robinson
N.F. Smith, Lt.(jg)
Donald M. Walker, Lt.(jg), Ex. Off.

Enlisted Men:

Bartie Allen
Tom Allen
William H. Baker, MM2c
John A. Barrett, SF1c
Karl P. Behrendt, CSF
Paul J. Bier, CM1c
Etoise P. Blackwell, Cox
Roy M. Bracken, Jr., Cox
James H. Broome, Jr., Cox
Conrad Brummett
Edward R. Bryson, Jr., Cox
William O. Butler, Cox

Karl A. Kinsaul, Cox
Carl La Zarr, MM1c
Raymond LeBlanc
John T. Lynch, QM3c
Arthur W. Magee, SM2c
E.J. Marietta, Chief Petty Off.
Frank E. Mattson
Raymond McCaw, MoMM1c
Thomas L. McElwee, MM2c
Edward L. McIntire, CMM
Roger E. Miller, EM2c
Walter R. Miller, EM3c

Robert N. Carlson, Chief Petty Officer
Oakley B. Cline, Jr.
Ernest R. Comer, Chief Petty Officer
Marvin Cooper, GM2c
William J. Cran, CM2c
William R. Crandell, RM3c
T.E. Crowder, SF2c
Andrew Cusimano, BM1c
Daniel A. Delgrosso
Edward N. Deringer, QM3c
Kenneth J. Dollinger, GM3c
Raymond J. Edwards
Stuart O. Eisentrager
Ralph D. Emerson, CPhM
Alton E. Evans
Tauren A. First
Walter R. Flathers, RM3c
Samuel P. Fore, Cox
William D. Foreman, GM3c
Glen Frey, BM2c
Leslie H. Goode
George Gregory, Jr.
Ralph R. Grimes, GM3c
S. J. Gunshefski, GM3c
J.L. Hoffman, Jr., GM2c
Daniel H. Holihan
L. A. Johnson, SK2c
Harold Jordan William
Albert N. King, BM1c
Robert E. King, BM2c

James C. Moore, BM2c
Keith R. Moore
Russell J. Morrow, QM3c
Francis Musick, Jr., GM3c
Thomas E. Owens, Cox
Donald J. Patton
Patrick J. Phelan, SM3c
Donald J. Presson, GM3c
Gary J. Price, GM3c
Sherman G. Prince, GM3c
Gilbert A. Reimer, SM2c
Bennie M. Rice, MM2c
Howard J. Rice, BM2c
Edward P. Robinson
C. Rudy, Jr., BM1c
George Rush, BM1c
P.S. Shoemaker, Cox
John E. Stone, Cox
Michael J. Sulik, Cox
V.G. Taraborelli, Cox
Donald P. Taylor, MM1c
Ervin H. Taylor, EM3c
Paul Toy, Cox
Orbin J. Tuttle, Cox
Duryee Van Wagenen
Frank Walker
Robert D. Ward
P. Whelan, Chief Petty Off.
R.M. Wilkinson, GM2c
Arnold D. Willardson

After the team was reformed in August, 1945 to train for the expected invasion of Japan, 28 replacements were added to the team, as follows:

Officers:

F.D. Fane, Lt. Comdr.
W.W. Spafford, Ensign

A.N. Weeden, Ensign
R.G. Armstrong, Ensign

Enlisted Men:

George Chancellor
R.F. Eagle, MM2c
R. Ellis, MM2c
L.W. Epperson, S1c
J.M. Gilleland, SF2c
J.W. Ingersoll, S1c
L.E. Jordan, GM1c
L.P. Kaicy, S1c
W.F. Kleindauf,Y2c
J.J. Kuipers, S1c
L. Limes, S1c
George Lindsey

W. Mansfield, WT3c
S.N. Moore, S1c
G. Nigh, AMM2c
H.A. Peddy, S1c
W.S. Reinbott, S1c
Francis Roos
J.E. Thomas, S1c
L.M. Thomas, CCM
R.C. Vause, StM1c
C. Welty, SC3c
William Winning
R.C. Ziegenfuss, S1c

APPENDIX E

NAVY RATING STRUCTURE
World War II

The US Navy's rating structure classifies enlisted men according to both rating (skill) and rate (skill level). Rating, or "trade" is denoted by a descriptive word or phrase while skill level (and seniority and pay grade) are indicated by a number or title. The following information was provided by Capt. A. Manly Bowen.

Non-rated Men

During WWII "non-rated men" were called either Seamen or Firemen, depending on whether they were in training for "engineering" ratings or "deck" ratings (anything other than engineering).

S2c	Seaman, second class	The non-rated "deck" trainee status assigned after completion of recruit training
S1c	Seaman, first class	The non-rated status to which an S2c could be promoted
F2c	Fireman second class	The non-rated engineering trainee status assigned after completion of recruit training
F1c	Fireman first class	The non-rated status to which an F2c could be promoted

Petty Officers (rated men)

The USS *Barr* had Petty Officers assigned with the ratings, or "trades" denoted by the descriptive words in the following table. These ratings were combined with skill levels (and pay-grade and seniority) to complete the classification:

Ratings of the USS *Barr's* personnel shown in the enlisted roster for 15 February 1944.

Abbr.	Rating	Duties
B	Boilerman	Maintained and operated ship's boilers.
Bkr	Baker	Kept the ship's messes supplied with baked goods.
BM	Boatswain's Mate	Assisted the First Lieutenant, in seamanship Evolutions such as mooring, anchoring, towing, underway replenishment of fuel ammunition and supplies, and maintaining and operating the ship's boats, cargo booms and other related to these evolutions.
Ck	Cook	Cooked for the officers' mess.
CM	Carpenter's Mate	Responsible for any required carpentry and Fire-fighting; and assisted the First Lieutenant in controlling and repairing battle damage.
CS	Commissary Steward	Assisted the ship's supply officer in managing the food supply and preparation.
Cox	Coxswain	The traditional name given to the lowest Boatswain's mate Rating (instead of BM3c).
EM	Electrician's Mate	Assisted the Engineer Officer in maintaining and operating the ship's electrical equipment including main propulsion generators, electrical service generators and distribution systems, and the ship's internal communication systems, including the gyrocompass and associated repeaters and wiring.
FC	Fire Controlman	Assisted the Gunnery Officer in maintaining

and operating the equipment and electrical circuits used to control the ship's guns and antisubmarine armament.

GM	Gunners Mate	Assisted the Gunnery Officer in maintaining and employing the ship's guns and caring for the magazines and their contents.
M	Metalsmith	Responsible for welding and other metalwork, and assisted the First Lieutenant in fire-fighting and control of battle damage.
MaM	Mail Man	Assisted the Executive Officer with postal matters.
MM	Machinist's Mate	Assisted the Engineer Officer in maintaining and operating the ship's steam engines and other engineering equipment not otherwise assigned.
MoMM	Motor Machinist's Mate	Maintained and operated gasoline and diesel engines.
PhM	Pharmacist's Mate	Physician's assistant. When no medical officer assigned was responsible for the health of the crew and for treatment of battle casualties.
QM	Quartermaster	Assisted the Navigator in determining the ship's navigational position and planned movement. Kept the ship's navigation chart allowance corrected and performed the daily calculation of the correction to be applied to the times shown on the ship's chronometers when navigating by celestial bodies.
RdM	Radarman	Assisted the CIC watch officer in tracking air and surface contacts using the ship's radar equipment and using the voice radios

		to exchange contact information with other ships and aircraft.
RM	Radioman	Assisted the Communications Officer in maintaining and operating the ship's radio equipment. Responsible for maintaining ship to shore radio communications and communications with other ships and aircraft. Copied the fleet broadcasts which were the primary source of orders and information from higher authority not in company with the ship.
RT	Radio Technician	Responsible for maintenance and repair of the ship's radar and electronics intercept equipment.
SC	Ship's Cook	Cooked for the crew's mess.
SF	Shipfitter	Responsible for any required metalworking, welding, the ship's plumbing, and assisting the First Lieutenant in fire-fighting and in control and repair of battle damage.
SK	Storekeeper	Assisted the Stores Officer, in Supply Department record keeping and ordering and accounting for all of the things needed to feed and supply the ship and her crew.
SM	Signalman	Handles visual communications (signal flags, semaphore, and flashing light).
SoM	Sonarman	Maintained and operated the ship's sonar equipment used in detecting and attacking submarines.
SSM	Ship's Serviceman	Responsible for maintaining and operating the ship's Laundry.
StM	Steward's Mate	Officers' mess attendant.

TM	Torpedoman	Responsible for the ship's antisubmarine armament (depth charges, hedgehogs and their launchers).
WT	Water Tender	Assisted the Engineer Officer in maintaining and operating the ship's boilers and associated auxiliary equipment, and managing the ship's fuel and water supply and storage.
Y	Yeoman	Assisted the Captain and Executive Officer in managing the ship's correspondence, keeping the ship's records, and other clerical matters.

Skill Levels

"Striker": a non-rated apprentice, e.g. Signalman Apprentice--S1c(SM)

Third Class Petty Officer: Lowest Petty Officer skill level, e.g. Sonarman third class--SoM3c

Second Class Petty Officer: Intermediate skill level, e.g. Boatswain's Mate second class--BM2c

First Class Petty Officer: Highest intermediate skill level, e.g. Shipfitter first class-SF1c

Chief Petty Officer: Top of the rating structure, e.g. Chief Water Tender--CWT

APPENDIX F

THE BARR RAG

An issue of the ship's paper included inside Yeoman Grenga's diary.

Vol. 1 No. 31

"THE BARR RAG"

Tuesday   **27 February 1945**

Undated - Pacific War:
Tank led devildogs of the fifth amphibious marine corps seized one runway of the central Iwo Jima bomber base Sunday and enveloped two thirds of the other as they continued to exact a four to one toll against bitterly resisting Japanese. Tokyo 750 miles to the north meanwhile felt the weight of a double barreled aerial assault as waves of carrier based planes and two hundred superforts swept in to give the capitals industrial and military area perhaps its heaviest poundings. New subterranean explosions rocked Corregidor fortress at the entrance of Manila Bay indicating more Japanese remnants sealed in the tunnels were committing suicide rather than face Yank cleanup crews. The fighting still was fierce on Iwo where Adm. Chester W. Nimitz reported 2827 dead had been counted. The American death toll is more than six hundred. In the Philippines with all but isolated pockets of enemy opposition eliminated within the ancient walled city of ravaged Manila while American doughboys were clearing enemy positions east of the city metropolis while others hit southward along Laguna De Bay. In the north spearheads were aimed toward Baguio the Philippines summer capital in the Benguet mountains. For the second time this month Adm Marc Mitscher took his carrier

task force into Japanese waters, most powerful fleet of its kind in the world and sent naval fliers against Tokyo region military objectives Sunday morning Japanese time. In the afternoon the two hundred B-29's largest superfort mission ever flown winged in on the Tokyo area. The bombardiers unloaded explosives through the clouds. Tokyo claimed the B-29 bombings were blind and came during a snowstorm and that imperial property was damaged slightly including the guard section of the royal palace. Premier Kuniaki Koiso was represented as angered and apologizing to Emperor Hirohito for the negligence. He reported to the emperor his person was in danger. Tokyo said the bombs started fires which were almost extinguished by nightfall. The Japanese claimed six hundred naval planes were in the morning attacks. On Iwo where the Leathernecks hold the whole of the central airfield the Japanese continued to resist fanatically. The guns of warships maintained their blistering fire on the inland positions. The Japanese were throwing their most modern weapons into the fight including one thousand pound rockets and heavy mortars. Flamethrowers were cleaning out Japanese caves, tunnels and pillboxes on southern Iwo's Mt. Suribachi. It was disclosed at Iwo that Navy Secretary James V. Forrestal witnessed the furious landing fights there and later went ashore to visit with the marines. The Secretary now is at Guam for conference with Fleet Admiral Chester W. Nimitz. Forrestal said he left Iwo with a feeling of tremendous admiration and reverence for the marines in battle there. He decried what he termed the great tendency to count our battles won before they are won and warned America has a real job ahead making this great ocean safe. In Manila some Japanese suicide troops held out in the walled city and nearby government buildings. Their end was near. To the east of Manila the yanks captured San Isidro and Montalban and were nearing the city of Antipolo. American bombers swept northern Luzon islands a shipping off the French Indo-China coast and off China. Allied heavy bombers pounded supply and troop areas at Myingyang southwest of Mandalay on the central Burma front. British forces on the Mandalay front beat off Japanese counterattacks and advanced in one sector.

London:

The Red army captured the Pomeranian stronghold of Preussich Friedland Sunday and drove to within sixty miles of the Baltic coast in a powerful new offensive aimed at the German province and sealing off thousands of troops in Danzig territory. Advancing up to seven miles near the Polish frontier southwest of Chojnice the Russians hurled the enemy from a ten mile stretch of the Berlin-Danzig highway and drove three miles beyond to seize Bichofswalee. In East Prussia other Soviet forces captured six localities as they tightened the narrow enemy pocket southwest of Koenigsberg and beat off large German counterattacks on Samland peninsula northwest of the half destroyed East Prussian capital the only sector mentioned in the brief Russian war bulletin.

London:

Overthrow of the Nicolae Radescu regime in Romania was predicted Sunday by Moscow dispatches in the wake of bloody rioting in Bucharest and other cities. A new national democratic front demonstrators were expected to take over. Moscow dispatches reported national democratic front demonstrators were fired upon by Romanian troops and gendarmes in the Capital and elsewhere.

Rome:

U.S. 10th mountain division troops repulsed German counterattacks Sunday near Mount Belvedere twenty nine miles southwest of Bologna and improved their positions on the flanks of a neighboring mountain. In support of allied strategy aimed at pinning down and destroying as many of Field Marshall Kesselring's troops as possible to prevent them from joining the main battle for Germany proper, a combined force of U.S., British and French warships have been heavily bombarding targets on the French-Italian frontier. Italian patriot forces behind the enemy lines recently attacked five military trains heading north from Genoa a communique on patriot activities broadcast from Lt. Gen. Clark's headquarters said. Brazilian troops on the 10th mountain division's right captured the villages of Bellavista and Laserra and took two hills the highest thirty one hundred feet. German troops struck back with three counterattacks and were partially successful. Heavy fighting was in progress La Serra. On the Adriatic sector Eighth army troops cleared out a stretch of the east bank of the Senio river southwest of Bagnacavallo and took up improved position.

Paris:

Duren key to the defenses of Cologne fell Sunday to U.S. infantry in a steamroller offensive that rumbled six miles or more out on the German Plain beyond the Roer river to within five miles of the enemy's last defense lines short of the Rhine. Fifteen miles ahead of the charging armies of General Eisenhower lay the western outskirts of Cologne city of 800,000 and symbol of German war might in the industrial Ruhr and Rhineland. The enemy was offering only slight to moderate resistance. The U.S. Ninth Army meanwhile on the north flank of the 25 mile front speared to within ten miles of Muenchen Gladbach and was threatening to encircle Erkelenz a highway center guarding the approaches to that Ruhr city of 200,000 population. The number of prisoners passed the 3300 mark and hundreds of warplanes were setting up more groups for the kill by blasting communications in the front of the moving mass of American troops and guns. Sixty miles south the U.S. Third Army broke across the Pruem river to two points within six miles of the enemy base at Bitburg and farther south pushed tanks across the Saar river in two synchronized thrusts toward the Rhine. The third army crushed the last resistance in a thirty two mile stretch of westwall east of the Duchy of

Luxembourg releasing forces for the eastward push. Fighting ebbed on the north end of the front held by the Canadian first army and the south end of the front held by the U.S. Seventh Army. Unable to match the Americans on the ground the Germans summoned considerable numbers of jet propelled planes which tried vainly to cut the bridges across the Roer.

London:
Reichleiter Xaver Schwartz treasurer of the Nazi party broadcast Sunday "it is possible that we will be destroyed but the national socialist idea will be preserved by the youth when all else has crumbled". Schwartz spoke to Nazi youth groups. The German radio said Hitler's proclamation yesterday on the 25th anniversary of the Nazi party was prominently displayed on the front pages of the Berlin Sunday morning papers.
Miscellaneous:
During the night RAF mosquitos rained block busters on Berlin in bright moonlight and tactical fighters flew several hundred sorties against Nazi communications.

Seattle:
Six male prisoners this morning bound and gagged their jailer and then slid eleven stories down greased elevator rails to effect a successful break from the King county jail. Twenty six other prisoners declined to join in the break.

New York:
Army and Navy clash on the basketball court at Annapolis this Saturday but instead of two unbeaten fives tangling the service clash no longer has a bearing on the national cage picture. The Annapolis middies went down to their first defeat yesterday when the Bainbridge Navy ended their twelve game winning streak 68 to 6(last number missing). Army's 27 game win streak was snapped by Penn a week ago.

San Francisco:
Delford G. Dulin Chief Fire Controlman somewhere in the Pacific is the father of a six pound fourteen and one half ounce baby born Feb. 24. Both Mrs. Dulin and baby are doing fine.

Cincinnati:
Lt. jg Walter L. Muller is the father of a five pound thirteen ounce girl born Feb. 13. Lt. Muller is somewhere in the South Pacific. Both Mrs. Muller and baby are doing fine.

GLOSSARY

See Appendix E, Navy Rating Structure, for additional abbreviations, e.g., QM2c.

AA: Antiaircraft.

AGC: Amphibious Force flagship.

AK: Cargo ship.

APA: Attack troop transport.

APD: High speed troop transport.

Ach-Ach: Antiaircraft fire.

BB: Battleship.

BOQ: Bachelor officers' quarters.

Betty Bomber: Japanese bomber.

Bogey (Bogie): Unidentified Aircraft (considered enemy until identified).

CAP: Combat Air Patrol.

CAT: Light observation planes.

CB: Construction Battalion.

CIC: Combat information center.

CO: Commanding officer.

CP: Command Post.

CV: Aircraft carrier.

CVE: Escort aircraft carrier (jeep carrier).

ComAdComPhibPac: Commander of the Pacific Fleet Amphibious Force Administrative Command.

Com Task Force: Task Force Commander.

Condition 2M: Readiness Condition 2 (Modified). The highest readiness condition was Condition 1, with battle stations fully manned and doors and hatches closed for maximum water tightness to limit flooding in case of battle damage. Condition 2 allowed half the crew to rest. Water tightness could be relaxed somewhat to permit access to living and messing spaces. For Condition 3 manning was reduced to about one-third, and water tightness was even more relaxed to permit ordinary activities. Any of these conditions could be "modified" (usually downward) if appropriate.

DD: Destroyer.

DE: Destroyer escort.

DMS: Fast mine sweeper.

Fantail: The weather (exposed) deck nearest the stern of the ship.

Fathometer: An instrument that measured depth by sound waves.

Fish: Torpedo.

Flash: Warning of air attack:
> Blue probable.
> Red - imminent.
> White - all clear.
> Control (Gun control orders):
>> Green -Friendly planes also in the air, fire only when attacked.
>> Yellow - no restrictions, fire at any plane.

Flying Bridge: The exposed ship control station, usually atop the wheelhouse. Visibility is much better from an open bridge, particularly for spotting attacking aircraft. So the discomforts of a station exposed to the weather were accepted during wartime.

Foc's'le (Forecastle): The weather (exposed) deck nearest the bow of the ship.

GQ: General quarters.

Hedgehogs: Small, ahead-thrown, antisubmarine weapons that exploded on contact with a submerged submarine. Hedgehog launchers projected a 24 charge pattern up to 200 yards ahead of the attacking ship. Ahead thrown weapons were more effective than stern dropped depth charges because the ship was still tracking the target when the weapons were fired. To reach a firing position for a stern dropped depth charge attack required the ship to pass over the submerged submarine, losing contact in the process. During the minute or more between losing contact and dropping the charges submarine evasive maneuvers could frustrate the attack.

JOOD (JOD): Junior officer of the deck.

Kamikaze: Japanese suicide plane.

K-gun: Stern mounted depth charge projector.

K-rations: Dried/canned field rations that required no preparation before being consumed.

LCI: Landing craft infantry.

LCIG: Landing craft infantry (gunboat).

LCPR: ˙Landing craft personnel/reconnaissance.

LCVP: Landing craft vehicle/personnel.

LSI: Landing ship infantry.

LSM: Landing ship medium.

LST: Landing ship tank.

OOD (OD): Officer of the deck.

P-38: Fighter aircraft (USAAF).

PT: Motor torpedo boat.

Quarter deck: The in port watch station of the officer or petty officer in charge of the watch, usually at the gangway or accommodation ladder that provided access to the ship.

Skunk: Unidentified surface contact, treated as enemy until identified.

Super-fort: B-29 heavy bomber.

TBM: Torpedo bomber.

TBS: Voice radio (talk between ships).

TG: Task group.

TU: Task unit.

U-boat: German Submarine.

Wheelhouse: The enclosed ship control, usually high in the ship and forward of the funnels and masts.

Wolfpack: Several German subs assembled to attack a convoy in concert. For both sides of the Battle of the Atlantic locating the enemy on the trackless ocean was a problem. The wolfpack was a German measure that took advantage of a known convoy location and projected movement. When a patrolling U-boat found a convoy, it didn't attack immediately, but instead began trailing it while other U-boats assembled for a combined attack. The Allies used the radio messages required to assemble the wolfpack to take countermeasures: diverting the convoy, and summoning a Hunter-Killer group.

XO: Executive officer, 2nd in command.

Zoomies: Slang for friendly pilots or planes.

INDEX

Page number in bold print refers to photograph.

San Miguel Island, 31
San Nicola Island, 31
San Salvador, 28
Sark, G.P., *Barr*, **12**, 13, 14, 245
Sark, W., wife of G.P. Sark, 13, 246
Schaffert, Lisa, daughter of J.E.
  Purgatorio, 244
Shangri-La CV38, 143
Shannon, D.J., *Barr*, **6, 94**, 107
Shawnee, OK, 82
Sheya Shima, 152
Shiogama, Japan, 188
Shoemaker, P.S., UDT #13, **49**
Sibunfan Island, 143
Sims APD50, 131, 141, 169, 174,
  177, 209, 243
Skotko, F.J., *Barr*, **6, 12**, 64, 107,
  246
"Skunks", 74, 141
Sliwinski, E.J., *Barr*, 130
Smith, N.F., UDT #13, **49**
Smith, "Pinetops", pianist, 183
Solomon Islands, 22, 238
Sonntag, H.G., *Barr*, **222**
Soucy, A.C., *Barr*, **6, 9**, 14, 16, 52,
  105, 108, **115**, 145, 146, 159, 172,
  173, 183, 197, 198, 201, 215, 216,
  224, 231, **232**, 246, 249
Southern Methodist University, 237
Southwest Texas State University,
  240
Stanford University, 246
Stassen, Cdr. Harold, USN, 194
Stein, W.C., *Barr*, **6**, 24, 143
Stillwell, General Joe, US Army,
  159
Stillwell, J.F., *Barr*, **94**
Stone, J.E., UDT #13, **49**
Storms, W.E., *Barr*, **6**
Stow, Massachusetts, 244
Stroud, Gloucestershire, England,

240
Swearer DE186, 125
Swearingen, E.L., *Barr*, 2, **8**, 33, **39**,
  41, 51, 62, 63, 84, 103, 105, 107,
  112, 133, 135, 162, 166, 172, 175,
  184, 196, 198, 215, 217, 231, **232**,
  246
Sweatt, R.J., *Barr*, 189, 191

Tallulah, Louisiana, 235
Taraborelli, V.G., UDT #13, **49**
Task Group 21.11, 9
Task Group 30.5, 169
Task Group 52.11, 56
Task Group 30.6, 169
Taylor, D.P., UDT #13, **49**
Taylor, E.H., UDT #13, **49**
Telfers Island, 28
Tennessee BB43, 235,
Teton AGC14, 27, 28, 30
Texas BB35, 55, 56, 62
Texas Tech University, 240
Theya, 159
Thomas, Lowell, war correspondent,
  51
Ticao Pass, 143
Tinty Town Club, 23
Tokashika Shima, 104
Tokyo, 7, 24, 55, 60, 79, 81, 87,
  165, 169, 171, 185-191, 193-195,
  198, 200, 205-208, 215, 216, 219,
  223-226, 229, 243
Tokyo Rose, 81, 146
Tori, 159
Toy, P., UDT #13, **49**
Tremont Hotel, 6
Truman, President Harry S., 166,
  173
Turner, Joe, pianist, 183
Tuttle, O.J., UDT #13, **49**

Order Form

I would like to order the following copies of the hard cover edition of

Movies on the Fantail
Helen E. Grenga

_____ copies @ $27.95 each: $_____

Georgia residents,
            add sales tax: $_____

Shipping costs: $_____
      1 copy $4.00
      2 copies $5.00
      3 copies $7.00
      4-7 copies $11.00
      8-10 copies $16.00

          TOTAL: $_____

SHIP TO (Please print)

NAME _____

ADDRESS _____

CITY_____ STATE _____ ZIP_____

MAIL ABOVE INFORMATION WITH CHECK OR MONEY ORDER MADE
PAYABLE TO YEOMAN PRESS

Yeoman Press
2 Pine Ridge Drive
Newnan, GA 30263-3317